SECOND EDITION

iOS Swift Game
Development Cookbook

Jonathon Manning and Paris Buttfield-Addison

Beijing · Cambridge · Farnham · Köln · Sebastopol · Tokyo

iOS Swift Game Development Cookbook, Second Edition

by Jonathon Manning and Paris Buttfield-Addison

Printed in the United States of America.

Published by O'Reilly Media, Inc., 1005 Gravenstein Highway North, Sebastopol, CA 95472.

O'Reilly books may be purchased for educational, business, or sales promotional use. Online editions are also available for most titles (*http://safaribooksonline.com*). For more information, contact our corporate/institutional sales department: 800-998-9938 or *corporate@oreilly.com*.

Editor: Rachel Roumeliotis	**Indexer:** WordCo Indexing Services, Inc.
Production Editor: Matthew Hacker	**Cover Designer:** Karen Montgomery
Copyeditor: Kim Cofer	**Interior Designer:** David Futato
Proofreader: Rachel Monaghan	**Illustrator:** Rebecca Demarest

April 2014:	First Edition
May 2015:	Second Edition

Revision History for the Second Edition:

2015-05-07:   First release

See *http://oreilly.com/catalog/errata.csp?isbn=9781491920800* for release details.

ISBN: 978-1-491-92080-0

[LSI]

Table of Contents

Preface.. ix

1. Laying Out a Game... 1
   1.1. Laying Out Your Engine   1
   1.2. Creating an Inheritance-Based Game Layout   2
   1.3. Creating a Component-Based Game Layout   4
   1.4. Calculating Delta Times   7
   1.5. Detecting When the User Enters and Exits Your Game   9
   1.6. Updating Based on a Timer   11
   1.7. Updating Based on When the Screen Updates   11
   1.8. Pausing a Game   13
   1.9. Calculating Time Elapsed Since the Game Start   14
   1.10. Working with Closures   15
   1.11. Writing a Method That Calls a Closure   17
   1.12. Working with Operation Queues   18
   1.13. Performing a Task in the Future   20
   1.14. Making Operations Depend on Each Other   21
   1.15. Filtering an Array with Closures   22
   1.16. Loading New Assets During Gameplay   22
   1.17. Adding Unit Tests to Your Game   24
   1.18. 2D Grids   26

2. Views and Menus.. 31
   2.1. Working with Storyboards   32
   2.2. Creating View Controllers   38
   2.3. Using Segues to Move Between Screens   45
   2.4. Using Constraints to Lay Out Views   49
   2.5. Adding Images to Your Project   51
   2.6. Slicing Images for Use in Buttons   53

2.7. Using UI Dynamics to Make Animated Views   55
2.8. Moving an Image with Core Animation   56
2.9. Rotating an Image   58
2.10. Animating a Popping Effect on a View   60
2.11. Theming UI Elements with UIAppearance   62
2.12. Rotating a UIView in 3D   63
2.13. Overlaying Menus on Top of Game Content   65
2.14. Designing Effective Game Menus   66

3. Input. 67
3.1. Detecting When a View Is Touched   68
3.2. Responding to Tap Gestures   69
3.3. Dragging an Image Around the Screen   70
3.4. Detecting Rotation Gestures   72
3.5. Detecting Pinching Gestures   75
3.6. Creating Custom Gestures   76
3.7. Receiving Touches in Custom Areas of a View   80
3.8. Detecting Shakes   81
3.9. Detecting Device Tilt   83
3.10. Getting the Compass Heading   85
3.11. Accessing the User's Location   87
3.12. Calculating the User's Speed   90
3.13. Pinpointing the User's Proximity to Landmarks   91
3.14. Receiving Notifications When the User Changes Location   92
3.15. Looking Up GPS Coordinates for a Street Address   95
3.16. Looking Up Street Addresses from the User's Location   97
3.17. Using the Device as a Steering Wheel   98
3.18. Detecting Magnets   99
3.19. Utilizing Inputs to Improve Game Design   101

4. Sound. 103
4.1. Playing Sound with AVAudioPlayer   103
4.2. Recording Sound with AVAudioRecorder   106
4.3. Working with Multiple Audio Players   108
4.4. Cross-Fading Between Tracks   109
4.5. Synthesizing Speech   111
4.6. Getting Information About What the Music App Is Playing   113
4.7. Detecting When the Currently Playing Track Changes   114
4.8. Controlling Music Playback   116
4.9. Allowing the User to Select Music   117
4.10. Cooperating with Other Applications' Audio   119
4.11. Determining How to Best Use Sound in Your Game Design   121

5. Data Storage... 123

 5.1. Saving the State of Your Game 123

 5.2. Storing High Scores Locally 126

 5.3. Using iCloud to Save Games 128

 5.4. Using the iCloud Key-Value Store 132

 5.5. Loading Structured Information 134

 5.6. Deciding When to Use Files or a Database 136

 5.7. Managing a Collection of Assets 137

 5.8. Storing Information in NSUserDefaults 139

 5.9. Implementing the Best Data Storage Strategy 141

 5.10. In-Game Currency 141

6. 2D Graphics and Sprite Kit... 143

 6.1. Getting Familiar with 2D Math 143

 6.2. Creating a Sprite Kit View 149

 6.3. Creating a Scene 150

 6.4. Adding a Sprite 152

 6.5. Adding a Text Sprite 153

 6.6. Determining Available Fonts 155

 6.7. Including Custom Fonts 156

 6.8. Transitioning Between Scenes 156

 6.9. Moving Sprites and Labels Around 158

 6.10. Adding a Texture Sprite 161

 6.11. Creating Texture Atlases 162

 6.12. Using Shape Nodes 162

 6.13. Using Blending Modes 163

 6.14. Using Image Effects to Change the Way That Sprites Are Drawn 165

 6.15. Using Bézier Paths 166

 6.16. Creating Smoke, Fire, and Other Particle Effects 167

 6.17. Shaking the Screen 168

 6.18. Animating a Sprite 170

 6.19. Parallax Scrolling 171

 6.20. Creating Images Using Noise 178

7. Physics.. 181

 7.1. Reviewing Physics Terms and Definitions 181

 7.2. Adding Physics to Sprites 183

 7.3. Creating Static and Dynamic Objects 184

 7.4. Defining Collider Shapes 185

 7.5. Setting Velocities 187

 7.6. Working with Mass, Size, and Density 188

 7.7. Creating Walls in Your Scene 189

7.8. Controlling Gravity   191
7.9. Keeping Objects from Falling Over   192
7.10. Controlling Time in Your Physics Simulation   192
7.11. Detecting Collisions   193
7.12. Finding Objects   194
7.13. Working with Joints   196
7.14. Working with Forces   197
7.15. Adding Thrusters to Objects   198
7.16. Creating Explosions   199
7.17. Using Device Orientation to Control Gravity   201
7.18. Dragging Objects Around   202
7.19. Creating a Car   205

8. 3D Graphics. 209
8.1. Working with 3D Math   210
8.2. Creating a GLKit Context   214
8.3. Drawing a Square Using OpenGL   216
8.4. Loading a Texture   224
8.5. Drawing a Cube   227
8.6. Rotating a Cube   231
8.7. Moving the Camera in 3D Space   232

9. Intermediate 3D Graphics. 235
9.1. Loading a Mesh   235
9.2. Parenting Objects   242
9.3. Animating a Mesh   246
9.4. Batching Draw Calls   249
9.5. Creating a Movable Camera Object   250

10. Advanced 3D Graphics. 255
10.1. Understanding Shaders   255
10.2. Working with Materials   259
10.3. Texturing with Shaders   265
10.4. Lighting a Scene   266
10.5. Using Normal Mapping   269
10.6. Making Objects Transparent   271
10.7. Adding Specular Highlights   273
10.8. Adding Toon Shading   276

11. Scene Kit. 279
11.1. Setting Up for Scene Kit   279
11.2. Creating a Scene Kit Scene   280

11.3. Showing a 3D Object   280
11.4. Working with Scene Kit Cameras   281
11.5. Creating Lights   282
11.6. Animating Objects   283
11.7. Working with Text Nodes   284
11.8. Customizing Materials   285
11.9. Texturing Objects   286
11.10. Normal Mapping   286
11.11. Constraining Objects   287
11.12. Loading COLLADA Files   288
11.13. Using 3D Physics   289
11.14. Adding Reflections   290
11.15. Hit-Testing the Scene   290

12. Artificial Intelligence and Behavior. **293**
12.1. Making Vector Math Nicer in Swift   293
12.2. Making an Object Move Toward a Position   295
12.3. Making Things Follow a Path   297
12.4. Making an Object Intercept a Moving Target   298
12.5. Making an Object Flee When It's in Trouble   299
12.6. Making an Object Decide on a Target   300
12.7. Making an Object Steer Toward a Point   301
12.8. Making an Object Know Where to Take Cover   302
12.9. Calculating a Path for an Object to Take   303
12.10. Finding the Next Best Move for a Puzzle Game   308
12.11. Determining If an Object Can See Another Object   309
12.12. Using AI to Enhance Your Game Design   311

13. Networking and Social Media. **313**
13.1. Using Game Center   313
13.2. Getting Information About the Logged-in Player   320
13.3. Getting Information About Other Players   320
13.4. Making Leaderboards and Challenges with Game Center   321
13.5. Finding People to Play with Using Game Center   325
13.6. Creating, Destroying, and Synchronizing Objects on the Network   327
13.7. Interpolating Object State   329
13.8. Handling When a Player Disconnects and Rejoins   331
13.9. Making Turn-Based Gameplay Work with Game Kit   332
13.10. Sharing Text and Images to Social Media Sites   335
13.11. Storing Saved Games in Game Center   336
13.12. Implementing iOS Networking Effectively   338
13.13. Implementing Social Networks Effectively   338

14. Game Controllers and External Screens. **341**
    14.1. Detecting Controllers   343
    14.2. Getting Input from a Game Controller   345
    14.3. Showing Content via AirPlay   347
    14.4. Using External Screens   348
    14.5. Designing Effective Graphics for Different Screens   350
    14.6. Dragging and Dropping   352

15. Performance and Debugging. **359**
    15.1. Improving Your Frame Rate   359
    15.2. Making Levels Load Quickly   361
    15.3. Dealing with Low-Memory Issues   363
    15.4. Tracking Down a Crash   365
    15.5. Working with Compressed Textures   366
    15.6. Working with Watchpoints   370
    15.7. Logging Effectively   371
    15.8. Creating Breakpoints That Use Speech   372

Index. **375**

Preface

Games rule mobile devices. The iPhone, iPad, and iPod touch are all phenomenally powerful gaming platforms, and making amazing games that your players can access at a moment's notice has never been easier. The iTunes App Store category with the most apps is Games; it includes games ranging from simple one-minute puzzle games to in-depth, long-form adventures. The time to jump in and make your own games has never been better. We say this having been in iOS game development since the App Store opened. Our first iOS game, in 2008, a little strategy puzzler named *Culture*, led us to working on hundreds of other awesome projects, ranging from a digital board game for museums to educational children's games, and everything in between! The possibilities for games on this platform are only becoming wider and wider.

This book provides you with simple, direct solutions to common problems found in iOS game programming using Swift. Whether you're stuck figuring out how to give objects physical motion, or how to handle Game Center, or just want a refresher on common gaming-related math problems, you'll find simple, straightforward answers, explanations, and sample projects. This book is part tutorial and part reference. It's something you'll want to keep handy to get new ideas about what's possible through a series of recipes, as well as for a quick guide to find answers on a number of topics.

Audience

We assume that you're a reasonably capable programmer, and that you know at least a little bit about developing for iOS: what Xcode is and how to get around in it, how to use the iOS Simulator, and the basics of the Swift programming language. We also assume you know how to use an iOS device. We don't assume any existing knowledge of game development on any platform, but we're guessing that you're reading this book with a vague idea about the kind of game you'd like to make.

This book isn't based on any particular genre of games—you'll find the recipes in it applicable to all kinds of games, though some will suit some genres more than others.

Organization of This Book

Each chapter of this book contains *recipes*: short solutions to common problems found in game development. The book is designed to be read in any order; you don't need to read it cover-to-cover, and you don't need to read any chapter from start to finish. (Of course, we encourage doing that, because you'll probably pick up on stuff you didn't realize you wanted to know.)

Each recipe is structured like this: the *problem* being addressed is presented, followed by the *solution*, which explains the technique of solving the problem (or implementing the feature, and so on). Following the solution, the recipe contains a *discussion* that goes into more detail on the solution, which gives you more information about what the solution does, other things to watch out for, and other useful knowledge.

Here is a concise breakdown of the material each chapter covers:

Chapter 1, Laying Out a Game
> This chapter discusses different ways to design the architecture and code layout of your game, how to work with timers in a variety of ways, and how blocks work in iOS. You'll also learn how to schedule work to be performed in the future using blocks and operation queues, and how to add unit tests to your project.

Chapter 2, Views and Menus
> This chapter focuses on interface design and working with UIKit, the built-in system for displaying user interface graphics. In addition to providing common objects like buttons and text fields, UIKit can be customized to suit your needs—for some kinds of games, UIKit might be the only graphical tool you'll need.

Chapter 3, Input
> In this chapter, you'll learn how to get input from the user so that you can apply it to your game. This includes touching the screen, detecting different types of gestures (such as tapping, swiping, and pinching), as well as other kinds of input like the user's current position on the planet, or motion information from the variety of built-in sensors in the device.

Chapter 4, Sound
> This chapter discusses how to work with sound effects and music. You'll learn how to load and play audio files, how to work with the user's built-in music library, and how to make your game's sound work well when the user wants to listen to his or her music while playing your game.

Chapter 5, Data Storage
> This chapter is all about storing information for later use. The information that games need to save ranges from the very small (such as high scores), to medium (saved games), all the way up to very large (collections of game assets). In this

chapter, you'll learn about the many different ways that information can be stored and accessed, and which of these is best suited for what you want to do.

Chapter 6, 2D Graphics and Sprite Kit

This chapter discusses Sprite Kit, the 2D graphics system built into iOS. Sprite Kit is both powerful and very easy to use; in this chapter, you'll learn how to create a scene, how to animate sprites, and how to work with textures and images. This chapter also provides you with info you can use to brush up on your 2D math skills.

Chapter 7, Physics

In this chapter, you'll learn how to use the two-dimensional physics simulation that's provided as part of Sprite Kit. Physics simulation is a great way to make your game's movements feel more realistic, and you can use it to get a lot of great-feeling game for very little programmer effort. You'll learn how to work with physics bodies, joints, and forces, as well as how to take user input and make it control your game's physical simulation.

Chapter 8, 3D Graphics

This chapter and the two that follow it provide a tutorial on OpenGL ES 2, the 3D graphics system used on iOS. These three chapters follow a slightly different structure than the rest of the book, because it's not quite as easy to explain parts of OpenGL in isolation. Instead, these chapters follow a more linear approach, and we recommend that you read the recipes in order so that you can get the best use out of them. Chapter 8 introduces the basics of OpenGL, and shows you how to draw simple shapes on the screen; at the same time, the math behind the graphics is explained.

Chapter 9, Intermediate 3D Graphics

This chapter is designed to follow on from the previous, and discusses more advanced techniques in 3D graphics. You'll learn how to load a 3D object from a file, how to animate objects, and how to make a camera that moves around in 3D space.

Chapter 10, Advanced 3D Graphics

This chapter follows on from the previous two, and focuses on shaders, which give you a tremendous amount of control over how objects in your game look. You'll learn how to write shader code, how to create different shading effects (including diffuse and specular lighting, cartoon shading, and more), and how to make objects transparent.

Chapter 11, Scene Kit

This chapter covers Scene Kit, Apple's new 3D framework. It has recipes for showing 3D objects with Scene Kit; working with cameras, lights, and textures; and using physics in 3D.

Chapter 12, Artificial Intelligence and Behavior
> This chapter discusses how to make objects in your game behave on their own, and react to the player. You'll learn how to make one object chase another, how to make objects flee from something, and how to work out a path from one point to another while avoiding obstacles.

Chapter 13, Networking and Social Media
> In this chapter, you'll learn about Game Center, the social network and match-making system built into iOS. You'll learn how to get information about the player's profile, as well as let players connect to their friends. On top of this, you'll also learn how to connect to nearby devices using Bluetooth. Finally, you'll learn how to share text, pictures, and other content to social media sites like Twitter and Facebook.

Chapter 14, Game Controllers and External Screens
> This chapter discusses the things that players can connect to their device: external displays, like televisions and monitors, and game controllers that provide additional input methods like thumbsticks and physical buttons. You'll learn how to detect, use, and design your game to take advantage of additional hardware where it's present.

Chapter 15, Performance and Debugging
> The last chapter of the book looks at improving your game's performance and stability. You'll learn how to take advantage of advanced Xcode debugging features, how to use compressed textures to save memory, and how to make your game load faster.

Additional Resources

You can download the code samples from this book (or fork using GitHub) at *http://www.secretlab.com.au/books/ios-game-dev-cookbook-swift*.

O'Reilly has a number of other excellent books on game development and software development (both generally and related to iOS) that can help you on your iOS game development journey, including:

- *Physics for Game Developers*
- *Learning Cocoa with Objective-C* (by us!)
- *Swift Development with Cocoa* (also by us!)
- *Programming iOS 8*

We strongly recommend that you add Gamasutra (*http://gamasutra.com*) to your regular reading list, due to its high-quality coverage of game industry news.

Game designer Marc LeBlanc's website (*http://8kindsoffun.com*) is where he collects various presentations, notes, and essays. We've found him to be a tremendous inspiration.

Finally, we'd be remiss if we didn't link to our own blog (*http://secretlab.com.au*).

Conventions Used in This Book

The following typographical conventions are used in this book:

Italic
> Indicates new terms, URLs, email addresses, filenames, and file extensions.

`Constant width`
> Used for program listings, as well as within paragraphs to refer to program elements such as variable or function names, databases, data types, environment variables, statements, and keywords.

`Constant width bold`
> Shows commands or other text that should be typed literally by the user.

`Constant width italic`
> Shows text that should be replaced with user-supplied values or by values determined by context.

 This element signifies a tip or suggestion.

 This element signifies a general note.

 This element indicates a warning or caution.

Using Code Examples

Supplemental material (code examples, exercises, etc.) is available for download at *http://www.secretlab.com.au/books/ios-game-dev-cookbook-swift*.

This book is here to help you get your job done. In general, if example code is offered with this book, you may use it in your programs and documentation. You do not need to contact us for permission unless you're reproducing a significant portion of the code. For example, writing a program that uses several chunks of code from this book does not require permission. Selling or distributing a CD-ROM of examples from O'Reilly books does require permission. Answering a question by citing this book and quoting example code does not require permission. Incorporating a significant amount of example code from this book into your product's documentation does require permission.

We appreciate, but do not require, attribution. An attribution usually includes the title, author, publisher, and ISBN. For example: "*iOS Swift Game Development Cookbook* by Jonathon Manning and Paris Buttfield-Addison (O'Reilly). Copyright 2015 Secret Lab, 978-1-449-92080-0."

If you feel your use of code examples falls outside fair use or the permission given above, feel free to contact us at *permissions@oreilly.com*.

Safari® Books Online

Safari Books Online is an on-demand digital library that delivers expert content in both book and video form from the world's leading authors in technology and business.

Technology professionals, software developers, web designers, and business and creative professionals use Safari Books Online as their primary resource for research, problem solving, learning, and certification training.

Safari Books Online offers a range of plans and pricing for enterprise, government, education, and individuals.

Members have access to thousands of books, training videos, and prepublication manuscripts in one fully searchable database from publishers like O'Reilly Media, Prentice Hall Professional, Addison-Wesley Professional, Microsoft Press, Sams, Que, Peachpit Press, Focal Press, Cisco Press, John Wiley & Sons, Syngress, Morgan Kaufmann, IBM Redbooks, Packt, Adobe Press, FT Press, Apress, Manning, New Riders, McGraw-Hill, Jones & Bartlett, Course Technology, and hundreds more. For more information about Safari Books Online, please visit us online.

How to Contact Us

Please address comments and questions concerning this book to the publisher:

O'Reilly Media, Inc.
1005 Gravenstein Highway North
Sebastopol, CA 95472
800-998-9938 (in the United States or Canada)
707-829-0515 (international or local)
707-829-0104 (fax)

We have a web page for this book, where we list errata, examples, and any additional information. You can access this page at *http://bit.ly/ios_game_dev_cookbook_swift*.

To comment or ask technical questions about this book, send email to *bookques tions@oreilly.com*.

For more information about our books, courses, conferences, and news, see our website at *http://www.oreilly.com*.

Find us on Facebook: *http://facebook.com/oreilly*

Follow us on Twitter: *http://twitter.com/oreillymedia*

Watch us on YouTube: *http://www.youtube.com/oreillymedia*

Acknowledgments

Jon thanks his mother, father, and the rest of his weirdly extended family for their tremendous support.

Paris thanks his mother, whose credit card bankrolled literally hundreds of mobile devices through his childhood—an addiction that, in all likelihood, created the gadget-obsessed monster he is today. He can't wait to read her upcoming novel.

Thank you to our editor, Rachel Roumeliotis, who kept the book under control and provided a ton of useful advice on content. We know it was a ton because we measured it. Likewise, all the O'Reilly Media staff and contractors we've worked with over the course of writing the book have been absolutely fantastic, and every one of them made this book better for having had them work on it. Thank you also to Brian Jepson, our first editor at O'Reilly.

A huge thank you to Tony Gray and the AUC for the monumental boost they gave us and many others listed on this page. We wouldn't be working in this industry, let alone writing this book, if it wasn't for Tony and the AUC community.

Thanks also to Neal Goldstein, who richly deserves all of the credit and/or blame for getting both of us into the whole book-writing racket.

We'd like to acknowledge the support of the goons at Maclab, who still know who they are and *still* continue to stand watch for Admiral Dolphin's inevitable apotheosis, as well as Professor Christopher Lueg, Dr Leonie Ellis, and the rest of the staff at the University of Tasmania for putting up with us.

Additional thanks to Tim N, Nic W, Andrew B, Jess L, and Rex S for a wide variety of reasons. Thanks also to Ash Johnson, for even more reasons.

Finally, very special thanks to Steve Jobs, without whom this book (and many others like it) would not have reason to exist.

CHAPTER 1

Laying Out a Game

Games are software, and the best software has had some thought put into it regarding how it's going to work. When you're writing a game, you need to keep in mind how you're going to handle the individual tasks that the game needs to perform, such as rendering graphics, updating artificial intelligence (AI), handling input, and the hundreds of other small tasks that your game will need to deal with.

In this chapter, you'll learn about ways you can lay out the structure of your game that will make development easier. You'll also learn how to organize the contents of your game so that adding more content and gameplay elements is easier, and find out how to make your game do multiple things at once.

1.1. Laying Out Your Engine

Problem

You want to determine the best way to lay out the architecture of your game.

Solution

The biggest thing to consider when you're thinking about how to best lay out your game is how the game will be updated. There are three main things that can cause the state of the game to change:

Input from the user

> The game may change state when the user provides some input, such as tapping a button or typing some text. Turn-based games are often driven by user input (e.g., in a game of chess, the game state might only be updated when the user finishes moving a piece).

Timers

The game state may change every time a timer goes off. The delay between timer updates might be very long (some web-based strategy games have turns that update only once a day), or very short (such as going off every time the screen finishes drawing). Most real-time games, like shooters or real-time strategy games, use very short-duration timers.

Input from outside

The game state may change when information from outside the game arrives. The most common example of this is some information arriving from the network, but it can also include data arriving from built-in sensors, such as the accelerometer.

Sometimes, this kind of updating is actually a specific type of timer-based update, because some networks or sensors need to be periodically checked to see if new information has arrived.

Discussion

None of these methods are mutually exclusive. You can, for example, run your game on a timer to animate content, and await user input to move from one state to the next.

Updating every frame is the least efficient option, but it lets you change state often, which makes the game look smooth.

1.2. Creating an Inheritance-Based Game Layout

Problem

You want to use an inheritance-based (i.e., a hierarchy-based) architecture for your game, which is simpler to implement.

Solution

First, define a class called `GameObject`:

```
class GameObject: NSObject {
    func update(deltaTime : Float) {

        // 'deltaTime' is the number of seconds since
        // this was last called.

        // This method is overriden by subclasses to update
        // the object's state - position, direction, and so on.
    }
}
```

When you want to create a new *kind* of game object, you create a subclass of the Game Object class, which inherits all of the behavior of its parent class and can be customized:

```
class Monster: GameObject {

    var hitPoints : Int = 10 // how much health we have
    var target : GameObject? // the game object we're attacking

    override func update(deltaTime: Float) {

        super.update(deltaTime)

        // Do some monster-specific updating

    }

}
```

Discussion

In an inheritance-based layout, as shown in Figure 1-1, you define a single base class for your game object (often called GameObject), which knows about general tasks like being updated, and then create subclasses for each specific type of game object. This hierarchy of subclasses can be multiple levels deep (e.g., you might subclass the Game Object class to make the Monster subclass, and then subclass *that* to create the Gob lin and Dragon classes, each of which has its own different kinds of monster-like behavior).

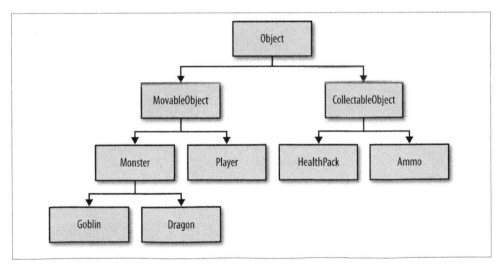

Figure 1-1. An inheritance-based layout

The advantage of a hierarchy-based layout is that each object is able to stand alone: if you have a Dragon object, you know that all of its behavior is contained inside that single object, and it doesn't rely on other objects to work. The downside is that you can often end up with a very deep hierarchy of different game object types, which can be tricky to keep in your head as you program.

1.3. Creating a Component-Based Game Layout

Problem

You want to use a component-based architecture for your game, which allows for greater flexibility.

Solution

First, define a Component class. This class represents components that are attached to game objects—it is a very simple class that, at least initially, only has a single method and a single property:

```
@class GameObject;
@interface Component : NSObject

- (void) update:(float)deltaTime;

@property (weak) GameObject* gameObject;
@end
```

Next, define a GameObject class. This class represents game objects:

```
class Component: NSObject {

    // The game object this component is attached to
    var gameObject : GameObject?

    func update(deltaTime : Float) {
        // Update this component
    }

}
```

The implementation for this class looks like this:

```
class GameObject: NSObject {

    // The collection of Component objects attached to us
    var components : [Component] = []

    // Add a component to this gameobject
    func addComponent(component : Component) {
        components.append(component)
```

```swift
        component.gameObject = self
}

// Remove a component from this game object, if we have it
func removeComponent(component : Component) {
    if let index = find(components, component) {
        component.gameObject = nil
        components.removeAtIndex(index)
    }
}

// Update this object by updating all components
func update(deltaTime : Float) {

    for component in self.components {
        component.update(deltaTime)
    }

}

// Returns the first component of type T attached to this
// game object
func findComponent<T: Component>() -> T?{

    for component in self.components {
        if let theComponent = component as? T {
            return theComponent
        }
    }

    return nil;
}

// Returns an array of all components of type T
// (this returned array might be empty)
func findComponents<T: Component>() -> [T?] {
    // NOTE: this returns an array of T? (that is,
    // optionals), even though it doesn't strictly need
    // to. This is because Xcode 6.1.1's Swift compiler
    // was crashing when this function returned an array of T
    // (that is, non-optionals). Your mileage may vary.

    var foundComponents : [T] = []

    for component in self.components {
        if let theComponent = component as? T {
            foundComponents.append(theComponent)
        }
    }

    return foundComponents
}
```

```
    }
```
Using these objects looks like this:

```
// Define a type of component
class DamageTaking : Component {
    var hitpoints : Int = 10

    func takeDamage(amount : Int) {
        hitpoints -= amount
    }
}

// Make an object - no need to subclass GameObject,
// because its behavior is determined by which
// components it has
let monster = GameObject()

// Add a new DamageTaking component
monster.addComponent(DamageTaking())

// Get a reference to the first DamageTaking component
let damage : DamageTaking? = monster.findComponent()
damage?.takeDamage(5)

// When the game needs to update, send all game
// objects the "update" message.
// This makes all components run their update logic.
monster.update(0.33)
```

Discussion

In a component-based architecture, as shown in Figure 1-2, each game object is made up of multiple components. Compare this to an inheritance-based architecture, where each game object is a subclass of some more general class (see Recipe 1.2).

A component-based layout means you can be more flexible with your design and not worry about inheritance issues. For example, if you've got a bunch of monsters, and you want one specific monster to have some new behavior (such as, say, exploding every five seconds), you just write a new component and add it to that monster. If you later decide that you want other monsters to also have that behavior, you can add that behavior to them, too.

In a component-based architecture, each game object has a list of components. When something happens to an object—for example, the game updates, or the object is added to or removed from the game—the object goes through all of its components and notifies them. This gives them the opportunity to respond in their own way.

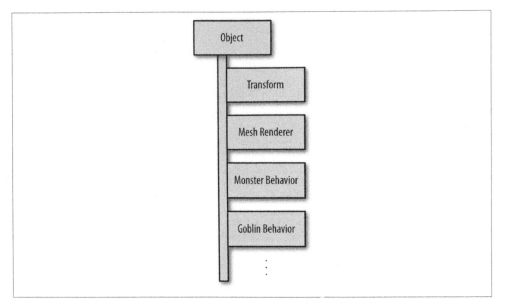

Figure 1-2. A component-based layout

The main problem with component-based architectures is that it's more laborious to create multiple copies of an object, because you have to create and add the same set of components every time you want a new copy.

 The findComponent and findComponents methods are worth a little explanation. These functions are designed to let you get a reference to a component, or an array of components, attached to the game object. The functions use *generics* to make them return an array of the type of component you expect. This means that you don't need to do any type casting in your code—you're guaranteed to receive objects that are the right type.

1.4. Calculating Delta Times

Problem

You want to know how many seconds have elapsed since the last time the game updated.

Solution

First, decide which object should be used to keep track of time. This may be a view controller, an SKScene, a GLKViewController, or something entirely custom.

Create an instance variable inside that object:

```
class TimeKeeper: NSObject {

    var lastFrameTime : Double = 0.0

}
```

Then, each time your game is updated, get the current time in milliseconds, and subtract lastFrameTime from that. This gives you the amount of time that has elapsed since the last update.

When you want to make something happen at a certain rate—for example, moving at 3 meters per second—multiply the rate by the delta time:

```
func update(currentTime : Double) {

    // Calculate the time since this method was last called
    let deltaTime = currentTime - lastFrameTime

    // Move at 3 units per second
    let movementSpeed = 3.0

    // Multiply by deltaTime to work out how far
    // an object needs to move this frame
    someMovingObject.move(distance: movementSpeed * deltaTime)

    // Set last frame time to current time, so that
    // we can calculate the delta time when we're next
    // called
    lastFrameTime = currentTime
}
```

Discussion

"Delta time" means "change in time." Delta times are useful for keeping track of how much time has elapsed from one point in time to another—in games, this means the time from one frame to the next. Because the game content changes frame by frame, the amount of time between frames becomes important.

Additionally, the amount of time between frames might change a little. You should always be aiming for a constant frame rate of 60 frames per second (i.e., a delta time of 16 milliseconds: $1 \div 60 = 0.0166$); however, this may not always be achievable, depending on how much work needs to be done in each frame. This means that delta time might vary slightly, so calculating the delta time between each frame becomes necessary if you want rates of change to appear constant.

Some engines give you the delta time directly. For example, CADisplayLink gives you a duration property (see Recipe 1.7), and GLKViewController gives you timeSince LastUpdate (see Recipe 8.6).

Some engines give you just the current time, from which you can calculate the delta time. For example, the SKScene class passes the currentTime parameter to the update: method (discussed further in Recipe 7.15).

In other cases (e.g., if you're doing the main loop yourself), you won't have easy access to either. In these cases, you need to get the current time yourself:

```
let currentTime = NSDate.timeIntervalSinceReferenceDate() as Double
```

1.5. Detecting When the User Enters and Exits Your Game

Problem

You want to detect when the user leaves your game, so that you can pause the game. You also want to know when the user comes back.

Solution

To get notified when the user enters and exits your game, you register to receive notifications from an NSNotificationCenter. The specific notifications that you want to receive are UIApplicationDidBecomeActiveNotification, UIApplicationWillEnter ForegroundNotification, UIApplicationWillResignActiveNotification, and UIAp plicationDidEnterBackgroundNotification:

```
override func viewDidLoad() {
    super.viewDidLoad()

    let center = NSNotificationCenter.defaultCenter()

    center.addObserver(self,
        selector: "applicationDidBecomeActive:",
        name: UIApplicationDidBecomeActiveNotification,
        object: nil)

    center.addObserver(self,
        selector: "applicationWillEnterForeground:",
        name: UIApplicationWillEnterForegroundNotification,
        object: nil)

    center.addObserver(self,
        selector: "applicationWillResignActive:",
        name: UIApplicationWillResignActiveNotification,
        object: nil)

    center.addObserver(self,
        selector: "applicationDidEnterBackground:",
        name: UIApplicationDidEnterBackgroundNotification,
        object: nil)
```

```
    }

    func applicationDidBecomeActive(notification : NSNotification) {
        NSLog("Application became active")
    }

    func applicationDidEnterBackground(notification : NSNotification) {
        NSLog("Application entered background - unload textures!")
    }

    func applicationWillEnterForeground(notification : NSNotification) {
        NSLog("Application will enter foreground - reload " +
            "any textures that were unloaded")
    }

    func applicationWillResignActive(notification : NSNotification) {
        NSLog("Application will resign active - pause the game now!")
    }

    deinit {
        // Remove this object from the notification center
        NSNotificationCenter.defaultCenter()
            .removeObserver(self)
    }
```

Discussion

On iOS, only one app can be the "active" application (i.e., the app that is taking up the screen and that the user is interacting with). This means that apps need to know when they become the active one, and when they stop being active.

When your game is no longer the active application, the player can't interact with it. This means that the game should pause (see Recipe 1.8). When the game resumes being the active application, the player should see a pause screen.

 Pausing, of course, only makes sense in real-time games, such as shooters, driving games, arcade games, and so on. In a turn-based game, like a strategy or puzzle game, you don't really need to worry about the game being paused.

In addition to being the active application, an application can be in the *foreground* or the *background*. When an application is in the foreground, it's being shown on the screen. When it's in the background, it isn't visible at all. Apps that are in the background become *suspended* after a short period of time to save battery power. Apps that enter the background should reduce their memory consumption as much as possible; if your app consumes a large amount of memory while it is in the background, it is more likely to be terminated by iOS.

1.6. Updating Based on a Timer

Problem

You want to update your game after a fixed amount of time.

Solution

Use an NSTimer to receive a message after a certain amount of time, or to receive an update on a fixed schedule.

First, add an instance variable to your view controller:

```
var timer : NSTimer?
```

Next, add a method that takes an NSTimer parameter:

```
func updateWithTimer(timer: NSTimer) {
    // Timer went off; update the game
    NSLog("Timer went off!")
}
```

Finally, when you want to start the timer:

```
// Start a timer
self.timer = NSTimer.scheduledTimerWithTimeInterval(0.5,
    target: self, selector: "updateWithTimer",
    userInfo: nil, repeats: true)
```

To stop the timer:

```
// Stop a timer
self.timer?.invalidate()
self.timer = nil
```

Discussion

An NSTimer waits for a specified number of seconds, and then calls a method on an object that you specify. You can change the number of seconds by changing the time Interval parameter.

You can also make a timer either fire only once or repeat forever, by changing the repeats parameter to false or true, respectively.

1.7. Updating Based on When the Screen Updates

Problem

You want to update your game every time the screen redraws.

Solution

Use a `CADisplayLink`, which sends a message every time the screen is redrawn.

First, `import` the `QuartzCore` framework:

```
import QuartzCore
```

Next, add an instance variable to your view controller:

```
var displayLink : CADisplayLink?
```

Next, add a method that takes a single parameter (a `CADisplayLink`):

```
func screenUpdated(displayLink : CADisplayLink) {
    // Update the game.
}
```

Finally, add this code when you want to begin receiving updates:

```
// Create and schedule the display link
displayLink = CADisplayLink(target: self, selector: "screenUpdated:")
displayLink?.addToRunLoop(NSRunLoop.mainRunLoop(), forMode: NSRunLoopCommonModes)
```

When you want to pause receiving updates, set the `paused` property of the `CADisplay Link` to YES:

```
// Pause the display link
displayLink?.paused = true
```

When you want to stop receiving updates, call `invalidate` on the `CADisplayLink`:

```
// Remove the display link; once done, you need to
// remove it from memory
displayLink?.invalidate()
displayLink = nil
```

Discussion

When we talk about "real-time" games, what comes to mind is objects like the player, vehicles, and other things moving around the screen, looking like they're in continuous motion. This isn't actually what happens, however—what's really going on is that the screen is redrawing itself every 1/60 of a second, and every time it does this, the locations of some or all of the objects on the screen change slightly. If this is done fast enough, the human eye is fooled into thinking that everything's moving continuously.

In fact, you don't technically *need* to update as quickly as every 1/60 of a second—anything moving faster than 25 frames per second (in other words, one update every 1/25 of a second) will look like motion. However, faster updates yield smoother-looking movement, and you should always aim for 60 frames per second.

You'll get the best results if you update your game at the same rate as the screen. You can achieve this with a CADisplayLink, which uses the Core Animation system to figure out when the screen has updated. Every time this happens, the CADisplayLink sends its target a message, which you specify.

It's worth mentioning that you can have as many CADisplayLink objects as you like, though they'll all update at the same time.

1.8. Pausing a Game

Problem

You want to be able to pause parts of your game, but still have other parts continue to run.

Solution

Keep track of the game's "paused" state in a Bool variable. Then, divide your game objects into two categories—ones that run while paused, and ones that don't run while paused:

```
for gameObject in self.gameObjects {

    // Update it if we're not paused, or if this game object
    // ignores the paused state
    if self.paused == false || gameObject.canPause == false {
        gameObject.update(deltaTime)
    }

}
```

Discussion

The simplest possible way to pause the game is to keep track of a pause state; every time the game updates, you check to see if the pause state is set to true, and if it is, you don't update any game objects.

However, you often don't want every single thing in the game to freeze. For example:

- The user interface may need to continue to animate.
- The network may need to keep communicating with other computers, rather than stopping entirely.

In these cases, having special objects that never get paused makes more sense.

1.9. Calculating Time Elapsed Since the Game Start

Problem

You want to find out how much time has elapsed since the game started.

Solution

When the game starts, create an NSDate object and store it:

```
// Store the time when the game started as a property
var gameStartDate : NSDate?

// When the game actually begins, store the current date
self.gameStartDate = NSDate()
```

When you want to find out how much time has elapsed since the game started, create a second NSDate and use the timeIntervalSinceDate method to calculate the time:

```
let now = NSDate()
let timeSinceGameStart = now
    .timeIntervalSinceDate(self.gameStartDate!)
NSLog("The game started \(timeSinceGameStart) seconds ago")
```

Discussion

NSDate objects represent moments in time. They're the go-to object for representing any instant of time that you want to be able to refer to again later, such as when your game starts. NSDate objects can refer to practically any date in the past or future and are very precise.

When you create an NSDate with the [NSDate date] method, you get back an NSDate object that refers to the current time (i.e., the instant when the NSDate object was created).

To determine the interval between two dates, you use timeIntervalSinceDate:. This method returns an NSTimeInterval, which is actually another term for a floating-point number. These values are represented in seconds, so it's up to your code to do things like determine the number of hours and minutes:

```
let hours = timeSinceGameStart / 3600.0 // 3600 seconds in an hour
let minutes = timeSinceGameStart % 3600.0 / 60.0 // 60 seconds in a minute
let seconds = timeSinceGameStart % 60.0 // remaining seconds

NSLog("Time elapsed: \(hours):\(minutes):\(seconds)")
```

1.10. Working with Closures

Problem

You want to store some code in a variable for later execution.

Solution

Closures are ideal for this:

```
class GameObject {
    // define a type of closure that takes a single GameObject
    // as a parameter and returns nothing
    var onCollision : (GameObject -> Void)?
}

// Create two objects for this example
let car = GameObject()
let brickWall = GameObject()

// Provide code to run when the car hits any another object
car.onCollision = { (objectWeHit) in
    NSLog("Car collided with \(objectWeHit)")
}

// later, when a character collides:
car.onCollision?(brickWall) // note the ? - this means that
                            // the code will only run if onCollision
                            // is not nil
```

Discussion

Closures are a language feature in Swift that allow you to store chunks of code in variables, which can then be worked with like any other variable.

Here's an example of a simple closure:

```
var multiplyNumber : Int -> Int   ❶

multiplyNumber = { (number) -> Int in   ❷

    return number * 2

}

multiplyNumber(2)   ❸
```

❶ This is how you define a closure. In this case, the closure returns an `Int`, is named `multiplyNumber`, and accepts a single `Int` parameter.

❷ Just like any other variable, once a closure is defined, it needs to be given a value. In this case, we're providing a closure that takes an `Int` and returns an `Int`, just like the variable's definition.

❸ Calling a closure works just like calling any other function.

How closures work

So far, this just seems like a very roundabout way to call a function. However, the real power of closures comes from two facts:

- Closures *capture the state* of any other variables their code references.
- Closures are objects, just like everything else. They stay around until you need them. If you store a closure, you can call it however often you like.

This is extremely powerful, because it means that your game doesn't need to carefully store values for later use; if a closure needs a value, it automatically keeps it.

You define a closure by describing the parameters it receives and the type of information it returns. To help protect against mistakes, you can also create a *type alias* for closures, which defines a specific type of closure. This allows you to declare variables with more easily understandable semantics:

```
typealias ErrorHandler = NSError -> Void

var myErrorHandler : ErrorHandler

myErrorHandler = { (theError) in
    // do work with theError
    NSLog("i SPILL my DRINK! \(theError)")
}
```

Closures and other objects

When a closure is created, the compiler looks at all of the variables that the closure is referencing. If a variable is a simple value, like an `int` or a `float`, that value is simply copied. However, if the variable is a Swift object, it can't be copied because it could potentially be very large. Instead, the object is *retained* by the closure. When a closure is freed, any objects retained by the closure are released.

This means that if you have a closure that references another object, that closure will keep the other object around. This is usually what you want, because it would be annoying to have to remember to keep the variables referenced by closures in memory. However, sometimes that's not what you want.

One example is when you want a closure to run in two seconds' time that causes an enemy object to run an attack animation. However, between the time you schedule the closure and the time the closure runs, the enemy is removed from the game. If the closure has a strong reference to the enemy, the enemy isn't actually removed from memory until the closure is scheduled to run, which could have unintended side effects.

To get around this problem, you use *weak references.* A weak reference is a reference that does not keep an object in memory; additionally, if the object that is being referred to is removed (because all owning references to it have gone away), the weak reference will automatically be set to `nil`. For more information on weak references, see *The Swift Programming Language*'s chapter on Automatic Reference Counting (*http://bit.ly/auto_ref_counting*).

1.11. Writing a Method That Calls a Closure

Problem

You want to write a method that, after performing its work, calls a closure to indicate that the work is complete.

For example, you want to tell a character to start moving to a destination, and then run a closure when the character finishes moving.

Solution

To create a method that takes a closure as a parameter, you just do this:

```
func moveToPosition(position : CGPoint, completion: (Void->Void)?) {

    // Do the actual work of moving to the location, which
    // might take place over several frames

    // Call the completion handler, if it exists
    completion?()
}

let destination = CGPoint(x: 5, y: 3)

// Call the function and provide the closure as a parameter
moveToPosition(destination) {
    NSLog("Arrived!")
}
```

Discussion

Methods that take a closure as a parameter are useful for when you're writing code that starts off a long-running process, and you want to run some code at the conclusion of that process but want to keep that conclusion code close to the original call itself.

Before closures were added to the Swift language, the usual technique was to write two methods: one where you started the long-running process, and one that would be called when the process completed. This separates the various parts of the code, which decreases the readability of your code; additionally, passing around variables between these two methods is more complicated (because you need to manually store them in a temporary variable at the start, and retrieve them at the end; with closures, you just use the variables without any additional work).

 If the last parameter that you pass to a function or method is a closure, you can place the closure outside the function call's parentheses. It can look a little cleaner.

1.12. Working with Operation Queues

Problem

You want to put chunks of work in a queue, so that they're run when the operating system has a moment to do them.

Solution

Use an NSOperationQueue to schedule closures to be run in the background without interfering with more time-critical tasks like rendering or accepting user input:

```
// Create a work queue to put tasks on
let concurrentQueue = NSOperationQueue()

// This queue can run 10 operations at the same time, at most
concurrentQueue.maxConcurrentOperationCount = 10

// Add some tasks
concurrentQueue.addOperationWithBlock {
    UploadHighScores()
}

concurrentQueue.addOperationWithBlock {
    SaveGame()
}

concurrentQueue.addOperationWithBlock {
    DownloadMaps()
}
```

Discussion

An operation queue is a tool for running chunks of work. Every application has an operation queue called the *main queue*. The main queue is the queue that normal application tasks (e.g., handling touches, redrawing the screen, etc.) are run on.

 Many tasks can only be run on the main queue, including updating anything run by UIKit. It's also a good idea to only have a single operation queue that's in charge of sending OpenGL instructions.

The main queue is a specific NSOperationQueue, which you can access using the mainQueue method:

```swift
let mainQueue = NSOperationQueue.mainQueue()

mainQueue.addOperationWithBlock { () -> Void in
    ProcessPlayerInput()
}
```

It's often the case that you want to do something in the background (i.e., on another operation queue), and then alert the user when it's finished. However, as we've already mentioned, you can only do UIKit or OpenGL tasks (e.g., displaying an alert box) on the main queue.

To address this, you can put tasks on the main queue from inside a background queue:

```swift
let backgroundQueue = NSOperationQueue()

backgroundQueue.addOperationWithBlock { () -> Void in

    // Do work in the background

    NSOperationQueue.mainQueue().addOperationWithBlock {

        // Once that's done, do work on the main queue

    }
}
```

An operation queue runs as many operations as it can simultaneously. The number of concurrent operations that can be run depends on several conditions, including the number of processor cores available and the different priorities that other operations may have.

By default, an operation queue determines the number of operations that it can run at the same time on its own. However, you can specify a maximum number of concurrent operations by using the maxConcurrentOperationCount property.

1.13. Performing a Task in the Future

Problem

You want to run some code, but you want it to happen a couple of seconds from now.

Solution

Use dispatch_after to schedule a closure of code to run in the future:

```
// Place a bomb, but make it explode in 10 seconds
PlaceBomb()

let delayTime : Float = 10.0

let dispatchTime = dispatch_time(DISPATCH_TIME_NOW,
    Int64(delayTime * Float(NSEC_PER_SEC)))

let queue = dispatch_get_global_queue(DISPATCH_QUEUE_PRIORITY_BACKGROUND, 0)

dispatch_after(dispatchTime, queue) { () -> Void in
    // Time's up. Kaboom.
    ExplodeBomb()
}
```

Discussion

NSOperationQueue is actually a higher-level wrapper around the lower-level features provided by the C-based *Grand Central Dispatch* API. Grand Central Dispatch, or GCD, works mostly with objects called "dispatch queues," which are basically NSOperation Queues. You do work with GCD by putting closures onto a queue, which runs the closures. Just as with NSOperationQueue, there can be many queues operating at the same time, and they can be serial or concurrent queues.

GCD provides a function called dispatch_after that runs a closure on an operation queue at a given time. To use the function, you first need to figure out the time when the closure should be run. GCD doesn't actually work in seconds, or even in nanoseconds, but rather with time units called dispatch_time_t, which Apple's documentation (*http://bit.ly/gcd_ref*) describes as "a somewhat abstract representation of time."

To work with dispatch_time_t, you use the function dispatch_time, which takes two parameters: a base time and an amount of time to be added on top, measured in nanoseconds.

Once you specify a time for the closure to run, you need to get a reference to a GCD dispatch_queue. You can get background queues using dispatch_get_glob al_queue, but you can also get the main queue using dispatch_get_main_queue.

Finally, you instruct GCD to run the closure.

1.14. Making Operations Depend on Each Other

Problem

You want to run some operations, but they need to run only after certain other operations are done.

Solution

To make an operation wait for another operation to complete, store each individual operation in a variable, and then use the addDependency: method to indicate which operations need to complete before a given operation begins:

```
let firstOperation = NSBlockOperation { () -> Void in
    NSLog("First operation")
}

let secondOperation = NSBlockOperation { () -> Void in
    NSLog("Second operation")
}

let thirdOperation = NSBlockOperation { () -> Void in
    NSLog("Third operation")
}

// secondOperation will not run until firstOperation and
// thirdOperation have finished
secondOperation.addDependency(firstOperation)
secondOperation.addDependency(thirdOperation)

NSOperationQueue.mainQueue().addOperations([firstOperation,
    secondOperation, thirdOperation], waitUntilFinished: true)
```

Discussion

You can add an operation to another operation as a *dependency*. This is useful for cases where you want one closure to run only after one or more operations have completed.

To add a dependency to an operation, you use the addDependency: method. Doing this doesn't run the operation, but just links the two together.

Once the operation dependencies have been set up, you can add the operations to the queue in any order that you like; operations will not run until all of their dependencies have finished running.

1.15. Filtering an Array with Closures

Problem

You have an array, and you want to filter it with your own custom logic.

Solution

Use the `filtered` method to create an array that only contains objects that meet certain conditions:

```
let array = ["One", "Two", "Three", "Four", "Five"]

NSLog("Original array: \(array)")

let filteredArray = filter(array) { (element) -> Bool in
    if element.rangeOfString("e") != nil {
        return true
    } else {
        return false
    }
}

NSLog("Filtered array: \(filteredArray)")
```

Discussion

The closure that you provide to the `filtered` method is called multiple times. Each time it's called, it takes an item in the array as its single parameter, and returns `true` if that item should appear in the filtered array.

1.16. Loading New Assets During Gameplay

Problem

You want to load new resources without impacting the performance of the game.

Solution

For each resource that needs loading, run an operation that does the loading into memory, and do it in the background. Then run a subsequent operation when all of the loads have completed.

You can do this by scheduling load operations on a background queue, and also running an operation on the main queue that depends on all of the load operations. This means that all of your images will load in the background, and you'll run code on the main queue when it's complete:

```
let imagesToLoad = ["Image 1.jpg", "Image 2.jpg", "Image 3.jpg"]

let imageLoadingQueue = NSOperationQueue()

// We want the main queue to run at close to regular speed, so mark this
// background queue as running in the background

// (Note: this is actually the default value, but it's good to know about
// the qualityOfService property.)
imageLoadingQueue.qualityOfService = NSQualityOfService.Background

// Allow loading multiple images at once
imageLoadingQueue.maxConcurrentOperationCount = 10

// Create an operation that will run when all images are loaded - you may want
// to tweak this
let loadingComplete = NSBlockOperation { () -> Void in
    NSLog("Loading complete!")
}

// Create an array for storing our loading operations
var loadingOperations : [NSOperation] = []

// Add a load operation for each image

for imageName in imagesToLoad {
    let loadOperation = NSBlockOperation { () -> Void in

        NSLog("Loading \(imageName)")

    }

    loadingOperations.append(loadOperation)

    // Don't run the loading complete operation until
    // this load (and all other loads) are done
    loadingComplete.addDependency(loadOperation)
}

imageLoadingQueue.addOperations(loadingOperations, waitUntilFinished: false)
imageLoadingQueue.addOperation(loadingComplete)
```

Discussion

When you create an NSOperationQueue, you can control its quality of service. By default, operation queues you create have the *background* quality of service, which indicates to the operating system that it's OK for higher-priority operations to take precedence. This is generally what you want for your asset loading routines, because it's important that you keep your application responsive to user input.

Depending on how much memory the rest of your game takes, you can also use this technique to load assets while the user is busy doing something else. For example, once the user reaches the main menu, you could start loading the resources needed for actual gameplay while you wait for the user to tap the New Game button.

1.17. Adding Unit Tests to Your Game

Problem

You want to test different parts of your game's code in isolation, so that you can ensure that each part is working.

Solution

You can write code that tests different parts of your app in isolation using unit tests. By default, all newly created projects come with an empty set of unit tests, in which you can add isolated testing functions.

 If you're working with an existing project, you can create a new set of unit tests by choosing File→New→Target and creating a Cocoa Touch Unit Testing Bundle.

You'll find your unit test files in a group whose name ends with `Tests`. For example, if your Xcode project is called `MyAwesomeGame`, your testing files will be in a group named `MyAwesomeGameTests`, and it will by default come with a file called *MyAwesomeGameTests.swift*.

When you want to add a test, open your test file (the *.swift* file) and add a method whose name begins with `test`:

```
func testDoingSomethingCool() {

    let object = SomeAwesomeObject()

    let succeeded = object.doSomethingCool()

    if succeeded == false {
        XCTFail("Failed to do something cool");
    }
}
```

When you want to run the tests, choose Product→Test or press Command-U. All of the methods in your testing classes that begin with `test` will be run, one after the other.

You can also add additional collections of tests, by creating a new *test suite*. You do this by choosing File→New→File and creating a new Swift test case class. When you create this new class, don't forget to make it belong to your testing target instead of your game target, or you'll get compile errors.

Discussion

Unit testing is the practice of writing small tests that test specific features of your code. In normal use, your code is used in a variety of ways, and if there's a bug, it can be difficult to track down exactly why your code isn't behaving the way you want it to. By using unit tests, you can run multiple tests of your code and check each time to see if the results are what you expect. If a test fails, the parts of your game that use your code in that particular way will also fail.

Each test is actually a method in a *test case*. Test cases are subclasses of `XCTestCase` whose names begin with `test`. The `XCTestCase` objects in a testing bundle make up a *test suite*, which is what's run when you tell Xcode to test your application.

When tests run, Xcode performs the following tasks for each test method, in each test case, in each test suite:

- Call the test case's `setUp` method.
- Call the test method itself, and note if the test succeeds or fails.
- Call the test case's `tearDown` method.
- Show a report showing which tests failed.

As you can see, the test case's `setUp` and `tearDown` methods are called for *each* test method. The idea behind this is that you use `setUp` to create whatever conditions you want to run your test under (e.g., if you're testing the behavior of an AI, you could use `setUp` to load the level in which the AI needs to operate). Conversely, the `tearDown` method is used to dismantle whatever resources are set up in `setUp`. This means that each time a test method is run, it's operating under the same conditions.

The contents of each test method are entirely up to you. Typically, you create objects that you want to test, run methods, and then check to see if the outcomes were what you expected. The actual way that you check the outcomes is through a collection of dedicated *assertion methods*, which flag the test as failing if the condition you pass in evaluates to false. The assertion methods also take a string parameter, which is shown to the user if the test fails.

For example:

```
// Fails if X is not nil
XCTAssertNil(X, "X should be nil")

// Fails if X IS nil
XCTAssertNotNil(X, "X should not be nil")

// Fails if X is not true
XCTAssertTrue(1 == 1, "1 really should be equal to 1")

// Fails if X is not false
XCTAssertFalse(2 != 3, "In this universe, 2 equals 3 apparently")

// Fails if X and Y are not equal (tested by calling X.equals(Y)])
XCTAssertEqualObjects((2), (1+1), "Objects should be equal")

// Fails if X and Y ARE equal (tested by calling X.equals(Y))
XCTAssertNotEqualObjects("One", "1", "Objects should not be equal")

// Fails, regardless of circumstances
XCTFail("Everything is broken")
```

There are several other assertion methods available for you to use that won't fit in this book; for a comprehensive list, see the file *XCTestAssertions.h* (press Command-Shift-O, type **XCTestAssertions**, and then press Enter).

1.18. 2D Grids

Problem

You want to store objects in a two-dimensional grid, as shown in Figure 1-3.

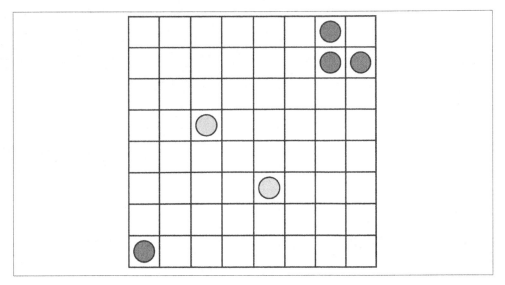

Figure 1-3. The grid: a digital frontier

Solution

Use a `Grid` class, which lets you store and look up objects.

Create an `NSObject` subclass called `Grid`, and put the following code in *Grid.swift*:

```swift
// A GridPoint is a structure that represents a location in the grid.
// This is Hashable, because it will be stored in a dictionary.
struct GridPoint : Hashable {
    var x: Int;
    var y: Int;

    // Returns a unique number that represents this location.
    var hashValue: Int {
        get {
            return x ^ (y << 32)
        }
    }

}


// If an object is Hashable, it's also Equatable. To conform
// to the requirements of the Equatable protocol, you need
// to implement the == operation (which returns true if two objects
// are the same, and false if they aren't)
func ==(first : GridPoint, second : GridPoint) -> Bool {
    return first.x == second.x && first.y == second.y
}
```

```swift
// Next: the grid itself
class Grid: NSObject {

    // The information is stored as a dictionary mapping
    // GridPoints to arrays of NSObjects
    var contents: [GridPoint: [NSObject]] = [:]

    // Returns the list of objects that occupy the given position
    func objectsAtPosition(position: GridPoint) -> [AnyObject] {

        // If we have a collection of objects at this position, return it
        if let objects = self.contents[position] {
            return objects
        } else {
            // Otherwise, create an empty collection
            self.contents[position] = []
            // And return it
            return []
        }

    }

    // Returns a GridPoint describing the position of an object, if it exists
    func positionForObject(objectToFind: NSObject) -> GridPoint? {

        for (position, objects) in contents {

            if find(objects, objectToFind) != nil {
                return position
            }

        }

        return nil

    }

    // Adds or moves the object to a location on the board
    func addObject(object: NSObject, atPosition position: GridPoint) {

        if self.contents[position] == nil {
            self.contents[position] = []
        }

        self.contents[position]?.append(object)

    }

    // Removes a given object from the board
    func removeObjectFromGrid(objectToRemove : NSObject) {

        var newContents = self.contents
```

```
        for (position, objects) in contents {
            newContents[position] = newContents[position]?.filter
            { (item) -> Bool in
                return item != objectToRemove
            }
        }
        self.contents = newContents
    }

    // Removes all objects at a given point from the board
    func removeAllObjectsAtPosition(position: GridPoint) {
        self.contents[position] = []
    }

    // Removes all objects from the board.
    func removeAllObjects() {
        self.contents = [:]
    }

}
```

Discussion

When working with 2D grids, you usually have two main tasks that you want to perform with it:

- You have a game object on the board, and want to work out *where* on the board it is.
- You have a location on the board, and you want to work out *what* object (or objects) are at that point on the board.

This Grid class doesn't require that you limit the board to a predefined size.

This class implements grids by using a dictionary to map locations to arrays of objects. When you add a piece to the board, the class works out which array should contain the object (and creates one if necessary) and inserts it. Later, when you want to get the objects at a given location, it simply looks up the location in the dictionary.

 For small boards (for example, those with a size of about 14-by-14), you can get away with a simple implementation. However, this implementation will slow down when you start having larger boards (especially with many objects on the board). In those cases, you'd be better off creating multiple dictionaries for different areas of the board (for example, one for the upper-left corner, one for the top-right, and so on). This improves the lookup speed of getting objects at a location, though it complicates your implementation.

CHAPTER 2

Views and Menus

When you fire up a game, you don't often get immediately dropped into the action. In most games, there's a lot of "nongame" stuff that your game will need to deal with first, such as showing a settings screen to let your player change volume levels and the like, or a way to let the player pick a chapter in your game to play.

Though it's definitely possible to use your game's graphics systems to show this kind of user interface, there's often no reason to re-create the built-in interface libraries that already exist on iOS.

UIKit is the framework that provides the code that handles controls like buttons, sliders, image views, and checkboxes. Additionally, UIKit has tools that let you divide up your game's screens into separate, easier-to-work-with units called *view controllers*. These view controllers can in turn be linked together using *storyboards,* which let you see how each screen's worth of content connects to the others.

The controls available to you in UIKit can also be customized to suit the look and feel of your game, which means that UIKit can fit right into your game's visual design. In addition to simply tinting the standard iOS controls with a color, you can use images and other material to theme your controls. This means that you don't have to reimplement standard stuff like sliders and buttons, which saves you a lot of time in programming your game.

To work with menus, it's useful to know how to work with storyboards. So, before we get into the meat of this chapter, we'll first talk about how to set up a storyboard with the screens you want.

2.1. Working with Storyboards

Problem

You need a way to organize the different screens of your game, defining how each screen links to other screens and what content is shown on each screen.

Solution

You can use storyboards to organize your screens:

1. Create a new single-view application. Call it whatever you like.

2. Open the *Main.storyboard* file. You're now looking at an empty screen.

3. Open the Utilities pane, if it isn't already open, by clicking the Utilities pane button at the far right of the toolbar.

   At the bottom of the pane, the objects library should be visible, showing a list of objects you can add to the storyboard (see Figure 2-1). If it isn't visible, click the "Show or hide object library" button (the button that looks like a circle containing a square, in the lower-right corner). Alternatively, press Control-Option-Command-3.

4. Scroll down in the objects library until you find the button, as shown in Figure 2-2. You can also type "button" into the search field at the bottom of the objects library.

5. Drag a button into the center of the window.

6. Center the button in the window by holding down the Control key and dragging from the button to the view in which it's contained. A list of constraints will appear; hold Shift, and click Center Horizontally In Container and Center Vertically In Container (see Figure 2-3). Press Enter, and Xcode will add centering contsraints to the button, which will center it on the screen no matter how big or small the screen is.

Figure 2-1. The objects library, at the bottom right of the window

Button - Intercepts touch events and sends an action message to a target object when it's tapped.

Bar Button Item - Represents an item on a UIToolbar or UINavigationItem object.

Fixed Space Bar Button Item - Represents a fixed space item on a UIToolbar object.

button

Figure 2-2. Finding the button in the objects library

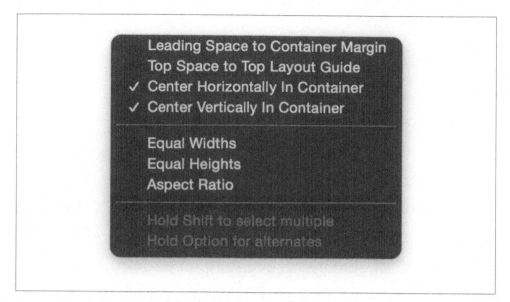

Figure 2-3. Adding the two centering constraints to the button

7. Run the application. A button will appear on the screen, as shown in Figure 2-4. You can tap it, but it won't do anything yet.

    Next, we'll set up the application so that tapping the button displays a new screen.

8. Find the navigation controller in the objects library by typing "navigation" into the search field. Drag one into the storyboard.

    Navigation controllers come with an attached Table View. We don't want this—select it and delete it.

9. The original screen currently has a small arrow attached to it. This indicates that it's the screen that will appear when the application begins. Drag this arrow from where it is right now to the navigation controller.

Figure 2-4. A button shown on the iPhone's screen

10. Hold down the Control key, and drag from the navigation controller to the first screen.

11. A window containing a list of possible "segues" will appear. Choose the "root view controller" option. When you do this, the two view controllers will be linked together, as shown in Figure 2-5.

Figure 2-5. The linked view controllers

When the application starts up, the navigation controller will appear, and inside it, you'll see the screen you designed. Next, we'll make it so that the button shows an additional screen when it's tapped:

1. Drag a new view controller into the storyboard.

   A new, empty screen will appear.

2. Hold down the Control key, and drag from the button to the new screen.

   Another list of possible segues will appear. Choose "show."

3. The two screens will appear linked with a line, as shown in Figure 2-6, which indicates that it's possible to go from one screen to the next.

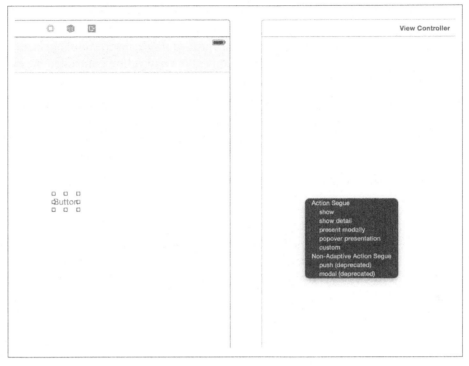

Figure 2-6. Selecting a segue

Because view controllers take up quite a bit of space on the screen, you might want to zoom out to get a bigger picture. Note that when you're zoomed out, you can't work with the views and controls inside a view controller.

4. Run the application.

   When you tap the button, a new screen will appear. A Back button will also appear in the navigation bar at the top of the screen.

When you create a new project, it will come with a storyboard file. *Storyboards* are files that define what *view controllers* are used in your application, and how those view controllers are linked together via *segues*.

A view controller is an object that contains the logic that controls an individual screen. Typically, you have one view controller per screen. For each type of screen that the user will see, you create a subclass of the `UIViewController` class, and you instruct the storyboard to use that subclass for specific screens. (For information on how to do this, see Recipe 2.2.)

In a storyboard, screens can be linked together using segues. A segue is generally a transition from one screen to the next. For example, a *show* segue tells the system that, when the segue is activated, the current view's *presentation context* should present a new view controller. Because the presentation context is a navigation controller, the navigation controller shows the new screen using a push animation.

Segues are also used to indicate relationships between different view controllers. For example, navigation controllers need to know which screen they should display when they're first shown; you do this by creating a *root view controller* segue.

2.2. Creating View Controllers

Problem

You have a project that has a storyboard, and you want to keep all of the logic for your screens in separate, easily maintainable objects. For example, you want to keep your main menu code separate from the high scores screen.

Solution

Follow these steps to create a new view controller:

1. Create a subclass of `UIViewController`.

   Choose New→File from the File menu. Select the Cocoa Touch category, and choose to make a Cocoa Touch class, as shown in Figure 2-7.

2. Create the new `UIViewController` subclass.

   Name the class `MainMenuViewController`, and set "Subclass of" to `UIView Controller`.

   Make sure that "Also create XIB file" is unchecked, as shown in Figure 2-8.

3. Create the file.

   Xcode will ask you where to put the newly created file. Choose somewhere that suits your particular purpose.

   Once this is done, a new file will appear in the Project Navigator: *MainMenuView-Controller.swift*. To actually use this new class, you need to indicate to the storyboard that it should be used on one of the screens. In this example, there's only one screen, so we'll make it use the newly created `MainMenuViewController` class.

Figure 2-7. Creating a new Cocoa Touch subclass

Figure 2-8. Setting up the new file

4. Open the storyboard.

   Find *Main.storyboard* in the Project Navigator, and click it.

5. Open the outline view.

The outline view lists all of the parts making up your user interface. You can open it either by choosing Show Document Outline from the Editor menu, or by clicking the Show Outline button at the bottom left of the Interface Builder.

6. Select the view controller.

You'll find it at the top of the outline view.

 If you just click the large blank white area in the storyboard, what you're actually selecting is just the *view* that the view controller manages, instead of the *view controller* itself. To select the view controller, click the little yellow circle icon, which you can find above the view or in the outline view.

7. Open the Identity Inspector.

You can do this by selecting the Identity Inspector at the top of the Utilities pane. It's the third icon from the left.

8. Change the class of the selected view controller to `MainMenuViewController`.

At the top of the Identity Inspector, you'll find the class of the currently selected view controller. Change it to `MainMenuViewController`, as shown in Figure 2-9. Doing this means that the `MainMenuViewController` class will be the one used for this particular screen.

Now that this is done, we'll add a text field to the screen and make the view controller class able to access its contents (on its own, a text field can't communicate with the view controller—you need an outlet for that). We'll also add a button to the screen, and make some code run when the user taps it.

9. Add a text field.

The objects library should be at the bottom of the Utilities pane, on the righthand side of the Xcode window. If it isn't visible, choose View→Utilities→Objects Library, or press Command-Control-Option-3.

Scroll down until you find the Text Field control. Alternatively, type "text field" into the search bar at the bottom of the objects library (as shown in Figure 2-10).

Drag and drop a text field into the top-left of the screen.

On its own, a text field can't communicate with the view controller—you need an *outlet* for that.

Figure 2-9. Changing the class of the view controller

Figure 2-10. Adding a text field to the screen

10. Open the view controller's code in the Assistant editor.

Open the Assistant editor by clicking the Assistant button at the top right of the Xcode window or by choosing View→Assistant Editor→Show Assistant Editor.

Once you've opened it, *MainMenuViewController.swift* should be visible in the editor. If it isn't, choose Automatic→*MainMenuViewController.swift* from the jump bar at the top of the Assistant editor (Figure 2-11).

Figure 2-11. Selecting MainMenuViewController.h in the Assistant editor

11. Add the outlet for the text field.

    Hold down the Control key, and drag from the text field into the `MainMenuView Controller` class. When you finish dragging, a dialog box will appear (see Figure 2-12) asking you what to name the variable.

    Type `textField`, and click the Connect button.

Figure 2-12. Creating an outlet for the text field

Finally, we'll add a button, which will run code when the button is tapped.

12. Add a button to the screen.

    Follow the same instructions for adding a text field, but this time, add a button.

13. Add the action.

    Hold down the Control key, and drag from the button into the `MainMenuViewCon troller` class.

Another dialog will appear, as shown in Figure 2-13, asking you what to name the action. Name it `buttonPressed`, and click Connect. A new method will be added to `MainMenuViewController`.

Figure 2-13. Creating an action

14. Add some code to the newly created method.

    We'll use the following code:

```
let alert = UIAlertController(title: "Button tapped",
    message: "The button was tapped",
    preferredStyle: UIAlertControllerStyle.Alert)

alert.addAction(UIAlertAction(title: "OK",
    style: UIAlertActionStyle.Default,
    handler: nil))

self.presentViewController(alert,
    animated: true, completion: nil)
```

Discussion

In almost every single case, different screens perform different tasks. A "main menu" screen, for example, has the task of showing the game's logo, and probably a couple of buttons to send the player off to a new game, to continue an existing game, to view the high scores screen, and so on. Each one of these screens, in turn, has its own functionality.

The easiest way to create an app that contains multiple screens is via a storyboard. However, a storyboard won't let you define the behavior of the screens—that's the code's job. So, how do you tell the application what code should be run for different screens?

Every view controller that's managed by a storyboard is an instance of the `UIView Controller` class. `UIViewControllers` know how to be presented to the user, how to show whatever views have been placed inside them in the Interface Builder, and how to do a few other things, like managing their life cycle (i.e., they know when they're about to appear on the screen, when they're about to go away, and when other important events are about to occur, like the device running low on memory).

However, `UIViewControllers` don't have any knowledge of what their role is—they're designed to be empty templates, and it's your job to create subclasses that perform the work of being a main menu, or of being a high scores screen, and so on.

When you subclass `UIViewController`, you override some important methods:

- `viewDidLoad` is called when the view has completed loading and all of the controls are present.

- `viewWillAppear` is called when the view is about to appear on the screen, but is not yet visible.

- `viewDidAppear` is called when the view has finished appearing on the screen and is now visible.

- `viewWillDisappear` is called when the view is about to disappear from the screen, but is currently still visible.

- `viewDidDisappear` is called when the view is no longer visible.

- `applicationReceivedMemoryWarning` is called when the application has received a memory warning and will be force-quit by iOS if memory is not freed up. Your `UIViewController` subclass should free any objects that can be re-created when needed.

Additionally, your `UIViewController` is able to respond to events that come from the controls it's showing, and to manipulate those controls and change what they're doing.

This is done through outlets and actions. An *outlet* is a property on the `UIViewController` that is connected to a view; once `viewDidLoad` has been called, each outlet property has been connected to a view object. You can then access these properties as normal.

To define an outlet, you create a property that uses the special keyword `IBOutlet`, like so:

```
@IBOutlet weak var textField: UITextField!
```

Actions are methods that are called as a result of the user doing something with a control on the screen. For example, if you want to know when a button has been tapped, you create an action method and connect the button to that method. You create similar action methods for events such as the text in a text field changing, or a slider changing position.

Action methods are defined in the `@interface` of a class, like this:

```
@IBAction func buttonPressed(sender: AnyObject) {
```

Note that IBAction isn't really a return type—it's actually another name for void. However, Xcode uses the IBAction keyword to identify methods that can be connected to views in the Interface Builder.

In the preceding example, the action method takes a single parameter: an id (i.e., an object of any type) called sender. This object will be the object that triggered the action: the button that was tapped, the text field that was edited, and so on.

If you don't care about the sender of the action, you can just define the method with no parameters, like so:

```
@IBAction func actionWithNoParameters() {

}
```

2.3. Using Segues to Move Between Screens

Problem

You want to use segues to transition between different screens.

Solution

We'll step through the creation of two view controllers, and show how to create and use segues to move between them:

1. Create a new single-view project.
2. Open *Main.storyboard*.
3. Add a new view controller.

   You can do this by searching for "view controller" in the objects library.
4. Add a button to the first view controller.

   Label it "Automatic Segue."
5. Add a segue from the button to the second view controller.

   Hold down the Control key, and drag from the button to the second view controller. A menu will appear when you finish dragging, which shows the possible types of segues you can use. Choose "present modally."
6. Run the application.

   When you tap the button, the second (empty) view controller will appear.

Currently, there's no way to return to the first one. We'll now address this:

1. Open *ViewController.swift*.

This is the class that powers the first screen.

2. Add an exit method.

   Add the following method to ViewController's code:

   ```
   @IBAction func closePopup(segue: UIStoryboardSegue) {
       NSLog("Second view controller was closed!")
   }
   ```

3. Add an exit button to the second view controller.

   Add a button to the second view controller, and label it "Exit."

   Then, hold down the Control key, and drag from the button to the Exit icon underneath the screen. It looks like a little orange box.

   A menu will appear, listing the possible actions that can be run. Choose "closePopup:."

4. Run the application.

   Open the pop-up screen, and then tap the Exit button. The screen will disappear, and the console will show the "Second view controller was closed!" text.

Finally, we'll demonstrate how to manually trigger a segue from code. To do this, we'll first need a named segue in order to trigger it. One already exists—you created it when you linked the button to the second view controller:

1. Give the segue an identifier.

   In order to be triggered, a segue must have a name. Click the segue you created when you linked the button to the second view controller (i.e., the line connecting the first view controller to the second).

   In the Attributes inspector (choose View→Utilities→Show Attributes Inspector, or press Command-Option-4), set the identifier of the segue to "ShowPopup," as shown in Figure 2-14.

Figure 2-14. Naming the segue

 Make sure you use the same capitalization as we've used here. "ShowPopup" isn't the same as "showpopup" or even "ShowPopUp."

2. Add a button that manually triggers the segue.

   Add a new button to the first view controller. Label it "Manual Segue."

   Open *ViewController.swift* in the Assistant editor.

   Hold down the Control key, and drag from the new button into ViewController's section. Create a new method called showPopup—note the capitalization.

   Add the following code to this new method:

   ```
   @IBAction func showPopup(sender: AnyObject) {
       self.performSegueWithIdentifier("ShowPopup",
           sender: self)
   }
   ```

3. Run the application.

   Now, tapping the Manual Segue button shows the second screen.

Discussion

A segue is an object that describes a transition from one view controller to the next.

When you run a segue, the segue takes care of presenting the new view controller for you. For example, if you create a push segue, the segue will handle creating the view controller and pushing the new view controller onto the navigation controller's stack.

A segue performs its work of transitioning between view controllers when it's *triggered*. There are two ways you can trigger a segue: you can connect it to a button in the Interface Builder, or you can trigger it from code.

When you hold down the Control key and drag from a button to a different screen, you create a segue. This new segue is set up to be triggered when the button is tapped.

Triggering a segue from code is easy. First, you need to give the segue an *identifier*, which is a string that uniquely identifies the segue. In our example, we set the identifier of the segue to "ShowPopup."

Once that's done, you use the `performSegueWithIdentifier(_sender:)` method. This method takes two parameters—the name of the segue you want to trigger, and the object that was responsible for triggering it.

You can trigger any segue from code, as long as it has an identifier. You don't need to create multiple segues from one view controller to the next.

When a view controller is about to segue to another, the view controller that's about to disappear is sent the `prepareForSegue(_, sender:)` message. When you want to know about the next screen that's about to be shown to the user, you implement this method, like so:

```
override func prepareForSegue(segue: UIStoryboardSegue, sender: AnyObject?) {
    NSLog("About to run \(segue.identifier)")
}
```

The method has two parameters: the segue that's about to run, and the object that triggered the segue. The segue object itself contains two particularly useful properties: the `identifier` of the segue, which allows you to differentiate between segues; and the `destinationViewController`, which is the view controller that's about to be displayed by the segue. This gives you an opportunity to send information to the screen that's about to appear.

Finally, *exit segues* are segues that allow you to return to a previously viewed view controller. You don't create these segues yourself; rather, you define an action method in the view controller that you'd like to return *to*, and then connect a control to the "exit" segue in the Interface Builder.

2.4. Using Constraints to Lay Out Views

Problem

You have a screen with another view (such as a button) inside it. You want the views to stay in the correct places when the screen rotates.

Solution

You use *constraints* to position views, as illustrated here:

1. Drag the view into the place you'd like to put it.

2. Add the constraint.

   Select the view, and open the Pin menu. This is the second button in the second group of buttons at the bottom right of the Interface Builder canvas (Figure 2-15).

Figure 2-15. The Constraints menu buttons (the Pin button is the second one from the left)

3. Apply the values you want to use for the new constraints.

   Let's assume that you want the view to always be 20 pixels from the top edge of the screen and 20 pixels from the left edge of the screen, as shown in Figure 2-16.

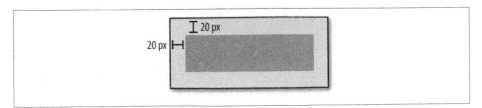

Figure 2-16. The view should always be 20 pixels from the top and left edges

Type **20** into the top field, and **20** into the left field.

Set "Update Frames" to "Items of New Constraints." This will reposition the view when the constraints are added (see Figure 2-17).

Figure 2-17. Creating the constraints

4. Add the constraints.

The button at the bottom of the menu should now read "Add 2 Constraints." Click it, and the button will be locked to the upper-right corner.

Discussion

To control the positioning and sizing of views, you use constraints. Constraints are rules that are imposed on views, along the lines of "Keep the top edge 10 pixels beneath the top edge of the container," or "Always be half the width of the screen." Without constraints, views don't change position when the size and shape of their superview changes shape (such as when the screen rotates).

Constraints can modify both the position and the size of a view, and will change these in order to make the view fit the rules.

 Another way that you can add constraints to views is to Control-drag from the view you want to constrain to another view. A pop-up menu will appear that lets you select the specific type of constraint you want to add. The specific types available for selection depend on the position of the two views; for example, if you have two buttons side by side, if you Control-drag from one to the other, you will be offered the option to constrain the horizontal space between the two.

2.5. Adding Images to Your Project

Problem

You want to add images to your game's project in Xcode, so that they can be used in your menu interface.

Solution

When you create a new project in Xcode, an *asset catalog* is created, which contains your images. Your code can then get images from the catalog, or you can use them in your interface.

If your project doesn't have one, or if you want a new one, choose File→New→File, choose Resource, and choose Asset Catalog.

Select the asset catalog in the Project Navigator, and then drag and drop your image into the catalog.

You can rename individual images by double-clicking the name of the image in the left pane of the asset catalog.

The easiest way to display an image is through a `UIImageView`. To add an image view, search for "image view" in the objects library, and add one to your screen. Then, select the new image view, open the Attributes inspector, and change the Image property to the name of the image you added (see Figure 2-18).

Figure 2-18. Setting the image for a UIImageView

You can also use images in your code. For example, if you've added an image called "Spaceship" to an asset catalog, you can use it in your code as follows:

```
let image = UIImage(named: "Spaceship")
```

Once you have this image, you can display it in a UIImageView, display it as a sprite, or load it as a texture.

Discussion

It's often the case that you'll need to use different versions of an image under different circumstances. The most common example of this is when working with devices that have a retina display, because such devices have a screen resolution that's double the density of nonretina-display devices.

In these cases, you need to provide two different copies of each image you want to use: one at regular size, and one at double the size.

Fortunately, asset catalogs make this rather straightforward. When you add an image to the catalog, you can add alternative representations of the same image, making available both 1x (nonretina) and 2x (retina) versions of the image. You can also add specific versions of an image for the iPhone and iPad; when you get the image by name, the correct version of the image is returned to you, which saves you having to write code that checks to see which platform your game is running on.

2.6. Slicing Images for Use in Buttons

Problem

You want to customize a button with images. Additionally, you want the image to not get distorted when the button changes size.

Solution

To customize your button, perform the following steps:

1. Add the image you want to use to an asset catalog.

   See Recipe 2.5 to learn how to do this.

2. Select the newly added image, and click Show Slicing.

   The button is at the bottom right of the asset catalog's view.

3. Click Start Slicing.

   Choose one of the slicing options. You can slice the image horizontally, vertically, or both horizontally and vertically, as shown in Figure 2-19.

4. Open your storyboard and select the button you want to theme.

5. Open the Attributes inspector and set the background.

   Select the name of the image that you added to the Xcode catalog. The button will change to use the new background image. You can also resize the image, and the background image will scale appropriately.

Discussion

One of the most effective ways to customize the look and feel of your game's user interface is to use custom images for buttons and other controls, which you can do by setting the "Background" property of your buttons.

Spaceship - 1x

Figure 2-19. The available slicing options are, from left to right, horizontal, both horizontal and vertical, and vertical

However, if you want to use background images, you need to take into account the size of the controls you're theming: if you create an image that's 200 pixels wide and try to use it on a button that's only 150 pixels wide, your image will be squashed. Do the reverse, and you'll end up with a repeating background, which may look worse.

To solve this issue, you can *slice* your images. Slicing divides your image into multiple regions, of which only some are allowed to squash and stretch or repeat.

In this solution, we looked at customizing a button; however, the same principles apply to other controls as well.

2.7. Using UI Dynamics to Make Animated Views

Problem

You want to make the views on your screen move around the screen realistically.

Solution

You can add physical behaviors to any view inside a view controller, using `UIDynamicAnimator`. In these examples, we'll assume that you've got a view called `ani matedView`. It can be of any type—button, image, or anything else you like.

First, create a `UIDynamicAnimator` object in your view controller. Add this property to your view controller's class:

```
var animator : UIDynamicAnimator?
```

Then, in your view controller's `viewDidLoad` method, add the following code:

```
self.animator = UIDynamicAnimator(referenceView: self.view)
```

We'll now talk about how you can add different kinds of physical behaviors to your views. Because these behaviors interact with each other, we'll go through each one and, in each case, assume that the previous behaviors have been added.

Adding gravity to views

Add the following code to your `viewDidLoad` method:

```
let gravity = UIGravityBehavior(items: [self.animatedView])

self.animator?.addBehavior(gravity)
```

Run the application. The view will move down the screen (and eventually fall off!).

Adding collision

Add the following code to your `viewDidLoad` method:

```
let collision = UICollisionBehavior(items: [self.animatedView])

collision.translatesReferenceBoundsIntoBoundary = true

self.animator?.addBehavior(collision)
```

Run the application. The button will fall to the bottom of the screen.

By default, the collision boundaries will be the same as the boundaries of the container view. This is what's set when `translatesRefer` `enceBoundsIntoBoundary` is changed to `true`. If you would prefer to create boundaries that are inset from the container view, use `set` `TranslatesReferenceBoundsIntoBoundaryWithInsets` instead:

```
collision.setTranslatesReferenceBoundsIntoBoundaryWithInsets(
    UIEdgeInsets(top: 10, left: 10, bottom: 10, right: 10))
```

Adding attachment

Add the following code to your `viewDidLoad` method:

```
// Anchor = top of the screen, centered
let anchor = CGPoint(x: self.view.bounds.width / 2, y: 0)

let attachment = UIAttachmentBehavior(item: self.animatedView,
    attachedToAnchor: anchor)

self.animator?.addBehavior(attachment)
```

Run the application. The button will swing down and hit the side of the screen.

When you create a `UIAttachmentBehavior`, you can attach your views to specific points, or to other views. If you want to attach your view to a point, you should use `UIAttach` `mentBehavior(item:, attachedToAnchor:)`, as shown in the previous example. If you want to attach a view to another view, you use `UIAttachmentBehavior(item:, atta` `chedToItem:)`, and provide another view as the second parameter.

Discussion

UIKit has a physics engine in it, which you can use to create a complex set of physically realistic behaviors.

The dynamic animation system is designed for user interfaces, rather than games—if you're interested in using physics simulation for games, use Sprite Kit (see Chapter 6).

Keep in mind that controls that move around too much may end up being disorienting for users, who are used to buttons generally remaining in one place. Additionally, if you're displaying your UI content on top of your game, you may end up with performance problems if you have lots of controls that use the dynamic animation system.

2.8. Moving an Image with Core Animation

Problem

You want an image to move around the screen, and smoothly change its position over time.

Solution

To animate your image, follow these steps:

1. Create a new single-view application for iPhone, named `ImageAnimation`.

2. Add an image of a ball to the project (one has been provided as part of the sample code):

   - Open *Main.storyboard*.

   - Add an image view to the screen. Set it to display the image you dragged in.

   - Connect the image view to an outlet called `ball` in your view controller's code (see Recipe 2.2).

   - Open *ViewController.swift*.

   - Add the following method to the code:

     ```
     UIView.animateWithDuration(2.0, animations: { () -> Void in
         self.ball.center = CGPoint(x: 0, y: 0)
     })
     ```

3. Run the application.

   When the app starts up, the ball will slowly move up to the upper-left corner of the screen.

Discussion

This application instructs a `UIImageView` to change its position over the course of two seconds.

Image views, being completely passive displays of images, have no means (nor any reason) to move around on their own, which means that something else needs to do it for them. That "something else" is the view controller, which is responsible for managing each view that's displayed on the screen.

For the view controller to be able to tell the image view to move, it first needs an outlet to that image view. An outlet is a variable in an object that connects to a view. When you hold the Control key and drag and drop from the image view into the code, Xcode recognizes that you want to add a connection and displays the "add connection" dialog.

When the application launches, the first thing that happens is that all connections that were created in the Interface Builder are set up. This means that all of your code is able to refer to properties like `self.ball` without having to actually do any of the work involved in setting them up.

Once the connection is established, the real work of moving the ball around on the screen is done in the viewWillAppear: method. This method is called, as you can probably tell from the name, when the view (i.e., the screen) is about to appear to the user. This snippet of code is where the actual work is done:

```
UIView.animateWithDuration(2.0, animations: { () -> Void in
    self.ball.center = CGPoint(x: 0, y: 0)
})
```

The animateWithDuration:animations method takes two parameters: the duration of the animation, and a block that performs the changes that should be seen during the animation.

In this case, the animation being run takes two seconds to complete, and a single change is made: the center property of whatever view self.ball refers to is changed to the point (0,0). Additional changes can be included as well. For example, try adding the following line of code between the two curly braces ({}):

```
self.ball.alpha = 0.0
```

This change causes the view's alpha setting (its opacity) to change from whatever value it currently is to zero, which renders it fully transparent. Because this change is run at the same time as the change to the view's position, it will fade out while moving.

2.9. Rotating an Image

Problem

You want to rotate an image on the screen.

Solution

To rotate an image view, use the transform property:

```
self.transformedView.transform = CGAffineTransformMakeRotation(CGFloat(M_PI_2))
```

In this example, self.rotatedView is a UIImageView. Any view can be rotated, though, not just image views.

Discussion

The transform property allows you to modify a view's presentation without affecting its contents. This allows you to rotate, shift, squash, and stretch a view however you want.

The value of transform is a CGAffineTransform, which is a 4-by-4 matrix of numbers. This matrix is multiplied against the four vertices that define the four corners of the view. The default transform is the identity transform, `CGAffineTransformIdentity`, which makes no changes to the presentation of the view.

To create a transform matrix that rotates a view, you use the `CGAffineTransform` `MakeRotation` method. This method takes a single parameter: the amount to rotate by, measured in radians. There are 2π radians in a circle; therefore, a rotation of one-quarter of a circle is $2\pi/4 = \pi/2$. This value is available via the built-in shorthand `M_PI_2`.

In our example, we have created a transform matrix using the `CGAffineTransform` `MakeRotation` function. Other functions you can use include:

`CGAffineTransformMakeTranslation`
  Adjusts the position of the view.

`CGAffineTransformMakeScale`
  Scales the view on the horizontal or vertical axis.

Once you've created a transform matrix, you can modify it by scaling, translating (moving), or rotating it. You can do this using the `CGAffineTransformScale`, `CGAffine` `TransformTranslate`, and `CGAffineTransformRotate` functions, which each take an existing transform and modify it. Once you're done making changes to the transform, you can then apply it.

For example:

```
var transform = CGAffineTransformIdentity  ❶
transform = CGAffineTransformTranslate(transform, 50, 0)  ❷
transform = CGAffineTransformRotate(transform, CGFloat(M_PI_2))  ❸
transform = CGAffineTransformScale(transform, 0.5, 2)  ❹

self.transformedView.transform = transform  ❺
```

This code does the following:

❶ Start with the default identity transform.

❷ Translate the transform 50 pixels to the right.

❸ Rotate the transform one quarter-circle clockwise.

❹ Scale the transform by 50% on the horizontal axis and 200% on the vertical axis.

❺ Apply the transform to a view.

The `transform` property of a view can be animated, just like its opacity and position. This lets you create animations where views rotate or squash and stretch.

2.10. Animating a Popping Effect on a View

Problem

You want the main menu of your game to feature buttons that appear with a visually appealing "pop" animation, which draws the player's eye (the object starts small, expands to a large size, and then shrinks back down to its normal size, as shown in Figure 2-20).

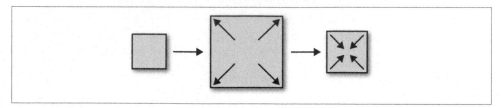

Figure 2-20. A "pop" animation

Solution

The solution to this problem makes use of features available in the Quartz Core framework. To use this framework, add this line near the top of your code:

```
import QuartzCore
```

Finally, add the following code at the point where you want the popping animation to happen:

```
let keyframeAnimation = CAKeyframeAnimation(keyPath: "transform.scale")

keyframeAnimation.keyTimes = [0.0, 0.7, 1.0]

keyframeAnimation.values = [0.0, 1.2, 1.0]

keyframeAnimation.duration = 0.4

keyframeAnimation.timingFunction =
    CAMediaTimingFunction(name: kCAMediaTimingFunctionEaseOut)

self.poppingView.layer.addAnimation(keyframeAnimation,
    forKey: "pop")
```

 In this example, `self.poppingView` is a `UIView`, but any view can be animated in this way.

Discussion

Every single view on the screen can be animated using Core Animation. These animations can be very simple, such as moving an item from one location to another, or they can be more complex, such as a multiple-stage "pop" animation.

You can achieve this behavior using a CAKeyframeAnimation. CAKeyframeAnimations allow you to change a visual property of any view over time, and through multiple stages. You do this by creating a CAKeyframeAnimation, providing it with the values that the property should animate through, and providing corresponding timing information for each value. Finally, you give the animation object to the view's CALayer, and the view will perform the animation.

Every animation object must have a "key path" that indicates what value should change when the animation runs. The key path used for this animation is transform.scale, which indicates that the animation should be modifying the scale of the view.

The values property is an array that contains the values that the animation should move through. In this animation, there are three values: 0, 1.2, and 1.0. These will be used as the scale values: the animation will start with a scale of zero (i.e., scaled down to nothing), then expand to 1.2 times the normal size, and then shrink back down to the normal size.

The keyTimes property is another array that must contain the same number of numbers as there are values in the values array. Each number in the keyTimes array indicates at which point the corresponding value in the values array will be reached. Each key time is given as a value from 0 to 1, with 0 being the start of the animation and 1 being the end.

In this case, the second value (1.2) will be reached at 70% of the way through the animation, because its corresponding key time is 0.7. This is done to make the first phase of the animation, in which the button expands from nothing, take a good amount of time, which will look more natural.

The duration of the animation is set to 0.4 seconds, and the timing function is set to "ease out." This means that the "speed" of the animation will slow down toward the end. Again, this makes the animation feel more organic and less mechanical.

Lastly, the animation is given to the view's layer using the addAnimation(_, forKey:) method. The "key" in this method is any string you want—it's an identifier to let you access the animation at a later time.

2.11. Theming UI Elements with UIAppearance

Problem

You want to change the color of views, or use background images to customize their look and feel.

Solution

You can set the color of a view by changing its tint color or by giving it a background image:

```
self.button.tintColor = UIColor.redColor()

let image = UIImage(named: "Ball")
self.button.setBackgroundImage(image,
    forState: UIControlState.Normal)
```

You can also set the tint color for most views in the Attributes inspector.

Discussion

Most (though not all) controls can be themed. There are two main ways you can change a control's appearance:

- Set a *tint color*, which sets the overall color of the control.
- Set a *background image*, which sets a background image.

To set a tint color for a specific control, you call one of the `setTintColor:` methods. Some controls have a single tint color, which you set with `setTintColor:`, while other controls can have multiple tint colors, which you set independently. For example, to tint a `UIProgressView`, do the following:

```
self.progressView.progressTintColor = UIColor.orangeColor()
```

You can also set the tint color for *all* controls of a given type, by accessing its *appearance proxy*. The appearance proxy is an object that you get from a class that has all of the same appearance-controlling properties—things like tint colors and background images—but applies those properties to *all* instances of that class. For example, to set *all* progress views to use orange as their progress tint color:

```
UIProgressView.appearance().progressTintColor = UIColor.purpleColor()
```

Background images for navigation bars work similarly:

```
UINavigationBar.appearance()
    .setBackgroundImage(image,
        forBarMetrics: UIBarMetrics.Default)
```

2.12. Rotating a UIView in 3D

Problem

You want to make a view rotate in 3D, and have a perspective effect as it does so (i.e., as parts of the view move away from the user, they get smaller, and as they get closer, they get larger).

Solution

To implement this functionality, you'll need to import the QuartzCore module at the top of your source code, just as in Recipe 2.10.

Then, when you want the animation to begin, you do this:

```
let animation = CABasicAnimation(keyPath: "transform.rotation.y")

animation.fromValue = 0.0
animation.toValue = M_PI * 2.0

animation.repeatCount = Float.infinity
animation.duration = 2.0

self.rotatingView.layer.addAnimation(animation, forKey: "spin")

var transform = CATransform3DIdentity
transform.m34 = 1.0 / 500.0
self.rotatingView.layer.transform = transform
```

To stop the animation, you do this:

```
self.rotatingView.layer
    .removeAnimationForKey("spin")
```

 In this example code, self.rotatingView is a UIView that's on the screen. This technique can be applied to any view, though—buttons, image views, and so on.

Discussion

CABasicAnimation allows you to animate a property of a view from one value to another. In the case of rotating a view, the property that we want to animate is its rotation, and the values we want to animate from and to are angles.

When you use CABasicAnimation(keyPath:) to create the animation, you specify the property you want to animate. In this case, the one we want is the rotation around the y-axis:

```
let animation = CABasicAnimation(keyPath: "transform.rotation.y")
```

The animation is then configured. In this example, we made the rotation start from zero, and proceed through to a full circle. In Core Animation, angles are measured in radians, and there are 2π radians in a full circle. So, the `fromValue` and `toValue` are set thusly:

```
animation.fromValue = 0.0
animation.toValue = M_PI * 2.0
```

Next, the animation is told that it should repeat an infinite number of times, and that the full rotation should take two seconds:

```
animation.repeatCount = Float.infinity
animation.duration = 2.0
```

You start the animation by adding it to the view's layer, using the `addAnimation(_, forKey:)` method. This method takes two parameters, the animation object that you want to use and a key (or name) to use to refer to the animation:

```
self.rotatingView.layer.addAnimation(animation, forKey: "spin")
```

Don't be confused by the similarity between the "key" that you use when you add the animation and the "key path" you use when creating the animation. The former is just a name you give the animation, and can be anything; the key path describes exactly what the animation modifies.

The last step is to give the rotating view a little perspective. If you run the code while omitting the last few lines, you'll end up with a view that appears to horizontally squash and stretch. What you want is for the edge that's approaching the user's eye to appear to get bigger, while the edge that's moving away from the user's eye appears to get smaller.

You do this by modifying the view's 3D transform. By default, all views have a transform matrix applied to them that makes them all lie flat over each other. When you want something to have perspective, though, this doesn't apply, and you need to override it:

```
var transform = CATransform3DIdentity
transform.m34 = 1.0 / 500.0
self.rotatingView.layer.transform = transform
```

The key to this part of the code is the second line: the one where the `m34` field of the transform is updated. This part of the transform controls the sharpness of the perspective. (It's basically how much the z coordinate gets scaled toward or away from the vanishing point as it moves closer to or farther from the "camera.")

2.13. Overlaying Menus on Top of Game Content

Problem

You want to overlay controls and views on top of your existing game content. For example, you want to overlay a pause menu, or put UIButtons on top of sprites. Additionally, you want to keep the interface for the pause menu in a separate file.

Solution

You can overlay any UIView you like on top of any other UIView. Additionally, both OpenGL views and Sprite Kit views are actually UIViews, which means anything can be overlaid on them.

To create a view that you can show, you can use *nibs*. A nib is like a storyboard, but only contains a single view.

To make a nib, choose File→New→File from the menu, choose User Interface, and choose View. Save the new file wherever you like. You can then edit the file and design your interface.

To instantiate the nib and use the interface you've designed, you first create a UINib object by loading it from disk, and then ask the nib to instantiate itself:

```
// Load the nib
let nib = UINib(nibName: "PauseMenu", bundle: nil)

// Instantiate a copy of the objects stored in the nib
let loadedObjects = nib.instantiateWithOwner(self,
    options: nil)
```

The instantiateWithOwner(_, options:) method returns an array that contains the objects that you've designed. If you've followed these instructions and created a nib with a single view, this array will contain a single object—the UIView object that you designed. Once you have this, you can add this view to your view controller using the addSubview: method:

```
// Try to get the first object, as a UIView
if let pauseMenuView = loadedObjects[0] as? UIView {
    // Add it to the screen and center it
    self.view.addSubview(pauseMenuView)
    pauseMenuView.center = self.view.center
}
```

Discussion

Keep in mind that if you overlay a view on top of Sprite Kit or OpenGL, you'll see a performance decrease. This is because the Core Animation system, which is responsible for compositing views together, has to do extra work to combine UIKit views with raw OpenGL.

That's not to say that you shouldn't ever do it, but be mindful of the possible performance penalty.

2.14. Designing Effective Game Menus

Problem

You want to build a game that uses menus effectively.

Solution

You should make your menus as simple and easy to navigate as possible. There's nothing worse than an iOS game that has an overly complicated menu structure, or tries to present too many options to the player. Menus should be simple and have the minimum amount of options required to make your game work.

Including only the minimum required set of options will make players feel more confident and in control of the game—ideally they'll be able to play through your entire game without ever using any menus beyond those necessary to start and end the game. And those menus should be super simple too!

Discussion

It's important to keep your game menus as simple as possible. When your game is the app running on a device, a simple and clear menu will ensure that the user is more likely to be playing the game than trying to configure it. You're building a game, not an elaborate set of menus!

CHAPTER 3

Input

Without a way to collect input from the user, your game is nothing but a pretty graphics demo. In this chapter, we'll look at common tasks that games often need to perform in order to get input from their players. The only way that a game can know about what the user wants to do is via the input that it collects, and the main way that the player provides that input is through the device's built-in touchscreen.

Behind the scenes, a touchscreen is a very complex piece of technology. However, the information that it provides to your game is rather simple: you get told when a touch lands on the screen, when a touch moves, and when a touch is lifted from the screen. This might not sound like much—everyone knows you can detect taps, for example— but the touch system built into iOS is able to use this information to determine when the user is dragging, pinching, rotating, and flicking, all of which can be used to interpret the user's will.

In addition to the touch system, iOS devices have a number of built in sensors that detect the current state of the hardware. These include an accelerometer (which detects force and movement), a gyroscope (which detects rotation), a magnetometer (which detects magnetic fields), and a receiver for the Global Positioning System, or GPS (which can calculate where on the planet the device is).

You can combine all of this information to learn a great deal about what the user's doing with the device, which can be used as input to your game. For example, it's possible to determine the user's speed by observing the distance traveled over time, which can give you an idea of whether the player is in a vehicle—which you can then use as part of your game's input.

3.1. Detecting When a View Is Touched

Problem

You want to know when the user touches a view.

Solution

You can override certain UIView methods that get called when a touch begins, moves, ends, and is cancelled.

Put this code in your view controller, or in your UIView subclasses:

```
override func touchesBegan(touches: Set<NSObject>,
    withEvent event: UIEvent) {

    for touch in touches as! Set<UITouch> {
        NSLog("A touch began at \(touch.locationInView(self.view))")
    }
}

override func touchesMoved(touches: Set<NSObject>,
    withEvent event: UIEvent) {

    for touch in touches as! Set<UITouch> {
        NSLog("A touch moved at \(touch.locationInView(self.view))")
    }
}

override func touchesEnded(touches: Set<NSObject>,
    withEvent event: UIEvent) {

    for touch in touches as! Set<UITouch> {
        NSLog("A touch ended at \(touch.locationInView(self.view))")
    }
}

override func touchesCancelled(touches: Set<NSObject>,
    withEvent event: UIEvent) {

    for touch in touches as! Set<UITouch> {
        NSLog("A touch was cancelled at \(touch.locationInView(self.view))")
    }
}
```

Discussion

A touch can be in one of four states:

Began
> The touch just landed on the screen.

Moved
> The touch moved from one location to another. (The related method is often called multiple times over the life of a touch.)

Ended
> The touch was lifted from the screen.

Cancelled
> The touch was interrupted by something, such as a gesture recognizer claiming the touch for itself (Recipe 3.2).

When a touch lands on the screen, iOS first determines which view should be responsible for handling that touch. It does this by first determining where the touch landed on the screen, and which view happens to contain that point; second, it determines if this view, or any of its subviews, is capable of handling the touch. This is determined by checking to see if the view (or any of its subviews) has implemented any of the touches Began, touchesMoved, touchesEnded, or touchesCancelled methods.

Each of these methods is called when a touch that belongs to the view changes state; because several touches can change state at the same time (e.g., two fingers being moved simultaneously over a view), each of the methods takes a Set that contains each of the UITouch objects that recently changed state.

 The touchesBegan, touchesMoved, touchesEnded, and touchesCancelled receive a Set<NSObject> as their first parameter, because the original Objective-C implementation receives an NSSet object. The NSSet type in Objective-C only knows about NSObjects, which means that you need to manually downcast the members by using as!.

3.2. Responding to Tap Gestures

Problem

You want to detect when the user taps a view.

Solution

A tap is when a finger lands on a view, and then lifts back up without having moved.

Use a UIGestureRecognizer (specifically, UITapGestureRecognizer):

```
override func viewDidLoad() {
    super.viewDidLoad()
```

```
    let tap = UITapGestureRecognizer(target: self,
        action: "tapped:")

    // In this case, we're adding it to the view controllers'
    // view, but you can add it to any view
    self.view.addGestureRecognizer(tap)
}

func tap(tapRecognizer : UITapGestureRecognizer) {
    if tapRecognizer.state == UIGestureRecognizerState.Ended {
        NSLog("View was tapped!")
    }
}
```

Discussion

Gesture recognizers are objects that you can attach to views that look for specific patterns of touches, such as pinches, taps, and drags.

UITapGestureRecognizer is a gesture recognizer that looks for taps—that is, a touch landing and then being lifted up quickly, without moving. Taps are the most common gesture performed on the iPhone or iPad.

When the gesture recognizer detects that the user has performed the gesture that it's looking for, it sends a message to a target object. You specify the message and the target object when you create the recognizer.

In this example, the message that's sent is tap. This method needs to be implemented on the target object (in this example, self). The method takes one parameter, which is the gesture recognizer itself.

By default, a tap gesture recognizer looks for a single finger that taps one time. However, you can configure the recognizer so that it looks for multiple taps (such as double taps, triple taps, or even the fabled quadruple tap), or taps with more than one finger at the same time (e.g., two-finger taps). These can also be combined to create, for example, double-fingered double-taps:

```
tap.numberOfTapsRequired = 2 // double tap
tap.numberOfTouchesRequired = 2 // with two fingers
```

3.3. Dragging an Image Around the Screen

Problem

You want to let the user directly manipulate the position of an image on the screen by dragging it around.

Solution

In this example, `self.draggedView` is a property that connects to a `UIView`. It can be any type of view that you like, but image views work particularly well:

```
override func viewDidLoad() {
    super.viewDidLoad()

    self.draggedView.userInteractionEnabled = true

    let drag = UIPanGestureRecognizer(target: self,
        action: "dragged:")
    self.draggedView.addGestureRecognizer(drag)
}

func dragged(dragGesture: UIPanGestureRecognizer) {

    if dragGesture.state == .Began ||
        dragGesture.state == .Changed {

            var newPosition = dragGesture.translationInView(dragGesture.view!)

            newPosition.x += dragGesture.view!.center.x
            newPosition.y += dragGesture.view!.center.y

            dragGesture.view!.center = newPosition

            dragGesture.setTranslation(CGPointZero,
                inView: dragGesture.view)
    }

}
```

Discussion

This code uses a gesture recognizer to detect and handle the user dragging a finger over the screen (a drag is when the user places a single finger on the screen within the bounds of the view, and then begins moving that finger).

The first thing that happens in this code is this:

```
self.draggedView.userInteractionEnabled = true
```

It's possible that the view may have interaction disabled by default. Some views do this, including `UIImageViews`. So, to be sure that it's going to work correctly, the view is set to allow user interaction.

The next two lines create and add the gesture recognizer:

```
let drag = UIPanGestureRecognizer(target: self,
    action: "dragged:")
self.draggedView.addGestureRecognizer(drag)
```

The `dragged` method is called when the recognizer changes state. For dragging, there are two states that we want to know about: when the drag begins, and when the drag changes. In both cases, we need to do the following:

1. Determine how much the drag has moved by.

2. Figure out where the view is on the screen.

3. Decide where it should now be, by adding the movement to the current position.

4. Make the view's position be this new position.

Pan gesture recognizers expose a value called *translation*, which is the amount of movement that they've seen. This value allows your code to work out a new position for the view:

```
func dragged(dragGesture: UIPanGestureRecognizer) {

    if dragGesture.state == .Began ||
       dragGesture.state == .Changed {

            var newPosition = dragGesture.translationInView(dragGesture.view!)

            newPosition.x += dragGesture.view!.center.x
            newPosition.y += dragGesture.view!.center.y

            dragGesture.view!.center = newPosition

            dragGesture.setTranslation(CGPointZero,
                inView: dragGesture.view)
    }

}
```

The translation value needs to be manually reset once you've done this, because when the gesture recognizer next updates, you want to update the view's position from its current position rather than its starting position.

3.4. Detecting Rotation Gestures

Problem

You want to let the user use two fingers to rotate something on the screen.

Solution

Use a `UIRotationGestureRecognizer`:

```swift
class ViewController: UIViewController {

    @IBOutlet weak var rotationView: UIView!
    @IBOutlet weak var rotationStatusLabel: UILabel!

    // The current angle of the rotation, in radians
    var angle : Float = 0.0

    // Converts self.angle from radians to degrees,
    // and wrap around at 360 degrees
    var angleDegrees : Float {
        get {
            return self.angle * 180.0 / Float(M_PI) % 360.0
        }
    }

    override func viewDidLoad() {
        super.viewDidLoad()

        // Set up the rotation gesture
        let rotationGesture = UIRotationGestureRecognizer(target: self,
            action: "rotated:")

        self.rotationView.userInteractionEnabled = true
        self.rotationView.addGestureRecognizer(rotationGesture)

        self.rotationStatusLabel?.text = "\(self.angleDegrees)°"
    }

    // When the rotation changes, update self.angle
    // and use that to rotate the view
    func rotated(rotationGesture : UIRotationGestureRecognizer) {

        switch rotationGesture.state {

        case .Changed:
            self.angle += Float(rotationGesture.rotation)

            rotationGesture.rotation = 0.0

            self.rotationView.transform =
                CGAffineTransformMakeRotation(CGFloat(self.angle))

        default: () // do nothing

        }

        // Display the rotation
        self.rotationStatusLabel?.text = "\(self.angleDegrees)°"

    }
```

```
    }
```

Discussion

The UIRotationGestureRecognizer is a *continuous* gesture recognizer (in other words, unlike a tap, rotation starts, changes over time, and then ends).

When a rotation gesture recognizer realizes that the user has begun a rotation—that is, when the user has placed two fingers on the view and begun to rotate them around a central point—it sends its target the message that it was configured with when it was created.

This method then checks the current state of the recognizer, and reacts accordingly. Recognizers can be in several different states. The states relevant to the rotation gesture recognizer are the following:

UIGestureRecognizerState.Began
> The recognizer enters this state when it determines that a rotation gesture is in progress.

UIGestureRecognizerState.Changed
> This state is entered when the angle of the rotation that the user is performing changes.

UIGestureRecognizerState.Ended
> This state is entered when the fingers are lifted from the screen, ending the rotation gesture.

UIGestureRecognizerState.Cancelled
> This state is entered when the gesture is interrupted by a system-wide event, such as a phone call or an alert box appearing. This can also occur when another gesture recognizer interrupts the gesture recognizer. For example, a long press gesture recognizer might be cancelled by a pan recognizer once the user starts moving his finger.

The UIRotationGestureRecognizer's key property is rotation, which is a measure of how far the rotation has changed since it was last reset, in radians.

In the example code, whenever the gesture changes, the rotation is measured and used to update an angle. Once that's done, the rotation property of the gesture recognizer is reset to zero.

3.5. Detecting Pinching Gestures

Problem

You want to track when the user pinches or spreads her fingers on the screen.

Solution

Use a `UIPinchGestureRecognizer` to detect when the user is pinching her fingers together, or spreading them apart:

```swift
class ViewController: UIViewController {

    @IBOutlet weak var scalingView: UIView!
    @IBOutlet weak var scalingStatusLabel: UILabel!

    // The current scale of the view (1.0 = normal scale)
    var scale : Float = 1.0

    override func viewDidLoad() {
        super.viewDidLoad()

        // Set up the rotation gesture
        let rotationGesture = UIPinchGestureRecognizer(target: self,
            action: "pinched:")

        self.scalingView.userInteractionEnabled = true
        self.scalingView.addGestureRecognizer(rotationGesture)

        self.scalingStatusLabel?.text = "\(self.scale)x"
    }

    // When the rotation changes, update self.angle
    // and use that to rotate the view
    func pinched(pinchGesture : UIPinchGestureRecognizer) {

        switch pinchGesture.state {

        case .Changed:
            self.scale *= Float(pinchGesture.scale)

            pinchGesture.scale = 1.0

            self.scalingView.transform =
                CGAffineTransformMakeScale(CGFloat(self.scale),
                                           CGFloat(self.scale))

        default: () // do nothing

        }
```

```
    // Display the current scale factor
    self.scalingStatusLabel?.text = "\(self.scale)x"

  }

}
```

Discussion

`UIPinchGestureRecognizer` is your friend in this situation. A pinch gesture recognizer looks for fingers moving away from each other, or closer to each other.

The key property for `UIPinchGestureRecognizer` is `scale`. This starts at 1 when the gesture begins, and moves toward 0 when the fingers get closer together, or toward infinity when the fingers move away from each other. This value is always relative to the *initial* scale—so, for example, if the user spreads her fingers so that the scale becomes 2, and then pinches *again*, the scale will reset to 1 when the pinch begins.

To see this in action, comment out the following line of code:

```
pinchGesture.scale = 1.0
```

3.6. Creating Custom Gestures

Problem

You want to create a gesture recognizer that looks for a gesture that you define.

Solution

Creating a new gesture recognizer means subclassing `UIGestureRecognizer`. To get started, create a new class that's a subclass of `UIGestureRecognizer`.

In this example, we'll create a new gesture recognizer that looks for a gesture in which the finger starts moving down, moves back up, and then lifts from the screen (see Figure 3-1). However, there's nothing stopping you from creating simpler or more complex gestures of your own.

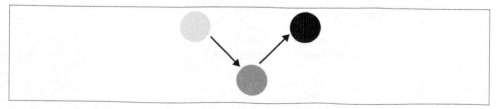

Figure 3-1. The gesture first goes down, then up again

This example shows a new `UIGestureRecognizer` called `DownUpGestureRecognizer`.

 To subclass `UIGestureRecognizer`, you need to add the following line to an Objective-C bridging header in your project:

```
#import <UIKit/UIGestureRecognizerSubclass.h>
```

Create a file called *DownUpGestureRecognizer.swift* with the following contents:

```swift
class DownUpGestureRecognizer: UIGestureRecognizer {

    // Represents the two phases that the gesture can be in:
    // moving down, or moving up after having moved down
    enum DownUpGesturePhase : Printable {
        case MovingDown, MovingUp

        // The 'Printable' protocol above means that this type
        // can be turned into a string.
        // This means you can say "\(somePhase)" and it will
        // turn into the right string
        // The following property adds support for this.
        var description: String {
            get {
                switch self {
                case .MovingDown:
                    return "Moving Down"
                case .MovingUp:
                    return "Moving Up"
                }
            }
        }
    }

    var phase : DownUpGesturePhase = .MovingDown

    override func touchesBegan(touches: Set<NSObject>,
        withEvent event: UIEvent!) {

        self.phase = .MovingDown

        if self.numberOfTouches() > 1 {

            // If there's more than one touch, this is not the type of gesture
            // we're looking for, so fail immediately
            self.state = .Failed
        } else {

            // Else, this touch could possibly turn into a down-up gesture
            self.state = .Possible
        }
```

```
}

override func touchesMoved(touches: Set<NSObject>,
    withEvent event:UIEvent) {

    // We know we only have one touch, beacuse touchesBegan will stop
    // recognizing when more than one touch is detected
    let touch = touches.first! as! UITouch

    // Get the current and previous position of the touch
    let position = touch.locationInView(touch.view)
    let lastPosition = touch.previousLocationInView(touch.view)

    // If the state is Possible, and the touch has moved down, the
    // gesture has Begun
    if self.state == .Possible {
        if position.y > lastPosition.y {
            self.state = .Began
        }
    }

    // If the state is Began or Changed, and the touch has moved, the
    // gesture will change state
    if self.state == .Began ||
        self.state == .Changed {

        // If the phase of the gesture is MovingDown, and the touch moved
        // down, the gesture has Changed
        if self.phase == .MovingDown && position.y >
            lastPosition.y {
                self.state = .Changed
        }
        // If the phase of the gesture is MovingDown, and the touch moved
        // up, the gesture has Changed; also, change the phase to MovingUp
        if self.phase == .MovingDown && position.y <
            lastPosition.y {
                self.phase = .MovingUp
                self.state = .Changed
        }
        // If the phase of the gesture is MovingUp, and the touch moved
        // down, then the gesture has Failed
        if self.phase == .MovingUp && position.y >
            lastPosition.y {
                self.state = .Failed
        }

    }
}

override func touchesEnded(touches: Set<NSObject>,
    withEvent event: UIEvent!) {
```

```
        // We know that there's only one touch.

        // If the touch ends while the phase is MovingUp, the gesture has
        // Ended. If the touch ends while the phase is MovingDown, the gesture
        // has Failed.

        if self.phase == .MovingDown {
            self.state = .Failed
        } else if self.phase == .MovingUp {
            self.state = .Ended
        }
    }

}
```

You can now use this gesture recognizer like any other. For example, here's a view controller that uses it:

```
class ViewController: UIViewController {

    @IBOutlet weak var customGestureView : UIView!
    @IBOutlet weak var customGestureStatusLabel : UILabel!

    override func viewDidLoad() {
        super.viewDidLoad()

        let downUpGesture = DownUpGestureRecognizer(target:self,
                                                    action:"downUp:")

        self.customGestureView.addGestureRecognizer(downUpGesture)

    }

    func downUp(downUpGesture: DownUpGestureRecognizer) {

        switch downUpGesture.state {
        case .Began:
            self.customGestureStatusLabel.text = "Gesture began"

        case .Changed:
            self.customGestureStatusLabel.text = "Gesture changed, phase = " +
            "\(downUpGesture.phase)"

        case .Ended:
            self.customGestureStatusLabel.text = "Gesture ended"

        case .Cancelled:
            self.customGestureStatusLabel.text = "Gesture cancelled"

        case .Possible:
            self.customGestureStatusLabel.text = "Gesture possible"

        case .Failed:
```

```
          self.customGestureStatusLabel.text = "Gesture failed"


      }
    }

  }
```

Discussion

The first step in creating a new `UIGestureRecognizer` is to import the Objective-C file *UIKit/UIGestureRecognizerSubclass.h*. This header file contains code that redefines the `state` property of the `UIGestureRecognizer` class as `readwrite`, which lets your subclass modify its own state. Everything else is simply watching touches, and changing state based on that.

A gesture recognizer works by receiving touches, via the `touchesBegan`, `touchesMoved`, `touchesEnded`, and `touchesCancelled` methods (much like a `UIView` does). A recognizer is responsible for keeping track of whatever information it needs to determine the state of the gesture.

Recognizers don't communicate directly with their targets; instead, they change the value of the `state` property, which controls whether they're in the `Began`, `Changed`, `Ended`, `Cancelled`, or other states.

When your recognizer decides that it's seen a gesture, it changes its state to `UIGestureRecognizerStateBegan`. This causes the gesture recognition system to send the recognizer's target object its action message. Similarly, your recognizer changes the `state` property to `UIGestureRecognizerStateChanged` when it decides that the gesture has changed.

An important state that you can set your recognizer to is `Failed`. For complex gestures, it's possible that the sequences of touches that the recognizer has been observing won't turn out to actually constitute the kind of gesture you're looking for. For example, if a drag gesture recognizer sees a touch land on the screen, it's possible that it's the start of a drag gesture, but it can't be sure—it's not a drag until the touch starts moving. If the touch immediately lifts up, the drag gesture recognizer changes to the `Failed` state. This allows other gesture recognizers to step in, if applicable.

3.7. Receiving Touches in Custom Areas of a View

Problem

By default, a `UIView` detects all touches that fall within its bounds. You want a view to receive touches in a different region.

Solution

To tell iOS that a point should be considered to be within the bounds of a view, you override the `pointInside(_, withEvent:)` method.

In a `UIView` subclass:

```swift
override func pointInside(point: CGPoint, withEvent event: UIEvent?) -> Bool {

    // A point is inside this view if it falls inside a rectangle that's 40pt
    // larger than the bounds of the view

    return CGRectContainsPoint(CGRectInset(self.bounds, -40, -40), point)
}
```

Discussion

When a touch lands on the screen, iOS starts checking all views to find out which view was touched. It does this by calling `pointInside(_, withEvent:)` on the top-level view, and finding out whether the touch is considered "inside" that view. It then begins asking each of the subviews inside that view whether the touch should be considered inside it, proceeding until the lowest-level view is reached.

By default, a point is considered "inside" the view if it's within the view's bounds rectangle. However, you can override this by providing your own implementation of `pointInside(_, withEvent:)`.

`pointInside(_, withEvent:)` takes a `CGPoint` in the coordinate space of the view, and returns `true` if the point should be considered inside the view and `false` if the point is outside of the view.

3.8. Detecting Shakes

Problem

You want to detect when the user's device is shaking.

Solution

Add this code to a view controller:

```swift
override func motionBegan(motion: UIEventSubtype, withEvent event: UIEvent) {

    // Show a label when shaking begins
    self.shakingLabel.hidden = false
}

override func motionEnded(motion: UIEventSubtype, withEvent event: UIEvent) {
```

```
        // Hide the label 1 second after shaking ends
        var delayInSeconds : Float = 1.0

        var popTime = dispatch_time(DISPATCH_TIME_NOW,
            (Int64)(delayInSeconds * Float(NSEC_PER_SEC)))

        dispatch_after(popTime, dispatch_get_main_queue()) {
            self.shakingLabel.hidden = true
        }
    }
}


    override func canBecomeFirstResponder() -> Bool {
        return true
    }
```

Discussion

Shaking is a kind of gesture that views and view controllers can detect. If you want a
view controller to detect it, you first need to indicate to the system that your view con‐
troller is capable of becoming the "first responder"—that is, that it's able to receive
motion gestures like shaking:

```
override func canBecomeFirstResponder() -> Bool {
    return true
}
```

When shaking begins, the view controller receives the motionBegan(_, withEvent:)
message. When shaking ends, the motionEnded(_, withEvent:) message is sent:

```
override func motionBegan(motion: UIEventSubtype, withEvent event: UIEvent) {

    // Show a label when shaking begins
    self.shakingLabel.hidden = false
}

override func motionEnded(motion: UIEventSubtype, withEvent event: UIEvent) {

    // Hide the label 1 second after shaking ends
    var delayInSeconds : Float = 1.0

    var popTime = dispatch_time(DISPATCH_TIME_NOW,
        (Int64)(delayInSeconds * Float(NSEC_PER_SEC)))

    dispatch_after(popTime, dispatch_get_main_queue()) {
        self.shakingLabel.hidden = true
    }
}
```

In the case of the example code, all we're doing is making a label become visible when
shaking begins, and making it invisible two seconds after shaking ends.

3.9. Detecting Device Tilt

Problem

You want to detect how the device has been tilted. For example, if you're making a driving game, you want to know how far the device is being turned, so that you can figure out how the user's car is being steered.

Solution

You get information about how the device is being moved and rotated by using the Core Motion framework. To add this framework to your code, you just need to `import` the CoreMotion module in the files you want to use it in:

```
@IBOutlet weak var pitchLabel : UILabel!
@IBOutlet weak var yawLabel : UILabel!
@IBOutlet weak var rollLabel : UILabel!

var motionManager = CMMotionManager()

override func viewDidLoad() {
    var mainQueue = NSOperationQueue.mainQueue()

    motionManager.startDeviceMotionUpdatesToQueue(mainQueue) {
        (motion, error) in

        var roll = motion.attitude.roll
        var rollDegrees = roll * 180 / M_PI

        var yaw = motion.attitude.yaw
        var yawDegrees = yaw * 180 / M_PI

        var pitch = motion.attitude.pitch
        var pitchDegrees = pitch * 180 / M_PI

        self.rollLabel.text = String(format:"Roll: %.2f°", rollDegrees)
        self.yawLabel.text = String(format: "Yaw: %.2f°", yawDegrees)
        self.pitchLabel.text = String(format: "Pitch: %.2f°", pitchDegrees)
    }

}
```

Discussion

Objects can be tilted in three different ways. As illustrated in Figure 3-2, they can *pitch*, *yaw*, and *roll*: that is, rotate around three different imaginary lines. When an object pitches, it rotates around a line drawn from its left edge to its right edge. When it yaws, it rotates around a line drawn from the top edge to the bottom edge. When it rolls, it rotates around a line drawn from the middle of its front face to the middle of the back face.

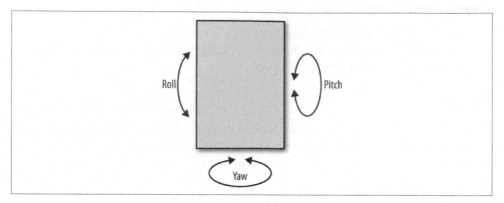

Figure 3-2. The three axes of rotation

Your app can get information regarding how the device is angled through the Core Motion framework. The main class in this framework is CMMotionManager, which allows you to sign up to be notified when the device is moved or tilted. So, to get started, you first need to create a CMMotionManager.

It's important to keep a reference to your CMMotionManager around. Without one, the automatic reference counting system will notice that there's no reason to keep the CMMotionManager in memory, and it'll be deallocated. This won't lead to a crash, but it will mean that you won't get any information from it when the device is rotated or moved.

That's why, in the example, we store the CMMotionManager in an instance variable. Doing this means that the view controller has a strong reference to the CMMotionManager, which will keep it in memory.

Once you've created your motion manager, you can start receiving information about the device's movement. To receive this information, you need to call startDeviceMotionUpdatesToQueue(_, withHandler:) on your CMMotionManager.

This method takes two parameters: an NSOperationQueue and a block. Every time the device moves, the motion manager will call the block, using the operation queue you provide. In our example, we're using the main queue (i.e., NSOperationQueue.mainQueue), so that the block is able to update the user interface.

Every time the block is called, it receives two parameters: a CMMotion object and an NSError object. The CMMotion object contains information about how the device is currently moving, and the NSError object either is nil if nothing's gone wrong, or contains information about what's gone wrong and why.

A CMMotion object contains a *lot* of information for you to work with:

- You can access accelerometer information, which tells you how the device is moving and in which direction gravity is, through the userAcceleration and gravity properties.

- You can access calibrated gyroscope information, which tells you how the device is oriented and how fast it's currently rotating, through the attitude and rotation Rate properties.

- You can access calibrated magnetic field information, which tells you about the total magnetic field that the device is in (minus device bias), through the magnetic Field property.

 The magneticField property is really cool. It's not too tricky to write an app that watches the magnetic field—once you've made that, wave your device near something made of iron or steel. Congratulations, you've just turned your phone into a metal detector! See Recipe 3.18.

In this particular example, we care most about the device's *attitude*. The attitude of an object means how it's oriented in space. The attitude of a device is represented by three angles, *pitch*, *yaw*, and *roll*, measured in radians—if you remember your high school math, there are 2π radians in a circle.

 To convert from radians to degrees, and vice versa, use these formulas:

```
degrees = radians / π * 180

radians = degrees * π / 180
```

This recipe talks about how you can access tilt across all axes; to use this information for steering, take a look at Recipe 3.18.

3.10. Getting the Compass Heading

Problem

You want to know which direction the user is facing, relative to north.

Solution

First, add the Core Motion framework to your project and set up a `CMMotionManager`, as per Recipe 3.9.

Then, when you ask the system to start delivering device motion information to your application, use the `startDeviceMotionUpdatesUsingReferenceFrame(_, to Queue:withHandler:)` method and pass in `CMAttitudeReferenceFrame.XTrueNorthZ Vertical` as the first parameter:

```
motionManager.startDeviceMotionUpdatesUsingReferenceFrame(
    CMAttitudeReferenceFrame.XTrueNorthZVertical,
    toQueue: mainQueue) { (motion, error) in
    var yaw = motion.attitude.yaw

    var yawDegrees = yaw * 180 / M_PI

    self.directionLabel.text = String(format:"Direction: %.0f°", yawDegrees)

}
```

Discussion

When you begin receiving device motion information, all attitude information is relative to a *reference frame*. The reference frame is your "zero point" for orientation.

By default, the zero point is set when you activate the device motion system. That is, the first attitude information you receive will indicate that the device is oriented at the zero point. As you rotate the device, the attitude information will change relative to the zero point.

The default reference frame is able to determine the device's pitch and roll by measuring the direction of gravity. That is, it's always possible to know what direction "down" is. However, it isn't possible for a gyroscope and accelerometer to measure the *yaw*, for the same reason that you don't have a constant, innate knowledge of which direction is north.

To get this information, a magnetometer is needed. Magnetometers sense magnetic fields, which allows you to figure out where the north pole of the strongest magnet near you is. In other words, a magnetometer is able to function as a compass.

Magnetometers require additional power to use, as well as additional CPU resources necessary to integrate the magnetic field data with the accelerometer and gyroscope data. By default, therefore, the magnetometer is turned off. However, if you need to know where north is, you can indicate to the Core Motion system that you need this information.

With the `startDeviceMotionUpdatesUsingReferenceFrame(_, toQueue:withHan` `dler:)` method, you have a choice regarding what reference frame you can use. The options available are as follows:

`CMAttitudeReferenceFrame.XArbitraryZVertical`
Yaw is set to zero when the device motion system is turned on.

`CMAttitudeReferenceFrame.XArbitraryCorrectedZVertical`
Yaw is set to zero when the device motion system is turned on, and the magnetometer is used to keep this stable over time (i.e., the zero point won't drift as much).

`CMAttitudeReferenceFrame.XMagneticNorthZVertical`
The zero yaw point is magnetic north.

`CMAttitudeReferenceFrame.XTrueNorthZVertical`
The zero yaw point is true north. The system needs to use the location system to figure this out.

If you need the most accuracy, `CMAttitudeReferenceFrame.XTrueNorthZVertical` should be used. This uses the most battery power, and takes the longest time to get a fix. If you don't really care about which direction north is, go with `CMAttitudeReferenceFrame.XArbitraryZVertical` or `CMAttitudeReference` `Frame.XArbitraryCorrectedZVertical`.

3.11. Accessing the User's Location

Problem

You want to determine where on the planet the user currently is.

Solution

When you want to work with user location data, you need to explain to the user for what purpose the location data is going to be used:

1. Go to the project's information screen by clicking the project at the top of the Project Navigator (at the left of the Xcode window).

2. Go to the Info tab.

3. Add a new entry in the list of settings that appears: "Privacy - Location Usage Description." In the Value column, add some text that explains what the user location will be used for. (In this example, it can be something like "the app will display your coordinates.")

On iOS 8, the way you provide the explanation of how the app will use user location data is different:

- If your app will use the user's location only when the app is running—that is, it's running in the foreground—you add an entry with the key NSLocationWhenInUseUsageDescription.

- If your app will use the user's location even when the app is closed, add an entry with the key NSLocationAlwaysUsageDe scription.

Adding this information is mandatory. If you don't explain why you need access to the user's location, Apple will likely reject your app from the App Store.

The reason for this is that the user's location is private information, and your app needs to have a good reason for using it. That's not to say that you shouldn't make games that ask for the user's location— far from it! But don't get the user's location just so that you can gather statistics about where your users live.

To actually get the user's location and work with it, you import the CoreLocation module and use a CLLocationManager:

```
import UIKit
import CoreLocation

class ViewController: UIViewController, CLLocationManagerDelegate {

    var locationManager = CLLocationManager()

    @IBOutlet weak var latitudeLabel : UILabel!
    @IBOutlet weak var longitudeLabel : UILabel!
    @IBOutlet weak var locationErrorLabel : UILabel!

    override func viewDidLoad() {
        super.viewDidLoad()

        locationManager.delegate = self

        locationManager.requestWhenInUseAuthorization()

        locationManager.startUpdatingLocation()

        self.locationErrorLabel.hidden = true
    }

    func locationManager(manager: CLLocationManager!,
        didUpdateLocations locations: [AnyObject]!) {
        self.locationErrorLabel.hidden = true
```

```
        var location = locations.last as! CLLocation

        var latitude = location.coordinate.latitude
        var longitude = location.coordinate.longitude

        self.latitudeLabel.text = String(format: "Latitude: %.4f", latitude)
        self.longitudeLabel.text = String(format: "Longitude: %.4f", longitude)
    }

    func locationManager(manager: CLLocationManager!,
        didFailWithError error: NSError!) {
        self.locationErrorLabel.hidden = false
    }

}
```

Discussion

A CLLocationManager, once set up and configured, sends messages to a delegate object,
notifying it of the user's location.

To receive messages from a CLLocationManager, an object needs to conform to the
CLLocationManagerDelegate protocol:

```
class ViewController: UIViewController, CLLocationManagerDelegate {
```

To set up a CLLocationManager, you create an instance of the class. You'll also need to
create and keep a strong reference to the CLLocationManager object, to keep it from
being freed from memory, and indicate to it what object should receive location updates.
Finally, you need to tell the CLLocationManager that it should activate the GPS system,
request permission from the user, and begin telling the delegate object about the user's
location:

```
locationManager.delegate = self

locationManager.requestWhenInUseAuthorization()

locationManager.startUpdatingLocation()
```

Once you've told the location manager that you want to start receiving location information, you then need to implement one of the methods in the CLLocationManager
Delegate protocol: locationManager(_, didUpdateLocations:). This method is
called every time the location manager decides that the user has changed location. It
receives two parameters: the CLLocationManager itself, and an array containing one or
more CLLocation objects.

There can be more than one CLLocation object in the array. This can happen when, for
some reason, your application hasn't been able to receive location updates (e.g., it may

have been in the background). In these cases, you'll receive a bunch of CLLocations, which are delivered in the order in which they occurred. The last object in the array is always the most recent location at which the device was observed. You can access it through array's last method:

```
var location = locations.last as! CLLocation
```

A CLLocation object represents the user's current location on the planet. It contains, among other information, the user's latitude, longitude, and altitude.

The user's latitude and longitude, which are almost always the only things you want to know about, can be accessed through the CLLocation's coordinate property, which is a CLLocationCoordinate2D. A CLLocationCoordinate2D contains two things:

```
var latitude = location.coordinate.latitude
var longitude = location.coordinate.longitude
```

 The user's location is not guaranteed to be precise—the GPS system is good, but it's not accurate enough to pinpoint the location down to the nearest centimeter (unless you're in the U.S. military, in which case, greetings!).

Therefore, each CLLocation object contains a horizontalAccuracy property, which represents the "radius of uncertainty" of the location, measured in meters.

For example, if the horizontalAccuracy of a CLLocation is 5, this means that the user is within 5 meters of the location indicated by the latitude and longitude.

3.12. Calculating the User's Speed

Problem

You want to determine how fast the user is moving.

Solution

This information can be gained through the Core Location framework.

First, set up a CLLocationManager, as discussed in the previous recipe, and start receiving updates to the user's location:

```
func locationManager(manager: CLLocationManager!,
    didUpdateLocations locations: [AnyObject]!) {

    let lastLocation = locations.last as! CLLocation

    if lastLocation.speed > 0 {
```

```
        self.speedLabel.text = String(format:"Currently moving at %.0fms",
            lastLocation.speed)
    }

}
```

Discussion

CLLocation objects contain a speed property, which contains the speed at which the device is traveling. This is measured in meters per second.

 If you want to convert meters per second to kilometers per hour, you can do this:

```
var kPH = location.speed * 3.6
```

If you want to convert meters per second to miles per hour, you can do this:

```
var mPH =  location.speed * 2.236936;
```

3.13. Pinpointing the User's Proximity to Landmarks

Problem

You want to calculate how far away the user is from a location.

Solution

We'll assume that you already know the user's location, represented by a CLLocation object. If you don't already have this information, see Recipe 3.11.

We'll also assume that you have the latitude and longitude coordinates of the location from which you want to measure the distance. You can use this information to determine the proximity:

```
var userLocation : CLLocation = ... // get the user's location from CoreLocation
var latitude : Float = ... // latitude of the other location
var longitude : Float = ... // longitude of the other location

var otherLocation = CLLocation(latitude:latitude
                              longitude:longitude)

var distance = userLocation.distanceFromLocation(otherLocation)
```

Discussion

The distanceFromLocation method returns the distance from the other location, measured in meters.

It's important to note that the distance is not a direct straight-line distance, but rather takes into account the curvature of the earth. Also keep in mind that the distance traveled doesn't take into account any mountains or hills between the user's location and the other location.

3.14. Receiving Notifications When the User Changes Location

Problem

You want to be notified when the user enters a specific region, or exits it.

Solution

This code requires adding the Core Location framework to your application (see Recipe 3.9 for instructions on adding a framework). Additionally, it requires using iOS 7 or higher.

Your application can receive updates to the user's location even when it's not running. To enable this, follow these steps:

1. Go to your project's Info screen by clicking the project at the top of the Project Navigator (at the left of the Xcode window; see Figure 3-3).

Figure 3-3. The project, at the top of the Project Navigator

2. Click the Capabilities tab.
3. Turn on "Background Modes."
4. Check the "Location updates" checkbox, as shown in Figure 3-4.

Figure 3-4. Adding the "Location updates" background mode

Additionally, you will need to add the key NSLocationAlwaysUsageDescription to your app's Info dictionary, and provide an explanation of how the app will be using the user's location.

Make *ViewController.swift* look like the following code:

```swift
import UIKit
import CoreLocation

class ViewController: UIViewController, CLLocationManagerDelegate {

    var locationManager = CLLocationManager()
    var regionToMonitor : CLCircularRegion?


    override func viewDidLoad() {
        locationManager.delegate = self;

        locationManager.requestAlwaysAuthorization()

        locationManager.startUpdatingLocation()


    }

    func locationManager(manager: CLLocationManager!,
        didUpdateLocations locations: [AnyObject]!) {
```

```
            if regionToMonitor == nil {

                var location = locations.last as! CLLocation

                regionToMonitor = CLCircularRegion(center: location.coordinate,
                    radius: 20.0, identifier: "StartingPoint")

                locationManager.startMonitoringForRegion(regionToMonitor)

                println("Now monitoring region \(regionToMonitor)")

            }
        }

        func locationManager(manager: CLLocationManager!,
            monitoringDidFailForRegion region: CLRegion!,
            withError error: NSError!) {
            println("Failed to start monitoring region!")

        }

        func locationManager(manager: CLLocationManager!,
            didEnterRegion region: CLRegion!) {
            println("Entering region!")
        }

        func locationManager(manager: CLLocationManager!,
            didExitRegion region: CLRegion!) {
            println("Exiting region!")
        }


    }
```

Discussion

Your application can be notified when the user enters or exits a region. A region is defined by a central point and a radius—that is to say, regions are always circular.

You register a region by creating a CLRegion object and giving it a center point (latitude and longitude) and radius, as well as a name (a string that you will use to refer to the region):

```
var latitude  : Float = ...  // latitude
var longitude : Float = ...  // longitude
var radius    : Float = ...  // radius
var name = "My Region"       // something to call the region

var coordinate = CLCoordinate2DMake(latitude, longitude)

var region = CLCircularRegion(center:coordinate,
                    radius: radius, identifier: name)
```

The maximum allowed radius for a region might vary from device to device. You can check what the maximum allowed radius is by asking the CLLocation Manager class for its maximumRegionMonitoringDistance property:

```
var maximumRegionRadius = locationManager.maximumRegionMonitoringDistance
```

Once the region has been created, you indicate to your CLLocationManager that you want to be notified when the user enters and exits the region:

```
locationManager.startMonitoringForRegion(regionToMonitor)
```

Once this is done, the CLLocationManager's delegate will receive a locationManager(_, didEnterRegion:) message when the user enters the region, and a locationManager(_, didExitRegion:) message when the user exits.

You can only register 20 regions at a time. You can ask the location manager to give you an array of all of the CLRegions you've registered via the monitoredRegions method:

```
var monitoredRegions = locationManager.monitoredRegions
```

When you no longer want to receive notifications regarding a region, you send the CLLocationManager the stopMonitoringForRegion message:

```
locationManager.stopMonitoringForRegion(regionToMonitor)
```

Finally, a word about how precise regions can be. Later devices tend to be more precise, which means that on devices earlier than the iPhone 4S, you shouldn't create regions with a radius of less than 400 meters. Additionally, when the user enters or exits a region, it generally takes about 3 to 5 minutes for the device to notice it and send a notification to your application. This means that using smaller regions may mean that your app receives notifications well after the user has left the area. To report region changes in a timely manner, the region monitoring service requires network connectivity.

3.15. Looking Up GPS Coordinates for a Street Address

Problem

You have a street address, and you want to get latitude and longitude coordinates for it. For example, you have a game that involves players moving from one named location to another, and you want to get the coordinates so you can monitor when they get close.

Solution

iOS has a built-in system that lets you convert between coordinates and street addresses. *Geocoding* is the process of converting a human-readable address (like "1 Infinite Loop, Cupertino, California") into latitude and longitude coordinates, which you can then use with the location system.

First, import the `CoreLocation` module (see Recipe 3.9).

Next, create a `CLGeocoder` instance variable (in this example, we've named it `geocoder`), and call `geocodeAddressString`:

```
let addressString = self.addressTextView.text // get the address from somewhere

geocoder.geocodeAddressString(addressString) { (placemarks, error) -> Void in
    if error != nil {
        self.latitudeLabel.text = "Error!"
        self.longitudeLabel.text = "Error!"
    } else {
        let placemark = placemarks.last as! CLPlacemark

        let latitude = placemark.location.coordinate.latitude
        let longitude = placemark.location.coordinate.longitude

        self.latitudeLabel.text = String(format: "Latitude: %.4f", latitude)
        self.longitudeLabel.text = String(format: "Longitude: %.4f", longitude)
    }
}
```

Discussion

To use geocoding, you create a `CLGeocoder` object. A `CLGeocoder` object communicates with Apple's geocoding server, and runs the completion handler block that you provide when the geocoding request returns. This means that your device needs to be on the network in order to use geocoding.

When the geocoding request returns, you'll either receive an array that contains `CLPlacemark` objects, or an `NSError` that describes what went wrong. You might get more than one `CLPlacemark` object; for example, if the geocoding server is unsure about the exact location you meant, it may return a few different options.

`CLPlacemark` objects describe a location, and they contain quite a lot of information for you to use. The specific contents available for each placemark vary, but they include things like the name of the location, the street name, the town or city, country, and so on.

Additionally, every `CLPlacemark` contains a property called `location`, which is a `CLLocation` object that you can use to get the latitude and longitude.

3.16. Looking Up Street Addresses from the User's Location

Problem

You know the user's location, and you want to find the street address using his coordinates.

Solution

First, add the Core Location framework to your project (see Recipe 3.9).

Next, create a `CLGeocoder` instance variable (in this example, we've named it `geocoder`), and call `reverseGeocodeLocation` on it:

```swift
func locationManager(manager: CLLocationManager!,
    didUpdateLocations locations: [AnyObject]!) {
    let location = locations.last as! CLLocation

    geocoder.reverseGeocodeLocation(location, completionHandler: {
        (placemarks, error) -> Void in
        let addressString =
            (placemarks.first as! CLPlacemark).name

        self.labelTextView.text = addressString

    })
}
```

Discussion

A `CLGeocoder` object is able to perform both geocoding and *reverse* geocoding. Whereas geocoding involves taking a street address and returning coordinates, reverse geocoding means taking coordinates and providing a street address.

Reverse geocoding works in a very similar manner to geocoding: you create a `CLGeocoder`, provide it with input data and a block that you want to run when the work is complete, and set it off.

Also like with normal geocoding, reverse geocoding returns an array of `CLPlacemark` objects. However, there's no built-in method for converting a `CLPlacemark` into a string (not counting `description`, which includes all kinds of information that the user doesn't care about). It's therefore up to you to pull the information out of the `CLPlacemark` object and format it into a string for the user to see.

3.17. Using the Device as a Steering Wheel

Problem

You want to let the user use the device as a steering wheel, and get information on how far he's steering.

Solution

You can get information about how far the user is steering by deciding which axis you want to define as the "steering" axis, and using Core Motion to work out the rotation around that axis.

In most cases, games that involve steering are played in landscape mode. To make sure your game only appears in landscape, select the project at the top of the Project Navigator, and scroll down to Device Orientation. Make sure that only Landscape Left and Landscape Right are selected.

Next, import the Core Motion framework (see Recipe 3.9). Finally, add a CMMotion Manager, and add the following code to watch for device motion updates:

```
motionManager.startDeviceMotionUpdatesToQueue(NSOperationQueue.mainQueue()) {
    (motion, error) -> Void in

    // Maximum steering left is -50 degrees, maximum steering right is
    // 50 degrees
    var maximumSteerAngle = 50.0

    // When in landscape,
    var rotationAngle = motion.attitude.pitch * 180.0 / M_PI

    // -1.0 = hard left, 1.0 = hard right
    var steering = 0.0

    var orientation = UIApplication.sharedApplication().statusBarOrientation

    if orientation == UIInterfaceOrientation.LandscapeLeft  {
        steering = rotationAngle / -maximumSteerAngle
    } else if orientation == UIInterfaceOrientation.LandscapeRight {
        steering = rotationAngle / maximumSteerAngle
    }

    // Limit the steering to between -1.0 and 1.0
    steering = fmin(steering, 1.0)
    steering = fmax(steering, -1.0)

    println("Steering: \(steering)")
}
```

Discussion

In this solution, the code figures out how the device is being held and generates a number to represent how the user is "steering" the device: −1.0 means the device is being steered hard left, and 1.0 means hard right.

In landscape mode, "steering" the device means changing its pitch—that is, changing the angle of the line that extends from the left of the screen to the right of the screen. However, "landscape" can mean that the device is being held in two different ways: "landscape left" means that the home button is to the left of the screen, and "landscape right" means that the home button is to the right. In other words, landscape right is an upside-down version of landscape left.

This means that if we want −1.0 to always mean left, we have to know the orientation in which the device is being held. You can check this by asking the shared UIApplica tion object for the current statusBarOrientation.

3.18. Detecting Magnets

Problem

You want your game to detect when the device is near a magnet or other ferrous material.

Solution

First, you need to import the Core Motion framework. See Recipe 3.9 for instructions. Use the CMMotionManager class's startMagnetometerUpdatesToQueue(_,withHan dler:) method to register to receive information from the device's built-in magnetometer:

```
motionManager.startMagnetometerUpdatesToQueue(NSOperationQueue.mainQueue()) {
    (magnetometerData, error) -> Void in

    let magneticField = magnetometerData.magneticField

    let xValue = String(format:"%.2f", magneticField.x)
    let yValue = String(format:"%.2f", magneticField.y)
    let zValue = String(format:"%.2f", magneticField.z)

    let average = (magneticField.x + magneticField.y + magneticField.z) / 3.0

    let averageValue = String(format:"%.2f", average)

    self.magneticFieldXLabel.text = xValue
    self.magneticFieldYLabel.text = yValue
    self.magneticFieldZLabel.text = zValue
    self.magneticFieldAverageLabel.text = averageValue
```

```
}
```

Discussion

The built-in magnetometer in all devices shipped since the iPhone 3GS is used to find the heading of the device (i.e., the direction in which it's pointing). By getting a reading on the magnetic fields surrounding the device, the iPhone can determine which direction is north.

However, this isn't the only reason why magnetometers are cool. The magnetometer can be accessed directly, which gives you information on the presence of magnets (as well as ferromagnetic metals, like steel and iron) near the device.

When you want to start getting information about nearby magnetic fields, you use the `CMDeviceMotion` class's `startMagnetometerUpdatesToQueue(_,withHandler)` method. This method works in a manner very similar to when you want to get overall device motion (see Recipe 3.9); however, instead of receiving a `CMDeviceMotion` object, you instead get a `CMMagnetometerData` object.

The `CMMagnetometerData` object contains two properties: an `NSTimeInterval` that represents when the information was sampled, and a `CMMagneticField` structure that contains the data itself.

The information stored in the `CMMagneticField` is represented in microteslas, which are a measurement of magnetic flux density—that is, the strength of the magnetic field currently affecting the device.

When the device is near a planet—which, at the time of writing, is very likely to be the case—it will be subjected to that planet's magnetic field. Earth has a particularly strong magnetic field, which means that the measurements that come from the magnetometer will never be zero. Additionally, some components in the device itself are slightly magnetic, which contributes to the readings. Finally, the readings that you'll get from the magnetometer will be stronger when the sensor is *moving* through a magnetic field, as opposed to remaining stationary within one.

This means that you can't treat the information that comes from the magnetometer as absolute "near magnet"/"not near magnet" data. Instead, you need to interpret the information over time: if the values you're getting from the magnetometer are rising or falling quickly, the device is near something magnetic.

Magnetometers haven't seen much use in games to date, which means that there's a huge potential area for new kinds of gameplay. This is left as an exercise for the reader—what kind of gameplay can you create that's based on detecting metal?

3.19. Utilizing Inputs to Improve Game Design

Problem

You want to effectively utilize the inputs (some of them unique) that are available on iOS to make a better game.

Solution

When you're considering how your game is controlled, it pays to look at the environment in which iOS games are frequently played. The iPhone and iPad are, obviously, inherently mobile devices—they are used by people who are often out and about, or at work, lying in front of the television, or commuting to work on a loud train.

Because of this, iOS games should be simple and easy to control, and should use as much direct manipulation—dragging, touching, gestures—as possible. People are distracted, and they don't want to think about the myriad ways in which they could control something. If the obvious doesn't work, they'll go and play a different game—it's hard enough trying to play a game on the train anyway!

If a player can directly drag her character around, rather than using an on-screen directional control, then you should enable that. If your game requires the player to shake loose enemy boarders from a spacecraft, why not let her shake the device instead of tapping a button marked "shake"?

Discussion

Give users direct control and your game will feel more responsive, be more entertaining, and end up getting played a whole lot more often.

CHAPTER 4

Sound

Sound is a frequently overlooked part of games. Even in big-name titles, sound design and programming are sometimes left until late in the game development process. This is especially true on mobile devices—the user might be playing the game in a crowded, noisy environment and might not even hear the sounds and music you've put into it, so why bother putting in much effort?

However, sound is an incredibly important part of games. When a game sounds great, and makes noises in response to the visible parts of the game, the player gets drawn in to the world that the game's creating.

In this chapter, you'll learn how to use iOS's built-in support for playing both sound effects and music. You'll also learn how to take advantage of the speech synthesis features built into iOS.

Sound good?[1]

4.1. Playing Sound with AVAudioPlayer

Problem

You want to play back an audio file, as simply as possible and with a minimum of work.

Solution

The simplest way to play a sound file is using `AVAudioPlayer`, which is a class available in the AVFoundation framework. To use this feature, you first need to `import` the AVFoundation module in each file that uses the AVFoundation classes:

---

1. We apologize for the pun and have fired Jon, who wrote it.

```
import AVFoundation
```

You create an AVAudioPlayer by providing it with the location of the file you want it to play. This should generally be done ahead of time, before the sound needs to be played, to avoid playback delays.

In this example, audioPlayer is an optional AVAudioPlayer instance variable:

```
let soundFileURL = NSBundle.mainBundle().URLForResource("TestSound",
    withExtension:"wav")
var error : NSError? = nil

audioPlayer = AVAudioPlayer(contentsOfURL: soundFileURL, error: &error)

if (error != nil) {
    println("Failed to load the sound: \(error)")
}

audioPlayer?.prepareToPlay()
```

To begin playback, you use the play method:

```
audioPlayer?.play()
```

To make playback loop, you change the audio player's numberOfLoops property. To make an AVAudioPlayer play one time and then stop:

```
audioPlayer?.numberOfLoops = 0
```

To make an AVAudioPlayer play twice and then stop:

```
audioPlayer?.numberOfLoops = 1
```

To make an AVAudioPlayer play forever, until manually stopped:

```
audioPlayer?.numberOfLoops = -1
```

By default, an AVAudioPlayer will play its sound one time only. After it's finished playing, a second call to play will rewind it and play it again. By changing the numberOfLoops property, you can make an AVAudioPlayer play its file a single time, a fixed number of times, or continuously until it's sent a pause or stop message.

To stop playback, you use the pause or stop method (the pause method just stops playback, and lets you resume from where you left off later; the stop method stops playback completely, and unloads the sound from memory):

```
// To pause:
audioPlayer?.pause()
// To stop:
audioPlayer?.stop()
```

To rewind an audio player, you change the `currentTime` property. This property stores how far playback has progressed, measured in seconds. If you set it to zero, playback will jump back to the start:

```
audioPlayer.currentTime = 0
```

You can also set this property to other values to jump to a specific point in the audio.

Discussion

If you use an `AVAudioPlayer`, you need to keep a strong reference to it (using an instance variable) to avoid it being released from memory. If that happens, the sound will stop.

If you have multiple sounds that you want to play at the same time, you need to keep references to each (or use an array to contain them all). This can get cumbersome, so it's often better to use a dedicated sound engine instead of managing each player yourself.

Preparing an `AVAudioPlayer` takes a little bit of preparation. You need to either know the location of a file that contains the audio you want the player to play, or have an `NSData` object that contains the audio data.

`AVAudioPlayer` supports a number of popular audio formats. The specific formats vary slightly from device to device; the iPhone 5 supports the following formats:

- AAC (8 to 320 Kbps)
- Protected AAC (from the iTunes Store)
- HE-AAC
- MP3 (8 to 320 Kbps)
- MP3 VBR
- Audible (formats 2, 3, 4, Audible Enhanced Audio, AAX, and AAX+)
- Apple Lossless
- AIFF
- WAV

You shouldn't generally have problems with file compatibility across devices, but it's usually best to go with AAC, MP3, AIFF, or WAV.

In this example, it's assumed that there's a file called *TestSound.wav* in the project. You'll want to use a different name for your game, of course.

Use the `NSBundle`'s `URLForResource(_, withExtension)` method to get the location of a resource on disk:

```
let soundFileURL = NSBundle.mainBundle().URLForResource("TestSound",
    withExtension:"wav")
```

This returns an NSURL object that contains the location of the file, which you can give to your AVAudioPlayer to tell it where to find the sound file.

The initializer for AVAudioPlayer is AVAudioPlayer(contentsOfURL:, error:). The first parameter is an NSURL that indicates where to find a sound file, and the second is a pointer to an NSError reference that allows the method to return an error object if something goes wrong.

Let's take a closer look at how this works. First, you create an NSError variable and set it to nil:

```
var error : NSError? = nil
```

Then you call AVAudioPlayer(contentsOfURL:, error:) and provide the NSURL and the NSError variable, prefixed with an ampersand (&):

```
audioPlayer = AVAudioPlayer(contentsOfURL: soundFileURL, error: &error)
```

When this method returns, audioPlayer is either a ready-to-use AVAudioPlayer object, or nil. If it's nil, the NSError variable will have changed to be a reference to an NSError object, which you can use to find out what went wrong:

```
if (error != nil) {
    println("Failed to load the sound: \(error)")
}
```

Finally, the AVAudioPlayer can be told to preload the audio file before playback. If you don't do this, it's no big deal—when you tell it to play, it loads the file and then begins playing back. However, for large files, this can lead to a short pause before audio actually starts playing, so it's often best to preload the sound as soon as you can. Note, however, that if you have many large sounds, preloading everything can lead to all of your available memory being consumed, so use this feature with care.

4.2. Recording Sound with AVAudioRecorder

Problem

You want to record sound made by the player, using the built-in microphone.

Solution

AVAudioRecorder is your friend here. Like its sibling AVAudioPlayer (see Recipe 4.1), AVAudioRecorder lives in the AVFoundation framework, so you'll need to import that module in any files where you want to use it. You can then create an AVAudioRecorder as follows:

```
// destinationURL is the location of where we want to store our recording
var error : NSError?
```

```
audioRecorder = AVAudioRecorder(URL:destinationURL, settings:nil, error:&error)

if (error != nil) {
    println("Couldn't create a recorder: \(error)")
}

audioRecorder?.prepareToRecord()
```

To begin recording, use the `record` method:

```
audioRecorder?.record()
```

To stop recording, use the `stop` method:

```
audioRecorder?.stop()
```

When recording has ended, the file pointed at by the URL you used to create the AVAudioRecorder contains a sound file, which you can play using AVAudioPlayer or any other audio system.

Discussion

Like an AVAudioPlayer, an AVAudioRecorder needs to have at least one strong reference made to it in order to keep it in memory.

To record audio, you first need to have the location of the file where the recorded audio will end up. The AVAudioRecorder will create the file if it doesn't already exist; if it does, the recorder will erase the file and overwrite it. So, if you want to avoid losing recorded audio, either never record to the same place twice, or move the recorded audio somewhere else when you're done recording.

The recorded audio file needs to be stored in a location where your game is allowed to put files. A good place to use is your game's *Documents* directory; any files placed in this folder will be backed up when the user's device is synced.

To get the location of your game's *Documents* folder, you can use the NSFileManager class:

```
let documentsURL = NSFileManager.defaultManager()
    .URLsForDirectory(NSSearchPathDirectory.DocumentDirectory,
        inDomains:NSSearchPathDomainMask.UserDomainMask).last as! NSURL
```

Once you have the location of the directory, you can create a URL relative to it. Remember, the URL doesn't have to point to a real file yet; one will be created when recording begins:

```
return documentsURL.URLByAppendingPathComponent("RecordedSound.wav")
```

4.3. Working with Multiple Audio Players

Problem

You want to use multiple audio players, but reuse players when possible.

Solution

Create a manager object that manages a collection of AVAudioPlayers. When you want to play a sound, you ask this object to give you an AVAudioPlayer. The manager object will try to give you an AVAudioPlayer that's not currently doing anything, but if it can't find one, it will create one.

To create your manager object, create a file called *AVAudioPlayerPool.swift* with the following contents:

```
// An array of all players stored in the pool; not accessible
// outside this file
private var players : [AVAudioPlayer] = []

class AVAudioPlayerPool: NSObject {

    // Given the URL of a sound file, either create or reuse an audio player
    class func playerWithURL(url : NSURL) -> AVAudioPlayer? {

        // Try to find a player that can be reused and is not playing
        let availablePlayers = players.filter { (player) -> Bool in
            return player.playing == false && player.url == url
        }

        // If we found one, return it
        if let playerToUse = availablePlayers.first {
            println("Reusing player for \(url.lastPathComponent)")
            return playerToUse
        }

        // Didn't find one? Create a new one
        var error : NSError? = nil
        if let newPlayer = AVAudioPlayer(contentsOfURL:url, error:&error) {
            println("Creating new player for url \(url.lastPathComponent)")
            players.append(newPlayer)
            return newPlayer
        } else {
            // We might not be able to create one, so log and return nil
            println("Couldn't load \(url.lastPathComponent): \(error)")
            return nil
        }

    }
}
```

```
    }
```

You can then use it as follows:

```
if let url = NSBundle.mainBundle().URLForResource("TestSound",
    withExtension: "wav") {
    let player = AVAudioPlayerPool.playerWithURL(url)
    player?.play()
}
```

Discussion

AVAudioPlayers are allowed to be played multiple times, but aren't allowed to change the file that they're playing. If you want to reuse a single player, you have to use the same file; if you want to use a different file, you'll need a new player.

This means that the AVAudioPlayerPool object shown in this recipe needs to know which file you want to play.

Our AVAudioPlayerPool object does the following things:

1. It keeps a list of AVAudioPlayer objects in an array.

2. When a player is requested, it checks to see if it has an available player with the right URL; if it does, it returns that.

3. If there's no AVAudioPlayer that it can use—either because all of the suitable AVAudioPlayers are playing, or because there's no AVAudioPlayer with the right URL—it creates one, prepares it with the URL provided, and adds it to the list of AVAudioPlayers. This means that when this new AVAudioPlayer is done playing, it can be reused.

4.4. Cross-Fading Between Tracks

Problem

You want to blend multiple sounds by smoothly fading one out and another in.

Solution

This method slowly fades an AVAudioPlayer from a starting volume to an end volume, over a set duration:

```
func fadePlayer(player: AVAudioPlayer,
    fromVolume startVolume : Float,
    toVolume endVolume : Float,
    overTime time : Float) {
```

```
        // Update the volume every 1/100 of a second
        var fadeSteps : Int = Int(time) * 100
        // Work out how much time each step will take
        var timePerStep : Float = 1 / 100.0

        self.audioPlayer?.volume = startVolume;

        // Schedule a number of volume changes
        for step in 0...fadeSteps {

            let delayInSeconds : Float = Float(step) * timePerStep

            let popTime = dispatch_time(DISPATCH_TIME_NOW,
                Int64(delayInSeconds * Float(NSEC_PER_SEC)));
            dispatch_after(popTime, dispatch_get_main_queue()) {

                let fraction = (Float(step) / Float(fadeSteps))

                player.volume = startVolume +
                    (endVolume - startVolume) * fraction

            }
        }
    }
```

To use this method to fade in an AVAudioPlayer, use a startVolume of 0.0 and an endVolume of 1.0:

```
    fadePlayer(audioPlayer!, fromVolume: 0.0, toVolume: 1.0, overTime: 1.0)
```

To fade out, use a startVolume of 1.0 and an endVolume of 0.0:

```
    fadePlayer(audioPlayer!, fromVolume: 1.0, toVolume: 0.0, overTime: 1.0)
```

To make the fade take longer, increase the overTime parameter.

Discussion

When you want the volume of an AVAudioPlayer to slowly fade out, what you really want is for the volume to change very slightly but very often. In this recipe, we've created a method that uses Grand Central Dispatch to schedule the repeated, gradual adjustment of the volume of a player over time.

To determine how many individual volume changes are needed, the first step is to decide how many times per second the volume should change. In this example, we've chosen 100 times per second—that is, the volume will be changed 100 times for every second the fade should last:

```
    // Update the volume every 1/100 of a second
    var fadeSteps : Int = Int(time) * 100
```

```
// Work out how much time each step will take
var timePerStep : Float = 1 / 100.0
```

 Feel free to experiment with this number. Bigger numbers will lead to smoother fades, whereas smaller numbers will be more efficient but might sound worse.

The next step is to ensure that the player's current volume is set to be the start volume:

```
self.audioPlayer?.volume = startVolume;
```

We then repeatedly schedule volume changes. We're actually scheduling these changes all at once; however, each change is scheduled to take place slightly after the previous one.

To know exactly when a change should take place, all we need to know is how many steps into the fade we are, and how long the total fade should take. From there, we can calculate how far in the future a specific step should take place:

```
for step in 0...fadeSteps {

    let delayInSeconds : Float = Float(step) * timePerStep
```

Once this duration is known, we can get Grand Central Dispatch to schedule it:

```
let popTime = dispatch_time(DISPATCH_TIME_NOW,
    Int64(delayInSeconds * Float(NSEC_PER_SEC)));
dispatch_after(popTime, dispatch_get_main_queue()) {
```

The next few lines of code are executed when the step is ready to happen. At this point, we need to know exactly what the volume of the audio player should be:

```
let fraction = (Float(step) / Float(fadeSteps))

player.volume = startVolume + (endVolume - startVolume) * fraction
```

When the code runs, the for loop creates and schedules multiple blocks that set the volume, with each block reducing the volume a little. The end result is that the user hears a gradual lessening in volume—in other words, a fade out!

4.5. Synthesizing Speech

Problem

You want to make your app speak.

Solution

First, import the AVFoundation in your file (see Recipe 4.1).

Then, create an instance of AVSpeechSynthesizer:

```
var speechSynthesizer = AVSpeechSynthesizer()
```

When you have text you want to speak, create an AVSpeechUtterance:

```
let utterance = AVSpeechUtterance(string:self.textToSpeakField.text)
```

You then give the utterance to your AVSpeechSynthesizer:

```
self.speechSynthesizer.speakUtterance(utterance)
```

Discussion

The voices you use with AVSpeechSynthesizer are the same ones seen in the Siri personal assistant that's built into all devices released since the iPhone 4S, and in the VoiceOver accessibility feature.

You can send more than one AVSpeechUtterance to an AVSpeechSynthesizer at the same time. If you call speakUtterance while the synthesizer is already speaking, it will wait until the current utterance has finished before moving on to the next.

 Don't call speakUtterance with the same AVSpeechUtterance twice—you'll cause an exception, and your app will crash.

Once you start speaking, you can instruct the AVSpeechSynthesizer to pause speaking, either immediately or at the next word:

```
// Stop speaking immediately
self.speechSynthesizer.pauseSpeakingAtBoundary(AVSpeechBoundary.Immediate)
// Stop speaking after the current word
self.speechSynthesizer.pauseSpeakingAtBoundary(AVSpeechBoundary.Word)
```

Once you've paused speaking, you can resume it at any time:

```
self.speechSynthesizer.continueSpeaking()
```

If you're done with speaking, you can clear the AVSpeechSynthesizer of the current and pending AVSpeechUtterances by calling stopSpeakingAtBoundary. This method works in the same way as pauseSpeakingAtBoundary, but once you call it, anything the synthesizer was about to say is forgotten.

4.6. Getting Information About What the Music App Is Playing

Problem

You want to find out information about whatever song the Music application is playing.

Solution

To do this, you'll need to add the Media Player framework to your code by importing the `MediaPlayer` module in your file.

First, get an `MPMusicPlayerController` from the system, which contains information about the built-in music library. Next, get the currently playing `MPMediaItem`, which represents a piece of media that the Music app is currently playing. Finally, call `value ForProperty` to get specific information about that media item:

```
let musicPlayer = MPMusicPlayerController.systemMusicPlayer()

let currentTrack : MPMediaItem? = musicPlayer.nowPlayingItem
let title = currentTrack?.valueForProperty(MPMediaItemPropertyTitle)
    as? String ?? "None"
let artist = currentTrack?.valueForProperty(MPMediaItemPropertyArtist)
    as? String ?? "None"
let album = currentTrack?.valueForProperty(MPMediaItemPropertyAlbumTitle)
    as? String ?? "None"

self.titleLabel.text = title
self.artistLabel.text = artist
self.albumLabel.text = album
```

Once you've got this information, you can do whatever you like with it, including displaying it in a label, showing it in-game, and more.

Discussion

An `MPMusicPlayerController` represents the music playback system that's built into every iOS device. Using this object, you can get information about the currently playing track, set the currently playing queue of music, and control the playback (such as by pausing and skipping backward and forward in the queue).

There are actually *two* `MPMusicPlayerControllers` available to your app. The first is the *system music player*, which represents the state of the built-in Music application. The system music player is shared across all applications, so they all have control over the same thing.

The second music player controller that's available is the *application music player*. The application music player is functionally identical to the system music player, with a single difference: each application has its own application music player. This means that they each have their own playlist.

Only one piece of media can be playing at a single time. If an application starts using its own application music player, the system music player will pause and let the application take over. If you're using an app that's playing music out of the application music player, and you then exit that app, the music will stop.

To get information about the currently playing track, you use the nowPlayingItem property of the MPMusicPlayerController. This property returns an MPMediaItem, which is an object that represents a piece of media. Media means music, videos, audiobooks, podcasts, and more—not just music!

To get information about an MPMediaItem, you use the valueForProperty method. This method takes one of several possible property names. Here are some examples:

MPMediaItemPropertyAlbumTitle
  The name of the album.

MPMediaItemPropertyArtist
  The name of the artist.

MPMediaItemPropertyAlbumArtist
  The name of the album's main artist (for albums with multiple artists).

MPMediaItemPropertyGenre
  The genre of the music.

MPMediaItemPropertyComposer
  The composer of the music.

MPMediaItemPropertyPlaybackDuration
  The length of the music, in seconds.

 The media library is only available on iOS devices—it's not available on the iOS Simulator. If you try to use these features on the simulator, it just plain won't work.

4.7. Detecting When the Currently Playing Track Changes

Problem

You want to detect when the currently playing media item changes.

Solution

Use NSNotificationCenter to subscribe to the MPMusicPlayerControllerNowPlayin gItemDidChangeNotification notification. First, create a property of type AnyOb ject? to store a reference to the *observer object*:

```
var trackChangedObserver : AnyObject?
```

When you want to begin tracking when the now playing item changes, ask the notification center to begin observing the notification:

```
trackChangedObserver = NSNotificationCenter.defaultCenter()
    .addObserverForName(
        MPMusicPlayerControllerNowPlayingItemDidChangeNotification,
        object: nil, queue: NSOperationQueue.mainQueue()) { (notification)
            -> Void in
    self.updateTrackInformation()
}
```

Next, get a reference to the MPMusicPlayerController that you want to get notifications for, and call beginGeneratingPlaybackNotifications on it:

```
let musicPlayer = MPMusicPlayerController.systemMusicPlayer()

musicPlayer.beginGeneratingPlaybackNotifications()
```

When you begin observing notifications using addObserverForName, you're given a reference to an object: the *observer object*. You need to keep a reference to this object around, because when you want to tell the notification system to stop notifying you (and you *must* do this, or else you'll get bugs and crashes), you pass the object back to the NSNotificationCenter and call the removeObserver method. A common place to do this is in the view controller's deinit method:

```
deinit {
    NSNotificationCenter.defaultCenter().removeObserver(trackChangedObserver!)
}
```

Discussion

Notifications regarding the current item won't be sent unless beginGeneratingPlay backNotifications is called. If you stop being interested in the currently playing item, call endGeneratingPlaybackNotifications.

Note that you might not receive these notifications if your application is in the background. It's generally a good idea to manually update your interface whenever your game comes back from the background, instead of just relying on the notifications to arrive.

4.8. Controlling Music Playback

Problem

You want to control the track that the Music application is playing.

Solution

Use the `MPMusicPlayerController` to control the state of the music player:

```
let musicPlayer = MPMusicPlayerController.systemMusicPlayer()

musicPlayer?.play()
musicPlayer?.pause()
musicPlayer?.skipToBeginning()
musicPlayer?.skipToNextItem()
musicPlayer?.skipToPreviousItem()
musicPlayer?.beginSeekingForward()
musicPlayer?.beginSeekingBackward()
musicPlayer?.stop()
```

Discussion

Don't forget that if you're using the shared system music player controller, any changes you make to the playback state apply to all applications. This means that the playback state of your application might get changed by *other* applications—usually the Music application, but possibly by other apps.

You can query the current state of the music player by asking it for the `playback State`, which is one of the following values:

`MPMusicPlaybackStateStopped`
  The music player isn't playing anything.

`MPMusicPlaybackStatePlaying`
  The music player is currently playing.

`MPMusicPlaybackStatePaused`
  The music player is playing, but is paused.

`MPMusicPlaybackStateInterrupted`
  The music player is playing, but has been interrupted (e.g., by a phone call).

`MPMusicPlaybackStateSeekingForward`
  The music player is fast-forwarding.

`MPMusicPlaybackStateSeekingBackward`
  The music player is fast-reversing.

You can get notified about changes in the playback state by registering for the `MPMusic PlayerControllerPlaybackStateDidChangeNotification` notification, in the same way `MPMusicPlayerControllerNowPlayingItemDidChangeNotification` allows you to get notified about changes in the currently playing item.

4.9. Allowing the User to Select Music

Problem

You want to allow the user to choose some music to play.

Solution

You can display an `MPMediaPickerController` to let the user select music.

First, make your view controller conform to the `MPMediaPickerControllerDelegate`:

```
class ViewController: UIViewController, MPMediaPickerControllerDelegate {
```

Next, add the following code at the point where you want to display the media picker:

```
let picker = MPMediaPickerController(mediaTypes:MPMediaType.AnyAudio)

picker.allowsPickingMultipleItems = true
picker.showsCloudItems = true

picker.delegate = self

self.presentViewController(picker, animated:false, completion:nil)
```

Then, add the following two methods to your view controller:

```
func mediaPicker(mediaPicker: MPMediaPickerController!,
    didPickMediaItems mediaItemCollection: MPMediaItemCollection!) {

    for item in mediaItemCollection.items {
        let itemName = item.valueForProperty(MPMediaItemPropertyTitle)
            as? String
        println("Picked item: \(itemName)")
    }

    let musicPlayer = MPMusicPlayerController.systemMusicPlayer()

    musicPlayer.setQueueWithItemCollection(mediaItemCollection)

    musicPlayer.play()

    self.dismissViewControllerAnimated(false, completion:nil)
}

func mediaPickerDidCancel(mediaPicker: MPMediaPickerController!) {
```

```
    self.dismissViewControllerAnimated(false, completion:nil)
}
```

Discussion

An `MPMediaPickerController` uses the exact same user interface as the one you see in the built-in Music application. This means that your player doesn't have to waste time learning how to navigate a different interface.

When you create an `MPMediaPickerController`, you can choose what kinds of media you want the user to pick. In this recipe, we've gone with `MPMediaTypeAnyAudio`, which, as the name suggests, means the user can pick any audio: music, audiobooks, podcasts, and so on. Other options include:

- `MPMediaType.Music`
- `MPMediaType.Podcast`
- `MPMediaType.AudioBook`
- `MPMediaType.AudioITunesU`
- `MPMediaType.Movie`
- `MPMediaType.TVShow`
- `MPMediaType.VideoPodcast`
- `MPMediaType.MusicVideo`
- `MPMediaType.VideoITunesU`
- `MPMediaType.HomeVideo`
- `MPMediaType.AnyVideo`
- `MPMediaType.Any`

In addition to setting what kind of content you want the user to pick, you can also set whether you want the user to be able to pick multiple items or just one:

```
picker.allowsPickingMultipleItems = true
```

Finally, you can decide whether you want to present media that the user has purchased from iTunes, but isn't currently downloaded onto the device. Apple refers to this feature as "iTunes in the Cloud," and you can turn it on or off through the `showsCloudItems` property:

```
picker.showsCloudItems = true
```

When the user finishes picking media, the delegate of the `MPMediaPickerController` receives the `mediaPicker(_, didPickMediaItems:)` message. The media items that were chosen are contained in an `MPMediaItemCollection` object, which is basically an array of `MPMediaItems`.

In addition to getting information about the media items that were selected, you can also give the `MPMediaItemCollection` directly to an `MPMusicPlayerController`, and tell it to start playing:

```
let musicPlayer = MPMusicPlayerController.systemMusicPlayer()

musicPlayer.setQueueWithItemCollection(mediaItemCollection)

musicPlayer.play()
```

Once you're done getting content out of the media picker, you need to dismiss it, by using the `dismissViewControllerAnimated(_, completion:)` method. This also applies if the user taps the Cancel button in the media picker: in this case, your delegate receives the `mediaPickerDidCancel` message, and your application should dismiss the view controller in the same way.

4.10. Cooperating with Other Applications' Audio

Problem

You want to play background music only when the user isn't already listening to something.

Solution

You can find out if another application is currently playing audio by using the `AVAudioSession` class:

```
let session = AVAudioSession.sharedInstance()

if (session.otherAudioPlaying) {
    // Another application is playing audio. Don't play any sound that might
    // conflict with music, such as your own background music.
} else {
    // No other app is playing audio - crank the tunes!
}
```

Discussion

The `AVAudioSession` class lets you control how audio is currently being handled on the device, and gives you considerable flexibility in terms of how the device should handle things like the ringer switch (the switch on the side of the device) and what happens when the user locks the screen.

By default, if you begin playing back audio using `AVAudioPlayer` and another application (such as the built-in Music app) is playing audio, the other application will stop all sound, and the audio played by your game will be the only thing audible.

However, you might want the user to be able to listen to her own music while playing your game—the background music might not be a very important part of your game, for example.

To change the default behavior of muting other applications, you need to set the audio session's *category*. For example, to indicate to the system that your application should not cause other apps to mute their audio, you need to set the audio session's category to `AVAudioSessionCategoryAmbient`:

```
var error : NSError = nil
AVAudioSession.sharedInstance().setCategory(AVAudioSessionCategoryAmbient,
  error:&error)

if (error != nil) {
    println("Problem setting audio session: \(error)")
}
```

There are several categories of audio session available. The most important to games are the following:

`AVAudioSessionCategoryAmbient`
Audio isn't the most important part of your game, and other apps should be able to play audio alongside yours. When the ringer switch is set to *mute*, your audio is silenced, and when the screen locks, your audio stops.

`AVAudioSessionCategorySoloAmbient`
Audio is reasonably important to your game. If other apps are playing audio, they'll stop. However, the audio session will continue to respect the ringer switch and the screen locking.

`AVAudioSessionCategoryPlayback`
Audio is very important to your game. Other apps are silenced, and your app *ignores* the ringer switch and the screen locking.

When using AVAudioSessionCategoryPlayback, your app will still be stopped when the screen locks. To make it keep running, you need to mark your app as one that plays audio in the background. To do this, follow these steps:

1. Open your project's information page by clicking the project at the top of the Project Navigator.
2. Go to the Capabilities tab.
3. Turn on "Background Modes," and then turn on "Audio and AirPlay."

Your app will now play audio in the background, as long as the audio session's category is set to AVAudioSessionCategoryPlayback.

4.11. Determining How to Best Use Sound in Your Game Design

Problem

You want to make optimal use of sound and music in your game design.

Solution

It's really hard to make an iOS game that relies on sound. For one, you can't count on the user wearing headphones, and sounds in games (and everything else, really) don't sound their best coming from the tiny speakers found in iOS devices.

Many games "get around" this by prompting users to put on their headphones as the game launches, or suggesting that they are "best experienced via headphones" in the sound and music options menu, if it has one. We think this is a suboptimal solution.

The best iOS games understand and acknowledge the environment in which the games are likely to be played: typically a busy, distraction-filled environment, where your beautiful audio might not be appreciated due to background noise or the fact that the user has the volume turned all the way down.

The solution is to make sure your game works with, or without, sound. Don't count on the user hearing anything at all, in fact.

Discussion

Unless you're building a game that is based around music or sound, you should make it completely playable without sound. Your users will thank you for it, even if they never actually thank you for it!

CHAPTER 5

Data Storage

Games are apps, and apps run on data. Whether it's just resources that your game loads or saved-game files that you need to store, your game will eventually need to work with data stored on the flash chips that make up the storage subsystems present on all iOS devices.

In this chapter, you'll learn how to convert objects into saveable data, how to work with iCloud, how to load resources without freezing up the rest of the game, and more.

5.1. Saving the State of Your Game

Problem

You want game objects to be able to store their state, so that it can be loaded from disk.

Solution

Make your objects conform to the NSCoding protocol, and then implement encode WithCoder and init(coder:), like so:

```
class Monster: NSObject, NSCoding {

    // Game data
    var hitPoints = 0
    var name = "GameObject"

    // Initializer used when creating a brand new object
    override init() {

    }

    // Initializer used when loading the object from data
    required init(coder aDecoder: NSCoder) {
```

```
        self.hitPoints = aDecoder.decodeIntegerForKey("hitPoints")

        // Attempt to get the object with key "name" as a string;
        // if we can't convert it to a string or it doesn't exist,
        // fall back to "No Name"
        self.name = aDecoder.decodeObjectForKey("name") as? String ?? "No Name"
    }

    func encodeWithCoder(aCoder: NSCoder) {

        aCoder.encodeObject(self.name, forKey: "name")
        aCoder.encodeInteger(self.hitPoints, forKey: "hitPoints")

    }

}
```

When you want to store this information into an `NSData` object, for saving to disk or somewhere else, you use the `NSKeyedArchiver`:

```
let monster = Monster()

let monsterData = NSKeyedArchiver.archivedDataWithRootObject(monster)

// monsterData can now be saved to disk
```

If you have an `NSData` object that contains information encoded by `NSKeyedArchiver`, you can convert it back into a regular object with `NSKeyedUnarchiver`:

```
// Load monsterData (an NSData) from somewhere, and then:

let loadedMonster = NSKeyedUnarchiver
    .unarchiveObjectWithData(monsterData) as! Monster
```

Discussion

When you're enabling objects to save their state on disk, the first step is to figure out exactly what you *need* to save, and what can be safely thrown away. For example, a monster may need to save the amount of hit-points it has left, but may not need to save the direction in which its eyes are pointing. The less data you store, the better.

The `NSKeyedArchiver` class lets you store specific data in an archive. When you use it, you pass in an object that you want to be archived. This object can be any object that conforms to the `NSCoding` protocol, which many built-in objects in Cocoa Touch already do (such as strings, arrays, dictionaries, numbers, `NSDate`, and so on). If you want to archive a collection object, such as an array or dictionaries, it must only include objects that conform to `NSCoding`.

NSKeyedArchiver gives you an NSData object, which you can write to disk, upload to another computer, or otherwise keep around. If you load this data from disk, you can *unarchive* the data and get back the original object. To do this, you use NSKeyed Unarchiver, which works in a very similar way to NSKeyedArchiver.

The encodeWithCoder method is used by the archiving system to gather the actual information that should be stored in the final archive. This method receives an NSCoder object, which you provide information to. For each piece of info you want to save, you use one of the following methods:

- encodeInt(_, forKey:)
- encodeObject(_, forKey:)
- encodeFloat(_, forKey:)
- encodeDouble(_, forKey:)
- encodeBool(_, forKey:)

These encoding methods are only the most popular ones. Others exist, and you can find the complete list in the Xcode documentation for the NSCoder class (*http://bit.ly/nscoder*).

When you want to encode, for example, an integer named hitPoints, you call enco deInt(_, forKey:) like so:

```
self.hitPoints = aDecoder.decodeIntegerForKey("hitPoints")
```

When you use encodeObject(_, forKey:), the object that you provide *must* be one that conforms to NSCoding. This is because the encoding system will send it an encode WithCoder method of its own.

The encoding system will detect if an object is encoded more than one time and remove duplicates. If, for example, both object A and object B use encodeObject(_, forKey:) to encode object C, that object will be encoded only once.

Decoding is the process of getting back information from the archive. This happens when you use NSKeyedUnarchiver, which reads the NSData object you give it and creates all of the objects that were encoded. Each object that's been unarchived is sent the init(coder:) method, which allows it to pull information out of the decoder.

You get information from the decoder using methods that are very similar to those present in the encoder (again, this is just a sampling of the available methods):

- decodeObjectForKey
- decodeIntForKey
- decodeFloatForKey
- decodeDoubleForKey
- decodeBoolForKey

5.2. Storing High Scores Locally

Problem

You want to store high scores in a file, on disk.

Solution

First, put your high scores in dictionary objects, and then put those dictionaries in an array:

```
// Store each high score you want to save in a
// dictionary
let scoreDictionary = [
    "score": 1000,
    "date":NSDate(),
    "playerName": playerName
]

// Store the list of scores you want to save in an
// array. (In real life, you would probably have more
// than one high score to record)
let highScores = [scoreDictionary]
```

Next, determine the location on disk where these scores can be placed:

```
let fileManager = NSFileManager.defaultManager()
let documentsURL = fileManager.URLsForDirectory(
    NSSearchPathDirectory.DocumentDirectory,
    inDomains:NSSearchPathDomainMask.UserDomainMask).last as! NSURL

let highScoreURL = documentsURL
    .URLByAppendingPathComponent("HighScores.plist")
```

Finally, write out the high scores array to this location:

```
    // We need to cast the array to NSArray, in order to
    // get access to the writeToURL method
    (highScores as NSArray).writeToURL(highScoreURL, atomically:true)
```

You can load the high scores array by reading from the location:

```
    // Load the array as an array of dictionaries mapping Strings to
    // other objects
    // If it can't be loaded, or doesn't contain this type, result is nil
    if let loadedHighScores
        = NSArray(contentsOfURL: highScoreURL) as? [[String:AnyObject]] {
        println("Loaded high scores:\(loadedHighScores)")
    } else {
        println("Error loading high scores!")
    }
```

Discussion

When you're saving high scores, it's important to know exactly what information you want to save. This will vary from game to game, but common components include the score, the time when the score was earned, and any additional context needed for that score to make sense.

A very easy way to save information to disk is to put each score in a dictionary, and put each dictionary in an array. You can then write that array to disk, or load it back. Note that the method used to write the data to disk, writeToURL(_, atomically:), is part of the array class, and not built into the Swift array class. However, the Swift compiler is able to *bridge* from the Swift array type to NSArray, meaning that you can cast the array to NSArray using the syntax array as NSArray. You can then call writeToURL on the result of that cast.

An application in iOS is only allowed to read and write files that are inside the app's *sandbox*. Each app is limited to its own sandbox and is generally not allowed to access any files that lie outside of it. To get the location of an app's *Documents* folder, which is located inside the sandbox, you use the NSFileManager class to give you the NSURL. You can then construct an NSURL based on that, and give *that* URL to the array, using it to write to the disk.

You can then do the reverse to load the data from disk. Note that when you load the array from disk, you need to specify to Swift what the array contains. If you don't, Swift won't know the type of the array, and will present it as an array of AnyObject, meaning you'll need to individually cast each object that you get from the array to your desired type.

If you want to store your high scores online, you can use Game Center (see Recipe 13.4).

5.3. Using iCloud to Save Games

Problem

You want to save the player's game in iCloud.

Solution

 To work with iCloud, you'll need to have an active iOS Developer Program membership.

First, activate iCloud support in your app. To do this, select the project at the top of the Project Navigator, and ensure that your developer team is selected (and isn't None). If you happen to be a member of multiple developer teams, make sure the right one is selected, because enabling iCloud support means registering a new App ID with your developer team.

Next, switch to the Capabilities tab. Turn on the "iCloud" switch. Follow the prompts to add iCloud support.

 In iCloud, you store your app's information in *iCloud containers*. Usually, each of your apps has its own container, but you can make multiple apps share a single container. For example, if you have a Mac game and an iOS game, you can have them share their saved games by making them use the same iCloud container.

When you first enable iCloud support, only *key-value storage* is turned on by default. Turn on iCloud Documents as well, to enable support for saving files in iCloud. Xcode will do a little more work to add support for storing files in an iCloud container.

Saving the player's game in iCloud really means saving game data. This means that you need to have your data stored in an NSData object of some kind.

First, you need to check to see if iCloud is available. It may not be; for example, if the user hasn't signed in to an Apple ID or has deliberately disabled iCloud on the device. You can check to see if iCloud is available by doing the following:

```
// Get the saved data from somewhere
let saveData : NSData = self.saveGameData()

// If we aren't signed in to iCloud, then we must save locally
if NSFileManager.defaultManager().ubiquityIdentityToken == nil {
```

```
        saveGameLocally(saveData)
    }
```

To put a file in iCloud, you do this:

```
// This must always be done in the background, because
// locating the iCloud container on disk can involve
// setting it up, which can take time.
NSOperationQueue().addOperationWithBlock { () -> Void in

    let fileName = "Documents/MySavedGame.save"

    if let containerURL = NSFileManager.defaultManager()
        .URLForUbiquityContainerIdentifier(nil) {

        let fileURL = containerURL.URLByAppendingPathComponent(fileName)

        var error : NSError? = nil

        saveData.writeToURL(fileURL,
            options: NSDataWritingOptions.DataWritingAtomic,
            error: &error)

        if error != nil {
            println("Error saving file to iCloud!")
        }
    }
}
```

To find files that are in iCloud, you use the NSMetadataQuery class. This returns information about files that have been stored in iCloud, either by the current device or by another device the user owns. NSMetadataQuery works like a search—you tell it what you're looking for, and register to be notified when the search completes:

```
lazy var metadataQuery : NSMetadataQuery = [
    let query = NSMetadataQuery()

    // Search for all files whose name end in .save in the iCloud
    // container's Documents folder
    query.searchScopes = [NSMetadataQueryUbiquitousDocumentsScope]
    query.predicate = NSPredicate(format: "%K LIKE '*.save'",
        NSMetadataItemFSNameKey)

    let notificationCenter = NSNotificationCenter.defaultCenter()

    // Call the searchComplete method when this query
    // finds content (either initially, or when new
    //changes are discovered after the app starts)
    notificationCenter.addObserver(self,
        selector: "searchComplete",
        name: NSMetadataQueryDidFinishGatheringNotification,
        object: nil)
    notificationCenter.addObserver(self,
```

```
            selector: "searchComplete",
            name: NSMetadataQueryDidUpdateNotification,
            object: nil)

        return query
    }()

    deinit {
        // When this object is going away, tidy up after
        // the metadata query

        metadataQuery.stopQuery()


        let notificationCenter = NSNotificationCenter.defaultCenter()
        notificationCenter.removeObserver(self)
    }
```

When your app starts, you tell the query to start running:

```
metadataQuery.startQuery()
```

You then implement a method that's run when the search is complete:

```
func searchComplete() {
    for item in metadataQuery.results as! [NSMetadataItem] {
        // Find the URL for the item
        let url = item.valueForAttribute(NSMetadataItemURLKey) as! NSURL

        if item.valueForAttribute(
            NSMetadataUbiquitousItemHasUnresolvedConflictsKey)
            as! Bool == true {
            // Another device has got a conflicting version
            // of this file, and we need to resolve it.
            self.resolveConflictsForItemAtURL(url)
        }

        // Has the file already been downloaded?
        if item.valueForAttribute(NSMetadataUbiquitousItemDownloadingStatusKey)
            as! String
            == NSMetadataUbiquitousItemDownloadingStatusCurrent {
                // This file is downloaded and is the most current version;
                // do something with it (like offer to let the user load
                // the saved game)
                self.saveGameWasUpdated(url)

        } else {
            // The file is either not downloaded at all, or is out of date
            // We need to download the file from iCloud; when it finishes
            // downloading, NSMetadataQuery will call this method again
            var error : NSError? = nil

            // Ask iCloud to begin downloading.
            NSFileManager.defaultManager()
```

```
                    .startDownloadingUbiquitousItemAtURL(url, error:&error)

            // Check if starting the download didn't work:
            if error != nil {
                println("Problem starting download of \(url): \(error)")
            }
        }
    }
}
```

 An NSMetadataQuery runs until it's stopped. If you make a change to a file that the query is watching, you'll receive a new notification.

If you're done looking for files in iCloud, you can stop the query using the stopQuery method:

```
metadataQuery.stopQuery()
```

When a file is in iCloud and you make changes to it, iCloud will automatically upload the changed file, and other devices will receive the new copy. If the same file is changed at the same time by different devices, the file will be in conflict. You can detect this by checking the NSMetadataUbiquitousItemHasUnresolvedConflictsKey attribute on the results of your NSMetadataQuery; if this is set to true, then there are conflicts.

There are several ways you can resolve a conflict; one way is to simply say, "The version that I have locally is the correct version; ignore conflicts." To indicate this to the system, you do this:

```
func resolveConflictsForItemAtURL(url : NSURL) {

    // 'The version I have is correct; all others are wrong.'
    for conflictVersion in NSFileVersion
        .unresolvedConflictVersionsOfItemAtURL(url)
        as! [NSFileVersion] {
        // Mark these other versions as resolved; iCloud will tell other
        // devices to update their local copies
        conflictVersion.resolved = true
    }

    // Remove our conflicted copies
    NSFileVersion.removeOtherVersionsOfItemAtURL(url, error: nil)

}
```

Discussion

iCloud is a technology from Apple that syncs documents and information across the various devices that a user owns. "Devices," in this case, means both iOS devices and

Macs; when you create a document and put it in iCloud, the same file appears on all devices that you're signed in to. Additionally, the file is backed up by Apple on the Web.

To use iCloud, you need to have an active iOS Developer account, because all iCloud activity in an app is linked to the developer who created the app. You don't have to do anything special with your app besides have Xcode activate iCloud support for it—all of the setup is handled for you automatically.

It's worth keeping in mind that not all users will have access to iCloud. If they're not signed in to an Apple ID, or if they've deliberately turned off iCloud, your game still needs to work without it. This means saving your game files locally, and not putting them into iCloud.

Additionally, it's possible that the user might have signed out of iCloud, and a different user has signed in. You can check this by asking the `NSFileManager` for the `ubiquityI dentityToken`, which you can store; if it's different from the last time you checked, you should throw away any local copies of your saved games, and redownload the files from iCloud.

You should always perform iCloud work on a background queue. iCloud operations can frequently take several dozen milliseconds to complete, which can slow down your game if you run them on the main queue and look like your game is hanging.

5.4. Using the iCloud Key-Value Store

Problem

You want to store small amounts of information in iCloud.

Solution

Use `NSUbiquitousKeyValueStore`, which is like a dictionary whose contents are shared across all of the user's devices.

To get values out of the key-value store, you do this:

```
// Retrieve the value from the key-value store
let store = NSUbiquitousKeyValueStore.defaultStore()
return Int(store.longLongForKey("levelNumber"))
```

To store values in the key-value store, you do this:

```
// Store the value in the key-value store
let store = NSUbiquitousKeyValueStore.defaultStore()
store.setLongLong(Int64(value), forKey: "levelNumber")

// Ensure that these changes have been saved to disk
// (note: this doesn't sync the local iCloud container
```

```
// with the server, that happens later when the system decides
// it's time)
store.synchronize()
```

It's possible that the contents of the key-value store can change remotely. For example, if your player happens to be playing the game on two devices at the same time—which you can be guaranteed will happen!—then you need to update your game accordingly. To do this, you register to receive the NSUbiquitousKeyValueStoreDidChangeExternallyNotification:

```
// Register to be notified when the key-value store
// is changed by another device
NSNotificationCenter.defaultCenter().addObserver(self,
    selector: "ubiquitousKeyValueStoreUpdated",
    name: NSUbiquitousKeyValueStoreDidChangeExternallyNotification,
    object: nil);
```

Discussion

Many games don't need to store very much information in order to let the players keep their state around. For example, if you're making a puzzle game, you might only need to store the number of the level that the players reached. In these cases, the NSUbiquitous KeyValueStore is exactly what you need. The ubiquitous key-value store stores small amounts of data—strings, numbers, and so on—and keeps them synchronized.

 You'll need to activate iCloud support in your app for NSUbiquitous KeyValueStore to work. Additionally, you must call NSFile Manager's URLForUbiquityContainerIdentifier at least once before attempting to access the key-value store, in order to make sure that your app has access to the iCloud container. Don't forget, URL ForUbiquityContainerIdentifier must be called on a background queue. Finally, you also need to handle the case of the user not being signed into iCloud: if the user is not signed in, anything you store in the key-value store will disappear, and you'll need to store the information locally.

Unlike when you're working with files, conflict resolution in the ubiquitous key-value store is handled automatically for you by iCloud: the most recent value that was set wins. This can sometimes lead to problems. For example, consider the following user experience:

1. You have a puzzle game, and the highest level that's been unlocked is stored in the key-value store.

2. You play up to level 6 on your iPhone, and iCloud syncs the key-value store.

3. Later, you play the game on your iPad, but it's offline. You get up to level 2 on your iPad. Later, your iPad is connected to the Internet, and iCloud syncs this latest value. Because it's the latest value to be set, it overwrites the "older" value of 2.

4. You then play the game on your iPhone, and are very surprised to see that your progress has been "lost." You delete the app and leave a 1-star review on the App Store. The app developer goes bankrupt and dies alone in a gutter.

To solve this problem, you should keep data in the local user defaults, and update it only after comparing it to the ubiquitous store. When the store changes, compare it against the local user defaults; if the ubiquitous store's value is lower, copy the value from the local store into the ubiquitous store, overwriting it. If it's higher, copy the value from the ubiquitous store into the local store. Whenever you want to read the information, always consult the local store.

You're limited to 1 MB of data in the ubiquitous key-value store on a per-application basis. If you try to put more data than this into the key-value store, the value will be set to nil.

5.5. Loading Structured Information

Problem

You want to store and load structured information (e.g., arrays and dictionaries), in a way that produces files that are easy to read and write.

Solution

Use the NSJSONSerialization class to read and write JSON files.

To create and write out a file:

```
let informationToSave = [
    "playerName": "Grabthar",
    "weaponType": "Hammer",
    "hitPoints": 1000,
    "currentQuests": ["save the galaxy", "get home"]
]

let url : NSURL = locationToSaveTo()

var error : NSError? = nil

let dataToSave = NSJSONSerialization.dataWithJSONObject(informationToSave,
    options: NSJSONWritingOptions.allZeros, error: &error)

if error != nil {
    println("Failed to convert to JSON! \(error)")
```

```
}

    dataToSave?.writeToURL(url, atomically: true)
```

The file created by the preceding code looks like this:

```
{
    "playerName": "Grabthar",
    "weaponType": "Hammer",
    "hitPoints": 1000,
    "currentQuests": [
        "save the galaxy",
        "get home"
    ]
}
```

You can load this file back in and convert it back to its original type, as well:

```
// Load the data
if let loadedData = NSData(contentsOfURL: url) {

    // Attempt to convert it to a dictionary that
    // maps strings to objects:
    var error : NSError? = nil
    let loadedInformation =
        NSJSONSerialization.JSONObjectWithData(
            loadedData,
            options: NSJSONReadingOptions.allZeros,
            error: &error) as? [String:AnyObject]

    // If we couldn't load it, or we couldn't load it
    // as the right type, log an error
    if loadedInformation == nil {
        println("Error loading data! \(error)")
    }
}
```

Discussion

JSON, which is short for JavaScript Object Notation, is a simple, easy-to-read format for storing structured information like dictionaries and arrays. NSJSONSerialization is designed to provide an easy way to convert objects into JSON data and back again.

Note that JSON can only store certain kinds of data. Specifically, you can only store the following types:

- Strings
- Numbers
- Boolean values (i.e., true and false)
- Arrays

- Dictionaries (JSON calls these "objects")

This means that NSJSONSerialization can only be given strings, numbers, arrays, and dictionary objects to process. If you don't do this, the class won't produce JSON.

You can check to see if the object you're about to give to NSJSONSerialization is able to be converted to JSON by using the isValidJSONObject method:

```
// Checking to see if an object is convertible to JSON
let dictionaryToCheck = ["canIDoThis": true]

let canBeConverted =
        NSJSONSerialization.isValidJSONObject(dictionaryToCheck) // == true
```

5.6. Deciding When to Use Files or a Database

Problem

You want to decide whether to store information as individual files, or as a database.

Solution

Use individual files when:

- You know that you'll need the entire contents of the file all at the same time.
- The file is small.
- The file is easy to read and process, and won't take lots of CPU resources to get information out.

Use a database when:

- The file is large, and you don't need to load everything in at once.
- You only need a little bit of information from the file.
- You need to very quickly load specific parts of the file.
- You want to make changes to the file while continuing to read it.

Discussion

Games tend to load files for two different reasons:

- The file contains information that needs to be kept entirely in memory, because all of it is needed at once (e.g., textures, level layouts, and some sounds).

- The file contains a lot of information, but only parts of it need to be read at once (e.g., monster information, player info, dialogue).

Databases are much faster and more efficient at getting small amounts of information from a larger file, but the downside is *lots* of increased code complexity.

5.7. Managing a Collection of Assets

Problem

Your game has a large number of big files, and you want to load them into memory in the background, without the main thread getting slowed down.

Solution

Create a new class, called `AssetManager`. Put the following code in *AssetManager.swift*:

```
class AssetLoader: NSObject {

    class func loadAssetsAtURLs(urls: [NSURL],
        withEnumerationBlock loadingComplete: (NSURL, NSData?, NSError?)
            -> Void) {

        // Create a queue
        let loadingQueue = NSOperationQueue()

        // For convenience, define a loading result as a tuple
        // containing the URL of the resource that was loaded,
        // and either the loaded data or an error
        typealias LoadingResult = (url: NSURL, data: NSData?, error: NSError?)

        // Create an array of results
        var loadingResults : [LoadingResult] = []

        // The loading complete operation runs the loadingComplete block
        // when all loads are finished
        let loadingCompleteOperation = NSBlockOperation { () -> Void in

            NSOperationQueue.mainQueue().addOperationWithBlock { () -> Void in
                // Call the loadingComplete block for each result
                for result in loadingResults {
                    loadingComplete(result.url, result.data, result.error)
                }
            }
        }

        // Start loading the data at each URL
        for url in urls {
```

```
            // Create an operation that will load the data in the background
            let loadOperation = NSBlockOperation{ () -> Void in
                // Attempt to load the data
                var error : NSError? = nil
                var result : LoadingResult? = nil

                // If we got it, result contains the data
                if let data = NSData(contentsOfURL: url,
                    options: NSDataReadingOptions.allZeros, error: &error) {
                    result = (url: url, data: data, error:nil)
                } else {
                    // Else the result contains an error
                    result = (url: url, data: nil, error:error)
                }

                // On the main queue (to prevent conflicts),
                // add this operation's result to the list
                NSOperationQueue.mainQueue().addOperationWithBlock { ()
                        -> Void in
                    loadingResults.append(result!)
                }
            }

            // Add a dependency to the loading complete operation,
            // so that it won't run until this load (and all others)
            // have completed
            loadingCompleteOperation.addDependency(loadOperation)

            // Add this load operation to the queue
            loadingQueue.addOperation(loadOperation)
        }

        // Add the loading complete operation to the queue.
        // Because it has dependencies on the load operations,
        // it won't run until all files have been loaded
        loadingQueue.addOperation(loadingCompleteOperation)
    }

}
```

To use this code:

```
// Get the list of all .png files in the bundles
let urls = NSBundle.mainBundle()
    .URLsForResourcesWithExtension("png", subdirectory: nil)
    as! [NSURL]

// Load all these images
AssetLoader.loadAssetsAtURLs(urls,
    withEnumerationBlock: { (url, data, error) -> Void in

    // This block is called once for each URL
    if error != nil {
```

```
            println("Failed to load resource \(url.lastPathComponent): \(error!)")
        } else {
            println("Loaded resource \(url.lastPathComponent) " +
                "(\(data?.length) bytes)")
        }

    })
```

Discussion

Large files can take a long time to load, and you don't want the player to be looking at a frozen screen while resources are loaded from disk. To address this, you can use a class that handles the work of loading resources in the background. The AssetManager in this solution handles the work for you, by creating a new operation queue and doing the resource loading using the new queue. After the loading is complete, a block that you provide to the loading function is called (on the main thread) for each NSURL that was provided.

5.8. Storing Information in NSUserDefaults

Problem

You want to store small amounts of information, like the most recently visited level in your game.

Solution

The NSUserDefaults class is a very useful tool that lets you store small pieces of data—strings, dates, numbers, and so on—in the *user defaults* database. The user defaults database is where each app keeps its preferences and settings.

There's only a single NSUserDefaults object that you work with, which you access using the standardUserDefaults method:

```
let defaults = NSUserDefaults.standardUserDefaults()
```

Once you have this object, you can treat it like a dictionary:

```
defaults.setValue("A string", forKey: "mySetting")

let string = defaults.valueForKey("mySetting") as? String
```

You can store the following kinds of objects in the NSUserDefaults system:

- Numbers
- Strings
- NSData

- NSDate
- Arrays, as long as they only contain objects in this list
- Dictionaries, as long as they contain objects in this list

Discussion

When you store information into NSUserDefaults, it isn't stored to disk right away—instead, it's saved periodically, and at certain important moments (like when the user taps the home button). This means that if your application crashes before the information is saved, whatever you stored will be lost.

You can force the NSUserDefaults system to save to disk any changes you've made to NSUserDefaults by using the synchronize method:

```
defaults.synchronize()
```

Doing this will ensure that all data you've stored to that point has been saved. For performance reasons, you shouldn't call synchronize too often—it's really fast, but don't call it every frame.

Information you store in NSUserDefaults is backed up, either to iTunes or to iCloud, depending on the user's settings. You don't need to do anything to make this happen—this will just work.

Sometimes, it's useful for NSUserDefaults to provide you with a default value—that is, a value that you should use if the user hasn't already provided one of his own.

For example, let's say your game starts on level 1, and you store the level that your player has reached as currentLevel in NSUserDefaults. When your game starts up, you ask NSUserDefaults for the current level, and set up the game from there:

```
let levelNumber = defaults.integerForKey("currentLevel")
```

However, what should happen the first time the player starts the game? If no value is provided for the currentLevel setting, the first time this code is called, you'll get a value of 0—which is incorrect, because your game starts at 1.

To address this problem, you can register default values. This involves giving the NSUserDefaults class a dictionary of keys and values that it should use if no other value has been provided:

```
let defaultValues = ["currentLevel": 1]
defaults.registerDefaults(defaultValues)

let levelNumber = defaults.integerForKey("currentLevel")
// levelNumber will be either 1, or whatever was last stored in NSUserDefaults.
```

It's very, very easy for users to modify the information you've stored in NSUserDefaults. Third-party tools can be used to directly access and modify the information stored in the defaults database, making it very easy for people to cheat.

If you're making a multiplayer game, for example, and you store the strength of the character's weapon in user defaults, it's possible for players to modify the database and make their characters have an unbeatable weapon.

That's not to say that you shouldn't use NSUserDefaults, but you need to be aware of the possibility of cheating.

5.9. Implementing the Best Data Storage Strategy

Problem

You want to make sure your game stores data sensibly, and doesn't annoy your users.

Solution

The solution here is simple: don't drop data. If your game can save its state, then it should be saving its state. You can't expect the user to manually save in an iOS game, and you should always persist data at every available opportunity.

Discussion

Nothing is more annoying than losing your progress in a game because a phone call came in. Don't risk annoying your users: persist the state of the game regularly!

5.10. In-Game Currency

Problem

You want to keep track of an in-game resource, like money, which the player can earn and spend.

Solution

The requirements for this kind of functionality vary from game to game. However, having an in-game currency is a common element in lots of games, so here's an example of how you might handle it.

In this example, let's say you have two different currencies: *gems* and *gold*. Gems are permanent, and the player keeps them from game to game. Gold is temporary, and goes away at the end of a game.

To add support for these kinds of currencies, use a computed property to persist the value of the gem currency in NSUserDefaults, while keeping the gold currency in memory (and reset it to zero when the game ends):

```
class CurrencyManager: NSObject {

    var gold : Int = 0

    var gems : Int {
        set(value) {
            // Set the updated count of gems in the user defaults system
            NSUserDefaults.standardUserDefaults()
                .setInteger(value, forKey: "gems")
        }

        get {
            // Ask the user defaults system for the current number of gems
            return NSUserDefaults.standardUserDefaults().integerForKey("gems")
        }
    }

    func endGame() {
        // When the game is over, reset gold but leave gems alone
        gold = 0
    }

}
```

Discussion

In this solution, the gems property stores its information using the NSUserDefaults system, rather than simply leaving it in memory (as is done with the gold property). From the perspective of other objects, the property works like everything else:

```
let currency = CurrencyManager()

currency.gold = 45
currency.gems = 21

currency.endGame()
```

When data is stored in user defaults, it persists between application launches. This means that your gems will stick around when the application exits—something that players will appreciate. Note that data stored in the user defaults system can be modified by the user, which means cheating is not impossible.

CHAPTER 6

2D Graphics and Sprite Kit

Just about every game out there incorporates 2D graphics on some level. Even the most sophisticated 3D games use 2D elements, such as in the menu or in the in-game interface.

Creating a game that limits itself to 2D graphics is also a good way to keep your game simple. 2D is simpler than 3D, and you'll end up with an easier-to-manage game, in terms of both gameplay and graphics. Puzzle games, for example, are a category of game that typically use 2D graphics rather than more complex 3D graphics.

2D is simpler for a number of reasons: you don't need to worry about how objects are going to look from multiple angles, you don't need to worry as much about lighting, and it's often simpler to create a great-looking scene with 2D images than it is to create a 3D version of the same scene.

iOS comes with a system for creating 2D graphics, called *Sprite Kit*. Sprite Kit takes care of low-level graphics tasks like creating OpenGL contexts and managing textures, allowing you to focus on game-related tasks like showing your game's sprites on the screen.

 Sprite Kit was introduced in iOS 7, and is available on both iOS and OS X. The API for Sprite Kit is the same on both platforms, which makes porting your game from one platform to the other easier.

In this chapter, you'll learn how to work with Sprite Kit to display your game's graphics.

6.1. Getting Familiar with 2D Math

When you're working with 2D graphics, it's important to know at least a little bit of 2D math.

Coordinate System

In 2D graphics, you deal with a space that has two dimensions: *x* and *y*. The x-axis is the horizontal axis and goes from left to right, whereas the y-axis is the vertical axis and runs from top to bottom. We call this kind of space a *coordinate system*. The central point of the coordinate system used in graphics is called the *origin*.

To describe a specific location in a coordinate space, you just need to provide two numbers: how far away from the origin the location is on the horizontal axis (also known as the *x coordinate*), and how far away it is on the vertical axis (also known as the *y coordinate*). These coordinates are usually written in parentheses, like this: (*x* coordinate, *y* coordinate).

The coordinates for a location 5 units to the right of the origin and 2 units above it would be written as (5,2). The location of the origin itself is written as (0,0)—that is, zero units away from the origin on both the x- and y- axes.

 Coordinate spaces in 3D work in the exact same way as in 2D, with one difference: there's one more axis, called the *z-axis*. In this coordinate system, coordinates have one more number, as in (0,0,0).

Vectors

In the simplest terms, a *vector* is a value that contains two or more values. In games, vectors are most useful for describing two things: positions (i.e., coordinates) and velocities.

An empty two-dimensional vector—that is, one with just zeros—is written like this: [0, 0].

When you're working in iOS, you can use the `CGPoint` structure as a 2D vector, as illustrated in Figure 6-1:

```
let myPosition = CGPoint(x: 2, y: 2)
```

You can also use vectors to store *velocities*. A velocity represents how far a location changes over time; for example, if an object is moving 2 units right and 3 units down every second, you could write its velocity as [2, 3]. Then, every second, you would add the object's velocity to its current position.

Although you can store velocities in `CGPoint` structures, it's slightly more convenient to store them in `CGVector` structures (see Figure 6-2). These are 100% identical to `CGPoints`, but the fields of the structure are named differently: x is named dx, and y is named dy. The d prefix stands for "delta," which means "amount of change of." So, "dx" means "delta x"—that is, "amount of change of x":

```
let myVector = CGVector(dx: 2, dy: 3)
```

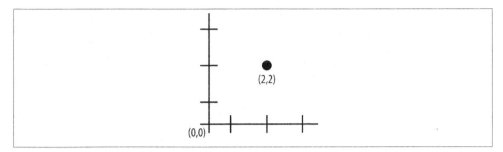

Figure 6-1. A vector used to define the position (2,2)

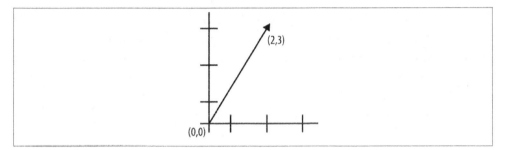

Figure 6-2. A vector used to define the direction (2,3)

Vector lengths

Let's say you've got a velocity vector [2, 3]. This means that in every second, it will move rightward 2 units, and upward 3 units. In a given second, how many units will it have travelled in total?

The first thing you might think of is to add the two values together, giving a value of 5. However, this isn't correct, because the object is traveling in a straight line, not traveling a certain distance, turning, and traveling the rest of the distance.

To get the *length* of a vector (also sometimes referred to as the *magnitude*), you square each component of the vector, add them all up, and take the square root of the result:

```
let length = sqrt(myVector.dx * myVector.dx + myVector.dy * myVector.dy)
// length = 3.60555127546399
```

You can use extensions to add convenience methods to types in Swift. This includes the CGVector type—so, if you wanted to be able to access a vector's length using a property instead of having to type out the equation every time, you can add it like so:

```
// Add a read-only property called 'length' to all CGVectors
extension CGVector {
```

```
    var length : Double {

        get {
            let dx = Double(self.dx)
            let dy = Double(self.dy)

            return sqrt(dx * dx +
                            dy * dy)
        }
    }
}

// Use it like this:
println(myVector.length)
```

Moving vectors

When you want to move a point by a given velocity, you need to add the two vectors together.

To add two vectors together (also known as *translating* a vector), you just add the respective components of each vector—that is, you sum the *x* coordinates, then the *y* coordinates (see Figure 6-3):

```
let vector1 = CGVector(dx: 1, dy: 2)
let vector2 = CGVector(dx: 1, dy: 1)

let combinedVector = CGVector(dx: vector1.dx + vector2.dx,
                              dy: vector1.dy + vector2.dy)

// combinedVector = [2, 3]
```

Figure 6-3. Adding vectors

You can also add an extension to the CGVector type that allows adding two vectors together using the + operator. You do this like so:

```
// Note: this function, like other operator functions,
// needs to be at the top level, and not in a class or extension
func + (left: CGVector, right: CGVector) -> CGVector {
```

```
        return CGVector(dx: left.dx + right.dx,
                        dy: left.dy + right.dy)
}

// Can now directly add using +:
let vectorAdding = vector1 + vector2
// = [2, 3]
```

The same thing applies to subtracting vectors: you just subtract the components, instead of adding them.

Rotating vectors

To rotate a vector, you first need to know the angle by which you want to rotate it.

In graphics, angles are usually given in *radians*. There are 2π radians in a full circle (and, therefore, π radians in half a circle, and $\pi/2$ radians in a quarter circle).

To convert from radians to degrees, multiply by 180 and divide by π:

```
let radians = 3.14159
let degrees = radians * 180.0 / M_PI
// degrees ~= 180.0
```

To convert from degrees to radians, divide by 180 and multiply by π:

```
let degrees = 45.0
let radians = degrees * M_PI / 180.0
// radians ~= 0.7854
```

When you have your angle in radians, you can rotate a vector like this:

```
let angle : Float = Float(M_PI) / 4.0 // = 45 degrees

let point = CGPoint(x: 4, y: 4)

let x = Float(point.x)
let y = Float(point.y)

var rotatedPoint : CGPoint = point
rotatedPoint.x = CGFloat(x * cosf(angle) - y * sinf(angle))
rotatedPoint.y = CGFloat(y * cosf(angle) + x * sinf(angle))
println(rotatedPoint)
// rotatedPoint = (0, 6.283)
```

Doing this will rotate the vector counterclockwise around the origin. If you want to rotate around another point, first subtract that point from your vector, perform your rotation, and then add the first point back.

Scaling vectors

Scaling a vector is easy—you just multiply each component of the vector by a value:

```
var scaledVector = CGVector(dx: 2, dy: 7)
scaledVector.dx *= 4
scaledVector.dy *= 4

// scaledVector = [8, 28]
```

Dot product

The *dot product* is a useful way to find out how much two vectors differ in the direction in which they point.

For example, let's say you've got two vectors, [2, 2] and [2, 1], and you want to find out how much of an angle there is between them (see Figure 6-4).

Figure 6-4. The dot product can be used to determine the angle between two vectors

You can figure this out by taking the dot product. The dot product can be calculated like this:

```
let v1 = CGPoint(x: 2, y: 2)
let v2 = CGPoint(x: 2, y: 1)

let dotProduct = (v1.x * v2.x + v1.y * v2.y)
```

In mathematical notation, the dot product operation is represented by the • character. Because Swift allows you to define entirely new operators, you can define your own operator that lets you dot two points together, like so:

```
// Declare the operator as having left associativity
// and the same level of precedence as the + operator
infix operator • { associativity left precedence 140 }
// (Typing Tip™: Press Option-8 to type the • character)

// Define what the • operator actually does
func • (left : CGPoint, right : CGPoint) -> Double {
    return Double(left.x * right.x + left.y * right.y)
}

// Use it like so:
v1 • v2
```

Defining your own operators in Swift is powerful, because it can save a lot of duplicate code, but can lead to problems. Unless your custom operators are understood by all of the people who read your code (including future versions of you, since you can forget things!) your code may be rendered *less* readable by the inclusion of arcane symbols.

In this particular case, using the • character is *usually* okay, because it's generally understood by people who are familiar with vector math notation. But, if you're unsure, consider extending the type and adding a dotProduct method instead of defining a new operator.

An interesting property of the dot product is that the dot product of any two vectors is the same as the result of multiplying their lengths together along with the cosine of the angle between them:

```
// A and B are vectors, a is the angle between them
A • B = |A| × |B| × cos a
```

This means that you can get the cosine of the angle by rearranging the equation as follows:

```
A • B ÷ (|A| × |B|) = cos a
```

which means you can get the angle itself by taking the arc cosine, like this:

```
acos(A • B ÷ (|A| × |B|)) = a
```

6.2. Creating a Sprite Kit View

Problem

You want to display a Sprite Kit view, which you can use for showing 2D graphics.

Solution

To use any element of Sprite Kit, you need to import the SpriteKit module by adding this line in the files in which you want to use Sprite Kit:

```
import SpriteKit
```

Go to your storyboard and select the view controller in which you want to show Sprite Kit content. Select the main view inside the view controller, and change its class to SKView.

You need to have added the `import SpriteKit` line of code to at least one file. If you don't, Xcode won't add the Sprite Kit framework to your code at build time, which means that when the view loads, the `SKView` class won't be found, and your app will crash.

Next, go to your view controller's implementation, and add the following code to the `viewDidLoad` method:

```
if let spriteView = self.view as? SKView {
    spriteView.showsDrawCount = true
    spriteView.showsFPS = true
    spriteView.showsNodeCount = true
}
```

Finally, run the application. You'll see an empty screen; however, as you begin to add content to your scene (which the rest of this chapter discusses!), down in the lower-right corner of the screen, you'll see additional information about how well your game is performing.

Discussion

An `SKView` is the area in which Sprite Kit content is drawn. All of your 2D graphics drawing happens inside this area.

An `SKView` is a subclass of `UIView`, which means you can work with it in the Interface Builder. Given that you'll most likely want to use the entire screen for your sprites, it makes sense to make the view used by the view controller an `SKView` (rather than, for example, adding an `SKView` as a subview of the view controller's main view).

By default, an `SKView` doesn't contain anything; you need to add content to it yourself. In this recipe, we've shown how to enable some debugging information: the frames per second (FPS), the number of draw calls that have been made, and the total number of nodes (items) in the scene. Note that these debugging displays don't appear if your scene is entirely empty—they'll only appear if your scene is actually rendering content.

6.3. Creating a Scene

Problem

You want to show a scene—that is, a collection of sprites—inside an `SKView`.

Solution

Create a new object, and make it a subclass of `SKScene`. In this example, we'll call it `TestScene`.

Add a new property to `TestScene`:

```
var contentCreated = false
```

Add the following methods to *TestScene.swift*:

```
override func didMoveToView(view: SKView) {
    if self.contentCreated == false {
        self.createSceneContents()
        self.contentCreated = true
    }
}

func createSceneContents() {
    self.backgroundColor = SKColor.blackColor()
    self.scaleMode = SKSceneScaleMode.AspectFit
}
```

Finally, implement the `viewWillAppear` method in your view controller, and add the following code:

```
let scene = TestScene()
scene.size = self.view.bounds.size
if let spriteView = self.view as? SKView {
    spriteView.presentScene(scene)
}
```

Discussion

When an `SKScene` is added to an `SKView`, it receives the `didMoveToView:` message. This is your scene's opportunity to prepare whatever content it wants to display.

However, it's important to keep in mind that an `SKScene` might be presented multiple times over its lifetime. For that reason, you should use a variable to keep track of whether the content of the scene has already been created:

```
override func didMoveToView(view: SKView) {
    if self.contentCreated == false {
        self.createSceneContents()
        self.contentCreated = true
    }
}
```

In the `createSceneContents` method, the actual content that appears in the scene is prepared. In this example, the scene is empty, but shows a black background:

```
self.backgroundColor = SKColor.blackColor()
```

The type of `backgroundColor` depends on which platform you're writing for. On OS X, it's an `NSColor`, and on iOS, it's a `UIColor` class. Both of these classes have very similar APIs, which means that it's a little easier to port code from iOS to OS X. If you use

SKColor, the compiler will use the correct color class for you depending on the platform you're building for.

Additionally, the scene's `scaleMode` is set. The scene's `scaleMode` property determines how the `SKView` scales the scene—because your scene might appear in different sizes (e.g., on iPhone screens versus iPad screens), it's important to know how the scene should be sized to fit into the `SKView`.

Several options exist for this:

SKSceneScaleMode.Fill
> The scene will be scaled to fill the `SKView`.

SKSceneScaleMode.AspectFill
> The scene will be scaled to fill the `SKView`, preserving the aspect ratio of the scene. Some areas of the scene might be clipped off in order to achieve this.

SKSceneScaleMode.AspectFit
> The scene will be scaled to fit inside the `SKView`. You might see some letterboxing (i.e., some blank areas at the top and bottom or sides).

SKSceneScaleMode.ResizeFill
> The scene will be resized—*not* scaled—in order to fill the `SKView`.

Once a scene has been prepared, it needs to be *presented* in order to appear in an `SKView`. This is quite straightforward—all you need to do is call `presentScene`, and pass in an `SKScene`:

```
let scene = TestScene()
scene.size = self.view.bounds.size
if let spriteView = self.view as? SKView {
    spriteView.presentScene(scene)
}
```

When you call `presentScene:`, the currently presented scene in the `SKView` is replaced with whatever you provided. Note that you have to cast `self.view` to an `SKView` before you can call `presentScene`. The safest way to do this is to use the `if-let` syntax, which attempts to cast the type, and will only attempt to run code if the cast succeeded.

6.4. Adding a Sprite

Problem

You want to display a sprite in a Sprite Kit scene.

Solution

To show a sprite to the player, you create an SKSpriteNode, configure its size and position, and then add it to your SKScene object:

```
let sprite = SKSpriteNode(color: UIColor.greenColor(),
    size: CGSize(width: 64, height: 64))

sprite.position = CGPoint(x: 100, y: 100)

myScene.addChild(sprite)
```

Discussion

SKSpriteNode is a *node*: an object that can be put inside a scene. There are several different kinds of nodes, all of which are subclasses of the SKNode class.

SKSpriteNode is a type of node that can display either a colored rectangle, or an image. In this recipe, we're focusing on just colored rectangles; to show an image, see Recipe 6.10.

To create a colored rectangle sprite, you just need to provide the color you'd like to use, as well as the size of the rectangle:

```
let sprite = SKSpriteNode(color: UIColor.greenColor(),
    size: CGSize(width: 64, height: 64))
```

The position of the sprite is controlled by the sprite's position property, which is a CGPoint. The position that you provide determines the location of the sprite's *anchor point*, which is the center point of the sprite:

```
sprite.position - CGPoint(x: 100, y: 100)
```

Sprites aren't visible unless they're inside an SKScene, which means you need to call the addChild method on the SKScene in which you want your sprite to appear:

```
myScene.addChild(sprite)
```

The position of a sprite—in fact, of any node—is determined relative to the position of the anchor point of the sprite's *parent*. This means that you can add sprites as children of *other sprites*. If you do this, the child sprites will move with their parents.

6.5. Adding a Text Sprite

Problem

You want to display some text in a Sprite Kit scene.

Solution

Create an `SKLabelNode`, and add it to your scene:

```
let textNode = SKLabelNode(fontNamed: "Zapfino")
textNode.text = "Hello, world!"
textNode.fontSize = 42
textNode.position = CGPoint(x: myScene.frame.midX, y: myScene.frame.midY)

textNode.name = "helloNode"

myScene.addChild(textNode)
```

Discussion

An `SKLabelNode` is a node that displays text. Just like with other kinds of nodes, you add it to a scene to make it visible to the player (see Recipe 6.4).

To create an `SKLabelNode`, all you need to provide is the font that the label should use:

```
let textNode = SKLabelNode(fontNamed: "Zapfino")
```

The specific font name that you provide to the `labelNodeWithFontNamed:` method needs to be one of the fonts that's included in iOS, or a custom font included with your application. To learn what fonts are available for use in your game, see Recipe 6.6; to learn how you can include a custom font in your app, see Recipe 6.7.

Once you've got an `SKLabelNode` to use, you just need to provide it with the text that it needs to display, as well as the font size that it should use and its position on screen:

```
textNode.text = "Hello, world!"
textNode.fontSize = 42
textNode.position = CGPoint(x: myScene.frame.midX, y: myScene.frame.midY)
```

By default, the text is aligned so that it's centered horizontally on the *x* coordinate of the node's `position`, and the baseline (i.e., the bottom part of letters that don't have a descender—letter like *e*, *a*, and *b*) of the text is set to the *y* coordinate. However, you can change this: all you need to do is change the `verticalAlignmentMode` or `horizontalAlignmentMode` properties.

The `verticalAlignmentMode` property can be set to one of the following values:

`SKLabelVerticalAlignmentMode.Baseline`
> The baseline of the text is placed at the origin of the node (this is the default).

`SKLabelVerticalAlignmentMode.Center`
> The center of the text is placed at the origin.

`SKLabelVerticalAlignmentMode.Top`
> The top of the text is placed at the origin.

SKLabelVerticalAlignmentMode.Bottom
    The bottom of the text is placed at the origin.

Additionally, the horizontalAlignmentMode property can be set to one of the following values:

SKLabelHorizontalAlignmentMode.Center
    The text is center-aligned (this is the default).

SKLabelHorizontalAlignmentMode.Left
    The text is left-aligned.

SKLabelHorizontalAlignmentMode.Right
    The text is right-aligned.

6.6. Determining Available Fonts

Problem

You want to know which fonts are available for your game to use.

Solution

The following code logs the name of every font available for use in your game to the debugging console:

```
for fontFamilyName in UIFont.familyNames() as! [String] {
    for fontName in UIFont.fontNamesForFamilyName(fontFamilyName) as! [String] {
        println("Available font: \(fontName)")
    }
}
```

Discussion

The UIFont class, which represents fonts on iOS, allows you to list all of the *font families* available to your code, using the familyNames method. This method returns an array of strings, each of which is the name of a font family.

However, a font family name isn't the same thing as the name of a usable font. For example, the font Helvetica is actually a *collection* of different fonts: it includes Helvetica Bold, Helvetica Light, Helvetica Light Oblique, and so on.

Therefore, to get a font name that you can use with an SKLabel (or, indeed, any other part of iOS that deals in font names), you pass a font family name to the fontNamesFor FamilyName method in UIFont. This returns *another* array of string objects, each of which is the name of a font you can use.

Alternatively, you can visit iOS Fonts (*http://iosfonts.com/*), which is a third-party site that lists all of the available fonts and includes additional information about which fonts are available on different versions of iOS.

6.7. Including Custom Fonts

Problem

You want to include a custom font in your game, so that you can show text using fancy letters.

Solution

First, you'll need a font file, in either TrueType or OpenType format—that is, a *.ttf* or *.otf* file.

Add the file to your project. Next, go to your project's Info tab, and add a new entry to the Custom Target Properties, called "Fonts provided by application." This is an array; for each of the fonts you want to add, create a new entry in this array.

For example, if you've added a font file called *MyFont.ttf*, add *MyFont.ttf* to the "Fonts provided by application" list.

Discussion

Any fonts you include in your application are available through `UIFont` (see Recipe 6.6); you don't have to do anything special to get access to them.

If you don't have a font, Dafont (*http://www.dafont.com*) is an excellent place to find free fonts—just be sure that any fonts you get are allowed to be used for commercial purposes.

6.8. Transitioning Between Scenes

Problem

You want to move from one scene to another.

Solution

Use the `presentScene:` method on an `SKView` to change which scene is being shown:

```
// newScene is an SKScene object that you want to switch to
self.view?.presentScene(newScene)
```

Using `presentScene:` immediately switches over to the new scene. If you want to use a transition, you create an `SKTransition`, and then call `presentScene(, transition:)`:

```
let crossFade = SKTransition.crossFadeWithDuration(0.5)
self.view?.presentScene(newScene, transition: crossFade)
```

Discussion

When an `SKScene` is presented, the scene that's about to be removed from the screen is sent the `willMoveFromView:` message. This gives the scene a chance to tidy up, or to remove any sprites that might take up a lot of memory. The `SKScene` that's about to be shown in the `SKView` is sent the `didMoveToView:` message, which is its chance to prepare the scene's content.

If you call `presentScene:`, the new scene will immediately appear. However, it's often good to use an animation to transition from one scene to another, such as a fade or push animation.

To do this, you use the `SKTransition` class, and provide that to the `SKView` through the `presentScene(_, transition:)` method.

You create an `SKTransition` through one of the factory methods, and provide any additional information that that type of transition needs. All transitions need to know how long the transition should run, and a few transitions need additional information, such as a direction. For example, you create a cross-fade transition like this:

```
let crossFade = SKTransition.crossFadeWithDuration(0.5)
```

There are a variety of transitions available for you to use, each with a corresponding method for creating it. Try them out! Options include:

Cross-fade (`crossFadeWithDuration`)
    The current scene fades out while the new scene fades in.

Doors close horizontal (`doorsCloseHorizontalWithDuration`)
    The new scene comes in as a pair of horizontal closing "doors."

Doors close vertical (`doorsCloseVerticalWithDuration`)
    The new scene comes in as a pair of vertical closing "doors."

Doors open horizontal (`doorsOpenHorizontalWithDuration`)
    The current scene splits apart, and moves off as a pair of horizontally opening "doors."

Doors open vertical (`doorsOpenVerticalWithDuration`)
    The current scene splits apart, and moves off as a pair of vertically opening "doors."

Doorway (doorwayWithDuration)
The current scene splits apart, revealing the new scene in the background; the new scene approaches the camera, and eventually fills the scene by the time the transition is complete.

Fade with color (fadeWithColor(_, duration))
The current scene fades out, revealing the color you specify; the new scene then fades in on top of this color.

Fade (fadeWithDuration)
The current scene fades to black, and then the new scene fades in.

Flip horizontal (flipHorizontalWithDuration)
The current scene flips horizontally, revealing the new scene on the reverse side.

Flip vertical (flipVerticalWithDuration)
The current scene flips vertically, revealing the new scene on the reverse side.

Move in (moveInWithDirection(_, duration:))
The new scene comes in from off-screen, and moves in on top of the current scene.

Push in (pushWithDirection(_, duration:))
The new scene comes in from off-screen, pushing the current scene off the screen.

Reveal (revealWithDirection(_, duration:))
The current scene moves off-screen, revealing the new scene underneath it.

`CIFilter` *transition (transitionWithCIFilter(_, duration:))*
You can use a `CIFilter` object to create a custom transition.

6.9. Moving Sprites and Labels Around

Problem

You want your sprites and labels to move around your scene.

Solution

You can use `SKAction` objects to make any node in the scene perform an *action*. An action is something that changes the position, color, transparency, or size of any node in your scene.

The following code makes a node move up and to the right while fading away, then runs some code, and finally removes the node from the scene:

```
// In this example, 'node' is any SKNode

// Move 100 pixels up and 100 pixels to the right over 1 second
```

```
    let moveUp = SKAction.moveBy(CGVector(dx: 100, dy: 100), duration: 1.0)

    // Fade out over 0.5 seconds
    let fadeOut = SKAction.fadeOutWithDuration(0.5)

    // Run a block of code
    let runBlock = SKAction.runBlock { () -> Void in
        println("Hello!")
    }

    // Remove the node
    let remove = SKAction.removeFromParent()

    // Run the movement and fading blocks at the same time
    let moveAndFade = SKAction.group([moveUp, fadeOut])

    // Move and fade, then run the block, then remove the node
    let sequence = SKAction.sequence([moveAndFade, runBlock, remove])

    // Run these actions on the node
    node.runAction(sequence)
```

Discussion

An SKAction is an object that represents an action that a node can perform. There are heaps of different kinds of actions available for you to use—too many for us to list here, so for full information, check out Apple's documentation for SKAction (*http://bit.ly/ skaction*).

Generally, an action is something that changes some property of the node to which it applies. For example, the moveBy(_, duration:) action in the preceding example changes the position of the node by making it move by a certain distance along the x- and y-axes (represented by a CGVector). Some actions don't actually change the node, though; for example, you can create an action that simply waits for an amount of time, or one that runs some code.

To run an action, you first create an SKAction with one of the factory methods. Then, you call runAction on the SKNode that you'd like to have perform that action.

You can add an action to multiple nodes—if you want several nodes to all do the same thing, just create the SKAction once and then call runAction: on each of the SKNodes that you want to perform the action.

Most actions are things that take place over a period of time: for example, moving, rotating, fading, changing color, and so on. Some actions take place immediately, however, such as running code or removing a node from the scene.

An action can work on its own, or you can combine multiple actions with *sequences* and *groups*. A sequence is an SKAction that runs *other* actions, one after the other. The first action is run, and once it's complete the next is run, and so on until the end; at this point, the sequence action is considered done. To create a sequence, use the `sequence` method, which takes an array of `SKAction` objects:

```
let sequence = SKAction.sequence([action1, action2, action3])
```

A group, by contrast, runs a collection of actions simultaneously. A group action is considered complete when the longest-running of the actions it's been given has completed. Creating groups looks very similar to creating sequences. To create a group, you pass an array of `SKAction` objects to the `group:` method:

```
let group = SKAction.group([action1, action2, action3])
```

You can combine groups and sequences. For example, you can make two sequences run at the same time by combining them into a group:

```
let sequence1 = SKAction.sequence([action1, action2])
let sequence2 = SKAction.sequence([action1, action2])

let groupedSequences = SKAction.group([sequence1, sequence2])
```

You can also create sequences that contain groups; if, for example, you have a sequence with two groups in it, the second group will not run until all actions in the first group have finished.

Some actions are able to be reversed. By sending the `reversedAction` message to these actions, you get back an `SKAction` that performs the opposite action to the original. Not all actions can be reversed; for details on which can and can't, check the documentation for `SKAction`.

As we've already mentioned, you start actions by calling `runAction` on an `SKNode`. You can also make Sprite Kit run a block when the action that you've submitted finishes running, using the `runAction(_, completion:)` method:

```
let action = SKAction.fadeOutWithDuration(1.0)

node.runAction(action, completion: { () -> Void in
    println("Action's done!")
})
```

You can add multiple actions to a node, which will all run at the same time. If you do this, it's often useful to be able to keep track of the actions you add to a node. You can do this with the `runAction(_, withKey:)` method, which lets you associate actions you run on an `SKNode` with a name:

```
node.runAction(action, withKey: "My Action")
```

If you add two actions with the same name, the old action is removed before the new one is added.

Once you've added an action with a name, you can use the `actionForKey` method to get the action back:

```
let theAction = node.actionForKey("My Action")
```

You can also remove actions by name, using the `removeActionForKey` method:

```
node.removeActionForKey("My Action")
```

Finally, you can remove *all* actions from a node in one line of code using the `removeAllActions` method:

```
node.removeAllActions()
```

 When you remove an action, the action stops whatever it was doing. However, any changes that the action had *already* made to the node remain.

For example, if you've added an action that moves the sprite, and you remove it before the action finishes running, the sprite will be left partway between its origin point and the destination.

6.10. Adding a Texture Sprite

Problem

You want to create a sprite that uses an image.

Solution

First, add the image that you want to use to your project (see Recipe 2.5).

Next, create an `SKSpriteNode` with the `SKSpriteNode(imageNamed:)` method:

```
let imageSprite = SKSpriteNode(imageNamed: "Spaceship")
```

Discussion

When you create a sprite with `SKSpriteNode(imageNamed:)`, the size of the sprite is based on the size of the image.

Once you've created the sprite, it works just like any other node: you can position it, add it to the scene, run actions on it, and so on.

6.11. Creating Texture Atlases

Problem

You want to use texture atlases, which save memory and make rendering more efficient.

Solution

Create a folder named *Textures.atlas* and put all of the textures that you want to group in it.

Then, add this folder to your project by dragging the folder into the Project Navigator.

Finally, go to the Build Settings by clicking the project at the top of the Project Navigator, and search for "Sprite Kit." Set Enable Texture Atlas Generation to Yes.

Discussion

A *texture atlas* is a texture composed of other, smaller textures. Using a texture atlas means that instead of several smaller textures, you use one larger texture. This atlas uses slightly less memory than if you were to use lots of individual textures, and more importantly is more efficient for rendering. When a sprite needs to be drawn, a subregion of the texture atlas is used for drawing.

If your game involves lots of sprites that each use different images, the Sprite Kit renderer needs to switch images every time it starts drawing a different sprite. Switching images has a small performance cost, which adds up if you're doing it multiple times. However, if multiple sprites share the same texture, Sprite Kit doesn't have to switch images, making rendering faster.

When you put images in a folder whose name ends with *.atlas*, and turn on Texture Atlas Generation, Xcode will automatically create a texture atlas for you based on whatever images are in that folder. Your images will be automatically trimmed for transparency, reducing the number of wasted pixels, and images are packed together as efficiently as possible.

When you're using texture atlases, your Sprite Kit code remains the same. The following code works regardless of whether or not you're using atlases:

```
let imageSprite = SKSpriteNode(imageNamed: "Spaceship")
```

6.12. Using Shape Nodes

Problem

You want to use shape nodes to draw vector shapes.

Solution

Use an SKShapeNode to draw shapes:

```
let path = UIBezierPath(roundedRect: CGRect(x: -100, y: -100,
                                            width: 200, height: 200),
                        cornerRadius: 20)

let shape = SKShapeNode(path: path.CGPath)

shape.strokeColor = SKColor.greenColor()
shape.fillColor = SKColor.redColor()

shape.glowWidth = 4

shape.position = CGPoint(x: myScene.frame.midX,
                         y: myScene.frame.midY)

myScene.addChild(shape)
```

Discussion

SKSceneNode draws *paths*, which are objects that represent shapes. A path can be a rectangle, a circle, or any shape you can possibly think of. For more information on working with paths, see Recipe 6.15.

The coordinates of the path that you provide are positioned relative to your node's anchor point. For example, a shape that has a line that starts at (–10,–10) and moves to (10,10) starts above and to the left of the node's position, and ends below and to the right of the position.

You can use the fillColor and strokeColor properties to change the colors used to draw the shape. Use SKColor to define the colors you want to use. The *fill color* is the color used to fill the contents of the shape, and the *stroke color* is the color used to draw the line around the outside of the shape. By default, the fill color is clear (i.e., no color, just empty space), and the stroke color is white.

Finally, you can specify how thick the line is. By default, the thickness is 1 point; Apple notes that specifying a line thickness of more than 2 points may lead to rendering problems. In these cases, you're better off using an SKSpriteNode. In addition, you can make the stroke line glow by setting the glowWidth property to a value higher than 0.

6.13. Using Blending Modes

Problem

You want to use different blending modes to create visual effects.

Solution

Use the `blendMode` property to control how nodes are blended with the rest of the scene:

```
shape.blendMode = SKBlendMode.Add
```

Discussion

When a node is drawn into the scene, the way that the final scene looks depends on the node's *blend mode*. When a node is blended into the scene, the Sprite Kit renderer looks at the color of each pixel of the node, and the color underneath each pixel, and determines what the resulting color should be.

By default, all `SKNodes` use the same blending mode: `SKBlendMode.Alpha`, which uses the alpha channel of the image multiplied by the sprite's `alpha` property to determine how much the node's color should contribute to the scene. This is generally the blending mode you want to use most of the time.

However, it isn't the *only* blending mode that you can use. Other options exist:

`SKBlendMode.Add`
> The colors of the node are added to the scene. This leads to a brightening, semi-transparent effect. (Good for lights, fires, laser beams, and explosions!)

`SKBlendMode.Subtract`
> The colors of the node are subtracted from the scene. This creates a rather weird-looking darkening effect. (Not very realistic, but it can lead to some interesting effects.)

`SKBlendMode.Multiply`
> The colors of the node are multiplied with the scene. This darkens the colors. (Very good for shadows, and for tinting parts of the scene.)

`SKBlendMode.MultiplyX2`
> The same as `SKBlendMode.Multiply`, but the colors of the sprite are doubled after the first multiplication. This creates a brighter effect than plain multiply.

`SKBlendMode.Screen`
> The colors of the node are added to the scene, multiplied by the inverse of the scene's color. This creates a more subtle brightening effect than `SKBlendMode.Add`. (Good for glosses and shiny areas.)

`SKBlendMode.Replace`
> The colors of the node replace the scene and are not blended with any existing colors. This means that any `alpha` information is completely ignored. This mode is also the fastest possible drawing mode, because no blending calculations need to take place.

6.14. Using Image Effects to Change the Way That Sprites Are Drawn

Problem

You want to use image effects on your sprites to create different effects.

Solution

Use an `SKEffectNode` with a `CIFilter` to apply visual effects to nodes:

```
let effect = SKEffectNode()

let filter = CIFilter(name: "CIGaussianBlur")
filter.setValue(20.0, forKey: "inputRadius")

effect.filter = filter;

myScene.addChild(effect)
effect.addChild(imageSprite)
```

Discussion

A `CIFilter` is an object that applies an effect to images. `CIFilter`s are incredibly powerful, and are used all over iOS and OS X. One of the most popular examples of where they're used is in the Photo Booth app, where they power the visual effects that you can apply to photos.

To use a `CIFilter` with Sprite Kit, you create an `SKEffectNode` and add any nodes that you want to have the effect apply to as children of that node. (Don't forget to add the `SKEffectNode` to your scene.)

Once you've done that, you get a `CIFilter`, configure it how you like, and provide it to the `SKEffectNode`. You get a `CIFilter` using the `filterWithName` method of the `CIFilter` class, which takes a string: the name of the filter you'd like to use.

Different filters have different properties, which you can configure using the `CIFilter`'s `setValue(_, forKey:)` method.

There are dozens of `CIFilter`s that you can use—lots more than we could sensibly list here. Here are a couple of especially cool ones:

CIGaussianBlur
> Applies a Gaussian blur. The default blur radius is 10.0; change it by setting `inputRadius` to something different.

`CIPixellate`
Makes the image all blocky and pixelated. The default pixel size is 8.0; change it by setting `inputScale` to something different.

`CIPhotoEffectNoir`
Makes the image black and white, with an exaggerated contrast. This filter has no parameters you can change.

6.15. Using Bézier Paths

Problem

You want to draw shapes using Bézier paths (custom shapes and lines).

Solution

Use the `UIBezierPath` class to represent shapes:

```
let rectangle = UIBezierPath(rect:CGRect(x: 0, y: 0,
    width: 100, height: 200))

let roundedRect = UIBezierPath(roundedRect:CGRect(x: -100, y: -100,
    width: 200, height: 200),
    cornerRadius:20)

let oval = UIBezierPath(ovalInRect:CGRect(x: 0, y: 0,
                                  width: 100, height: 200))

let customShape = UIBezierPath()
customShape.moveToPoint(CGPoint(x: 0, y: 0))
customShape.addLineToPoint(CGPoint(x: 0, y: 100))
customShape.addCurveToPoint(CGPoint(x: 0, y: 0),
    controlPoint1:CGPoint(x: 100, y: 100),
    controlPoint2:CGPoint(x: 100, y: 0))

customShape.closePath()
```

Discussion

`UIBezierPath` objects represent shapes, which you can display on the screen with an `SKShapeNode`.

Creating a rectangle, rounded rectangle, or oval is pretty easy—there are built-in factory methods for these. There's no built-in method for creating circles, but it's easy to make one—just create an oval inside a square rectangle (i.e., a rectangle with an equal width and height).

In addition to these basic shapes, you can also create your own custom shapes. You do this by using the `moveToPoint`, `addLineToPoint`, and `addCurveToPoint(_, control Point1: controlPoint2:)` methods.

When you're drawing a custom shape, it helps to imagine a virtual pen poised over a sheet of paper. When you call `moveToPoint`, you're positioning your hand over a specific point. When you call `addLineToPoint`, you place the pen down on the paper and draw a straight line from the pen's current location to the destination. You can call `moveToPoint` again to lift the virtual pen from the paper and reposition your hand somewhere else.

The `addCurveToPoint(_, controlPoint1:controlPoint2:)` method lets you draw a cubic Bézier curve. A Bézier curve is a curved line that starts at the pen's current location and moves toward the destination point you provide, bending toward the two control points. A Bézier curve is often useful for drawing smoothly curving things in games, such as roads.

When you're done creating a shape, you call `closePath`. Doing this draws a straight line from the pen's current position to the starting position.

To use a `UIBezierPath` with an `SKShapeNode`, you ask the `UIBezierPath` for its `CGPath` property, and give that to the `SKShapeNode`. For more information on how `SKShape Node` works, see Recipe 6.12.

6.16. Creating Smoke, Fire, and Other Particle Effects

Problem

You want to create fire, smoke, snow, or other visual effects.

Solution

You can use particle effects to simulate these kinds of effects. To create a particle effect, follow these steps:

1. From the File menu, choose New→File. Select Resource, and then select Sprite Kit Particle File.

2. You'll be asked to pick a template to start from. Pick whichever you like—Jon happens to like the Fire template.

3. Open the newly created file, and you'll enter the Emitter editor. This component of Xcode allows you to play with the various properties that define how the particle system looks, including how many particles are emitted, how they change over time,

and how they're colored. Additionally, you can click and drag to see how the particle system looks when it's moving.

Once you're done configuring the particle system, you can add the effect to your scene with the following code (adjust the filenames to suit your needs):

```
let fireNode = SKEmitterNode(fileNamed: "Fire.sks")

myScene.addChild(fireNode)
```

Discussion

Particle effects can be used for a variety of natural-looking effects that would be difficult to create with individual sprites. Individual particles in a particle system have much less overhead than creating the sprites yourself, so you can create rather complex-looking effects without dramatically affecting performance.

Because there are so many different parameters available to customize, creating a particle system that suits your needs is very much more an art than a science. Be prepared to spend some time playing with the available settings, and try the different built-in presets to get an idea of what's possible.

6.17. Shaking the Screen

Problem

You want the screen to shake—for example, an explosion has happened, and you want to emphasize the effect by rattling the player's view of the scene around.

Solution

Create an empty node, and call it cameraNode. Add it to the screen. Put all of the nodes that you'd normally put into the scene into this new node.

Add the following method to your scene's code:

```
func shakeNode(node: SKNode) {
    // Cancel any existing shake actions
    node.removeActionForKey("shake")

    // The number of individual movements that the shake will be made up of
    let shakeSteps = 15

    // How "big" the shake is
    let shakeDistance = 20.0

    // How long the shake should go on for
    let shakeDuration = 0.25
```

```
// An array to store the individual movements in
var shakeActions : [SKAction] = []

// Loop 'shakeSteps' times
for i in 0...shakeSteps  {

    // How long this specific shake movement will take
    let shakeMovementDuration : Double = shakeDuration / Double(shakeSteps)

    // This will be 1.0 at the start and gradually move down to 0.0
    let shakeAmount : Double = Double(shakeSteps - i) / Double(shakeSteps)

    // Take the current position - we'll then add an offset from that
    var shakePosition = node.position

    // Pick a random amount from -shakeDistance to shakeDistance
    let xPos = (Double(arc4random_uniform(UInt32(shakeDistance*2)))) -
               Double(shakeDistance)) * shakeAmount
    let yPos = (Double(arc4random_uniform(UInt32(shakeDistance*2)))) -
        Double(shakeDistance)) * shakeAmount
    shakePosition.x = shakePosition.x + CGFloat(xPos)
    shakePosition.y = shakePosition.y + CGFloat(yPos)

    // Create the action that moves the node to the new location, and
    // add it to the list
    let shakeMovementAction = SKAction.moveTo(shakePosition,
        duration:shakeMovementDuration)
    shakeActions.append(shakeMovementAction)

}

// Run the shake!
let shakeSequence = SKAction.sequence(shakeActions)
node.runAction(shakeSequence, withKey:"shake")


}
```

When you want to shake the screen, just call shakeNode and pass in cameraNode:

```
shakeNode(textNode)
```

Discussion

Shaking the screen is a really effective way to emphasize to the player that something big and impressive is happening. If something forceful enough to shake the *world* around you is going on, then you know it means business!

So, what does a shake actually mean in terms of constructing an animation? Well, a shake is when you start at a neutral resting point and begin moving large distances back and forth over that neutral point. An important element in realistic-looking shakes is that the shake gradually settles down, with the movements becoming less and less drastic as the shaking comes to an end.

To implement a shake, therefore, you need to construct several small movements. These can be implemented using SKActions: each step in the shake is an SKAction that moves the node from its current location to another location.

During the for loop, to attenuate the shake—that is, to make the movements smaller and smaller—subtract the number of steps taken from the total number of steps, producing the number of steps remaining. This is divided by the total number of steps, which gives us a number from 0 to 1, by which the movement is multiplied. Eventually, the amount of movement is multiplied by 0—in other words, the movement settles back down to the neutral position.

6.18. Animating a Sprite

Problem

You want to make a Sprite Kit animation using a collection of images. For example, you've got a "running" animation, and you want your sprite to play that animation.

Solution

In this solution, we're going to assume that you've already got all of your individual frames, and you've put them into a folder named *Animation.atlas*, which has been added to your project.

Use SKAction's animateWithTextures(_, timePerFrame:) method to animate a collection of sprites:

```
// Load the texture atlas that contains the frames
let atlas = SKTextureAtlas(named: "Animation")

// Get the list of texture names, and sort them
let textureNames = (atlas.textureNames as! [String]).sorted {
    (first, second) -> Bool in
    return first < second
}

// Load all textures
var allTextures : [SKTexture] = textureNames.map { (textureName) -> SKTexture in
    return atlas.textureNamed(textureName)
}

// Create the sprite, and give it the initial frame; position it
// in the middle of the screen
let animatedSprite = SKSpriteNode(texture:allTextures[0])
animatedSprite.position = CGPoint(x: self.frame.midX,
```

```
        y: self.frame.midY)
    self.addChild(animatedSprite)

    // Make the sprite animate using the loaded textures, at a rate of
    // 30 frames per second
    let animationAction = SKAction.animateWithTextures(allTextures,
        timePerFrame:(1.0/30.0))

    animatedSprite.runAction(SKAction.repeatActionForever(animationAction))
```

Discussion

The SKAction class is capable of changing the texture of a sprite over time. If you have a sequence of images that you want to use as an animation, all you need is an array containing each of the textures you want, with each one stored as an SKTexture.

When you create the animation action using animateWithTextures(_, timePer Frame:), you provide the array and the amount of time that each texture should be displayed. If you want to run your animation at 30 FPS, then each frame should be shown for 1/30 of a second (0.033 seconds per frame).

To get the SKTextures for display, you either need to load them using SKTexture's textureWithImageNamed: method, or else get them from a texture atlas that contains them. Texture atlases were discussed in Recipe 6.11, and are an excellent way to group the frames for your animation together. They're also better for memory, and ensure that all necessary frames are present for your animation—the game won't pause halfway through your animation to load more frames.

6.19. Parallax Scrolling

Problem

Using Sprite Kit, you want to show a two-dimensional scene that appears to have depth, by making more *distant* objects move slower than *closer* objects when the *camera* moves.

Solution

The specific approach for implementing parallax scrolling will depend on the details of your game. In this solution, we're creating a scene where there are four components, listed in order of proximity:

- A dirt path
- Some nearby hills
- Some further distant hills
- The sky

You can see the final scene in Figure 6-5. (Unless you have magic paper, or possibly some kind of hyper-advanced *computer reader* technology that is yet to be invented, the image below will not be scrolling.)

Figure 6-5. The final parallax scrolling scene

In this scene, we've drawn the art so that each of these components is a separate image. Additionally, each of these images can tile horizontally without visible edges. The art has been put in a texture atlas (see Recipe 6.11 to learn how to use these). The names of the textures for each of the components are *Sky.png*, *DistantHills.png*, *Hills.png*, and *Path.png* (shown in Figure 6-6).

Figure 6-6. The components of the parallax scene. Note that all four components can tile horizontally.

With that out of the way, here's the source code for the SKScene that shows these four components scrolling horizontally at different speeds:

```
class ParallaxScene: SKScene {

    // Sky
    var skyNode : SKSpriteNode
    var skyNodeNext : SKSpriteNode

    // Foreground hills
    var hillsNode : SKSpriteNode
    var hillsNodeNext : SKSpriteNode

    // Background hills
    var distantHillsNode : SKSpriteNode
    var distantHillsNodeNext : SKSpriteNode

    // Path
    var pathNode : SKSpriteNode
    var pathNodeNext : SKSpriteNode

    // Time of last frame
    var lastFrameTime : NSTimeInterval = 0
```

```
// Time since last frame
var deltaTime : NSTimeInterval = 0

override init(size: CGSize) {

    // Prepare the sky sprites
    skyNode = SKSpriteNode(texture:
        SKTexture(imageNamed: "Sky"))
    skyNode.position = CGPoint(x: size.width / 2.0,
        y: size.height / 2.0)

    skyNodeNext = skyNode.copy() as! SKSpriteNode
    skyNodeNext.position =
        CGPoint(x: skyNode.position.x + skyNode.size.width,
            y: skyNode.position.y)

    // Prepare the background hill sprites
    distantHillsNode = SKSpriteNode(texture:
        SKTexture(imageNamed: "DistantHills"))
    distantHillsNode.position =
        CGPoint(x: size.width / 2.0,
            y: size.height - 284)

    distantHillsNodeNext = distantHillsNode.copy() as! SKSpriteNode
    distantHillsNodeNext.position =
        CGPoint(x: distantHillsNode.position.x +
            distantHillsNode.size.width,
            y: distantHillsNode.position.y)

    // Prepare the foreground hill sprites
    hillsNode = SKSpriteNode(texture:
        SKTexture(imageNamed: "Hills"))
    hillsNode.position =
        CGPoint(x: size.width / 2.0,
            y: size.height - 384)

    hillsNodeNext = hillsNode.copy() as! SKSpriteNode
    hillsNodeNext.position =
        CGPoint(x: hillsNode.position.x + hillsNode.size.width,
            y: hillsNode.position.y)

    // Prepare the path sprites
    pathNode = SKSpriteNode(texture:
        SKTexture(imageNamed: "Path"))
    pathNode.position =
        CGPoint(x: size.width / 2.0,
            y: size.height - 424)

    pathNodeNext = pathNode.copy() as! SKSpriteNode
    pathNodeNext.position =
        CGPoint(x: pathNode.position.x +
```

```
                pathNode.size.width,
            y: pathNode.position.y)

    super.init(size: size)


    // Add the sprites to the scene
    self.addChild(skyNode)
    self.addChild(skyNodeNext)

    self.addChild(distantHillsNode)
    self.addChild(distantHillsNodeNext)

    self.addChild(hillsNode)
    self.addChild(hillsNodeNext)

    self.addChild(pathNode)
    self.addChild(pathNodeNext)
}

required init?(coder aDecoder: NSCoder) {
    fatalError("Not implemented")
}

// Move a pair of sprites leftward based on a speed value;
// when either of the sprites goes off-screen, move it to the
// right so that it appears to be seamless movement
func moveSprite(sprite : SKSpriteNode,
    nextSprite : SKSpriteNode, speed : Float) -> Void {
    var newPosition = CGPointZero

    // For both the sprite and its duplicate:
    for spriteToMove in [sprite, nextSprite] {

        // Shift the sprite leftward based on the speed
        newPosition = spriteToMove.position
        newPosition.x -= CGFloat(speed * Float(deltaTime))
        spriteToMove.position = newPosition

        // If this sprite is now offscreen (i.e., its rightmost edge is
        // farther left than the scene's leftmost edge):
        if spriteToMove.frame.maxX < self.frame.minX {

            // Shift it over so that it's now to the immediate right
            // of the other sprite.
            // This means that the two sprites are effectively
            // leap-frogging each other as they both move.
            spriteToMove.position =
                CGPoint(x: spriteToMove.position.x +
                    spriteToMove.size.width * 2,
                    y: spriteToMove.position.y)
        }
```

```
        }
    }

    override func update(currentTime: NSTimeInterval) {
        // First, update the delta time values:

        // If we don't have a last frame time value, this is the first frame,
        // so delta time will be zero.
        if lastFrameTime <= 0 {
            lastFrameTime = currentTime
        }

        // Update delta time
        deltaTime = currentTime - lastFrameTime

        // Set last frame time to current time
        lastFrameTime = currentTime

        // Next, move each of the four pairs of sprites.
        // Objects that should appear move slower than foreground objects.
        self.moveSprite(skyNode, nextSprite:skyNodeNext, speed:25.0)
        self.moveSprite(distantHillsNode, nextSprite:distantHillsNodeNext,
            speed:50.0)
        self.moveSprite(hillsNode, nextSprite:hillsNodeNext, speed:100.0)
        self.moveSprite(pathNode, nextSprite:pathNodeNext, speed:150.0)
    }

}
```

Discussion

Parallax scrolling is no more complicated than moving some things quickly and other things slowly. In Sprite Kit, the real trick is getting a sprite to appear to be continuously scrolling, showing no gaps.

In this solution, each of the four components in the scene—the sky, hills, distant hills, and path—are drawn with two sprites each: one shown onscreen, and one to its immediate right. For each pair of sprites, they both slide to the left until one of them has moved completely off the screen. At that point, it's repositioned so it's placed to the right of the other sprite.

In this manner, the two sprites are leap-frogging each other as they move. You can see the process illustrated in Figure 6-7.

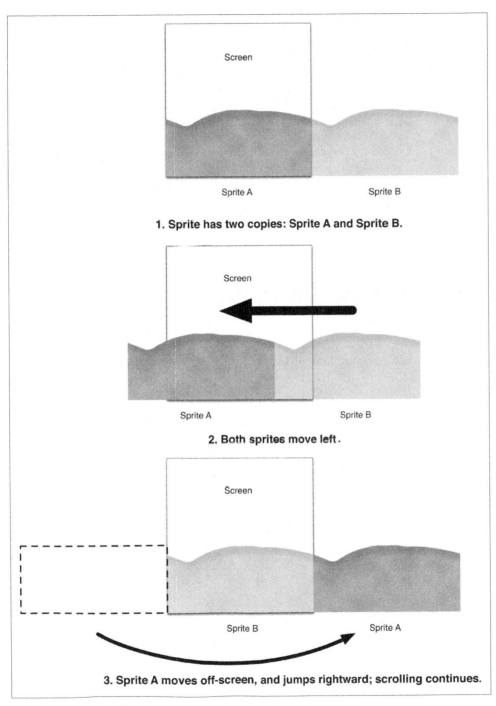

Figure 6-7. The scrolling process

Getting the speed values right for your scene is a matter of personal taste. However, it's important to make sure that the relationships between the speeds of the different layers makes sense: if you have an object that's in the foreground and is moving much, much faster than a relatively close background, it won't look right.

 Simulating perspective using parallax scrolling is a great and simple technique, but be careful with it. Your fearless authors wrote this recipe while in the back of a car that was driving down a winding road, and we developed a little motion sickness while testing the source code.

Motion sickness in games, sometimes known as "simulation sickness," is a real thing that affects many game players around the world. If you're making a game that simulates perspective—either in a 3D game or a 2D game where you're faking perspective—make sure you test with as many people as you can find.

6.20. Creating Images Using Noise

Problem

You want to create organic-looking textures and effects using visual noise.

Solution

Noise is *incredibly useful* in games, and it's especially useful in textures when natural-looking patterns are sought. You can see an example of a noise texture in Figure 6-8.

To generate an SKTexture filled with noise, you use the SKTexture(noiseWithSmoothness:, size, grayscale). You can then use this texture in a sprite, or combine it with other information:

```
let noiseTexture = SKTexture(noiseWithSmoothness: 0.2,
    size: CGSize(width: 200, height: 200), grayscale: true)
let noiseSprite = SKSpriteNode(texture: noiseTexture)
myScene.addChild(noiseSprite)
```

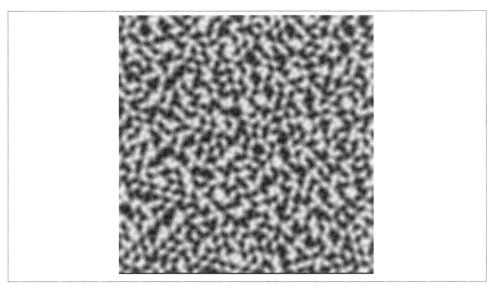

Figure 6-8. A noise texture

Discussion

Noise is an incredibly effective method for creating natural, organic-looking textures. You can use it for a number of things, including fire, fog, smoke, lightning—all you need to do is change the `smoothness` parameter. Noise works best when blended with other images.

A slightly more complex and better-looking type of noise is *Perlin* noise. Perlin was invented by Ken Perlin in 1985, and was based on earlier work done for the Disney film *Tron* (1982). Perlin himself later won an Academy Award for Technical Achievement in 1997 for his work on Perlin noise. You can see a full description, as well as links to implementations of the algorithm, at *http://en.wikipedia.org/wiki/Perlin_noise*.

CHAPTER 7

Physics

If, like us, you've visited a planet that has gravity, you'll be familiar with the fact that objects react to forces and collide with other objects. When you pick up an object and let go, it falls down until it hits something. When it hits something, it bounces (or shatters, depending on what you dropped). In games, we can make objects have this kind of behavior through *physics simulation*.

Physics simulation lets you do things like:

- Make objects have gravity and fall to the ground
- Give objects properties like weight, density, friction, and bounciness
- Apply forces to objects, and make them move around realistically
- Attach objects together in a variety of configurations

In short, adding physics simulation to your game often gives you a lot of realism for free.

Sprite Kit has built-in support for simulating physics in two dimensions, and we'll mostly be talking about physics in Sprite Kit in this chapter. (If you're not familiar with Sprite Kit yet, go check out Chapter 6.) Before we get to the recipes, though, let's go over some terminology.

7.1. Reviewing Physics Terms and Definitions

Physics simulation has its basis in math, and math people tend to like giving everything its own name. These terms are used by the physics simulation system built into iOS, and it's important to know what's being referred to when you encounter, say, a *polygon collision body*.

In this section, before we get into the recipes themselves, we're going to present a list of definitions that you'll very likely run into when working with physics. Some of these are terms that you've probably heard in other contexts, and others are fairly specific to physics:

World

A physics world is the "universe" in which all of your objects exist. If an object isn't in the world, it isn't being physically simulated, and nothing will interact with it. A physics world contains settings that apply to all objects in the world, such as the direction and strength of gravity.

Mass

Mass is a measure of how much stuff is inside an object. The more mass there is, the heavier it is.

Velocity

Velocity is a measure of how quickly an object is moving, and in which direction. In 2D physics, velocity has two components: horizontal velocity, or "x-velocity," and vertical velocity, or "y-velocity."

Body

A body is an object in the physics simulation. Bodies react to forces, and can collide with other bodies. Bodies have mass and velocity. You can optionally make a body be *static*, which means that it never reacts to forces and never moves.

Force

A force is something that causes a body to move. For example, when you throw a ball, your arm is imposing a force on the ball; when your hand releases the ball, the ball's got a large amount of built-up velocity, and it flies out of your hand. Gravity is another force, and it applies to all objects in your physics world. The amount of force needed to make an object move depends on how much mass is in that object. If you apply the exact same force to a heavy object and to a light object, the light object will move farther.

Friction

When an object rubs against something else, it slows down. This is because of friction. In the real world, friction converts kinetic energy (i.e., movement) into heat, but in Sprite Kit, the energy is just lost. You can configure how much friction an object has. For example, if you make an object have very low friction, it will be slippery.

Collider

A collider defines the shape of an object. Common shapes include squares, rectangles, circles, and polygons. In Sprite Kit, all bodies have a collider, which you define when you create the body. (In some other physics engines, bodies and colliders are separate entities.)

Edge collider

An edge collider is a collider that is composed of one or more infinitely thin lines. Edge colliders are useful for creating walls and obstacles, because they're simple to create and very efficient to simulate. A body with an edge collider never moves; it's always static.

Collision

A collision is when two objects come into contact. Note that a *collision* is different from a *collider*—a collision is an event that happens, whereas a collider is a shape. When a collision happens, you can get information about it, such as which objects collided, where they collided, and so on.

Joint

A joint is a relationship between two objects. Several different kinds of joints exist. Some common ones include "pin" joints, in which one object is allowed to rotate freely but isn't allowed to move away from a certain point relative to another body, and "spring" joints, in which one object is allowed to move away from another but, if it moves beyond a threshold, begins to be pushed back toward the first object.

7.2. Adding Physics to Sprites

Problem

You want to make sprites be affected by gravity and other physical forces.

Solution

To make an `SKSpriteNode` be physically simulated, create an `SKPhysicsBody` and then set the sprite's `physicsBody` property to it:

```
// 'scene' is an SKScene

let sprite = SKSpriteNode(color:SKColor.whiteColor(),
    size:CGSize(width: 100, height: 50))
sprite.position = CGPoint(x: self.frame.midX, y: self.frame.midY)
sprite.physicsBody = SKPhysicsBody(rectangleOfSize:sprite.size)

scene.addChild(sprite)
```

Discussion

When you add an SKPhysicsBody to an SKSpriteNode, Sprite Kit physically simulates the sprite's movement in the scene.

This has the following effects:

- The physics engine will start keeping track of physical forces that apply to the body, such as gravity.
- The position and rotation of the body will be updated every frame, based on these forces.
- The body will collide with other SKPhysicsBody objects.

When you run the sample code, you'll notice that the sprite falls off the bottom of the screen. This is because there's nothing for the sprite to land on—the physics body that you added to the sprite is the only physically simulated body in the entire scene. To learn how to create objects for your sprite's body to land on, see Recipe 7.3.

7.3. Creating Static and Dynamic Objects

Problem

You want to create an immobile object—one that never moves, but that other objects can collide with.

Solution

Set the dynamic property of your SKPhysicsBody to false:

```
let staticSprite = SKSpriteNode(color:SKColor.yellowColor(),
    size:CGSize(width: 200, height: 25))

staticSprite.position = CGPoint(x: self.frame.midX, y: self.frame.midY - 100)
staticSprite.physicsBody = SKPhysicsBody(rectangleOfSize:staticSprite.size)
staticSprite.physicsBody?.dynamic = false


scene.addChild(staticSprite)
```

Discussion

There are two kinds of physics bodies used in Sprite Kit:

- *Dynamic bodies* respond to physical forces, and move around the scene.
- *Static bodies* don't respond to physical forces—they're fixed in place, and dynamic bodies can collide with them.

When you set the `dynamic` property of an `SKPhysicsBody` to false, the body immediately stops responding to forces and stops moving and rotating. However, you can still reposition it by setting the sprite's `position` and `rotation`, or by using actions (see Recipe 6.9 to learn how to do this).

7.4. Defining Collider Shapes

Problem

You want to specify a custom shape for physics bodies.

Solution

To make your physics bodies use a shape other than a rectangle, you create them by using a different method, such as `SKPhysicsBody(circleOfRadius:)` or `SKPhysicsBody(polygonFromPath:)`, as shown here:

```
let circleSprite = SKShapeNode()
circleSprite.path =
    UIBezierPath(ovalInRect:CGRectMake(-50, -50, 100, 100)).CGPath
circleSprite.lineWidth = 1;
circleSprite.physicsBody = SKPhysicsBody(circleOfRadius:50)
circleSprite.position =
    CGPoint(x: self.frame.midX+40, y: self.frame.midY + 100);

self.addChild(circleSprite)
```

Discussion

There are a number of different ways that you can create an `SKPhysicsBody`. When you create one, you specify what sort of *collider* the body is using—that is, the actual shape of the body (a circle, a rectangle, or some other shape).

The easiest way to create a body is with the `bodyWithRectangleOfSize:` method, which lets you (as you might expect, given the name), create a rectangle given a size (you don't set the position of the body—that's determined by the position of the node to which the body's attached).

A circular collider is the simplest possible collider, and requires the least amount of computation to simulate. If you need to create a large number of colliders, consider making them circular where possible.

In addition to creating rectangular or circular colliders, you can define your own custom shapes by defining a path and creating an SKPhysicsBody with it:

```
let polygonSprite = SKShapeNode()

let path = UIBezierPath()
path.moveToPoint(CGPoint(x: -25, y: -25))
path.addLineToPoint(CGPoint(x: 25, y: 0))
path.addLineToPoint(CGPoint(x: -25, y: 25))
path.closePath()

polygonSprite.physicsBody = SKPhysicsBody(polygonFromPath:path.CGPath)
```

You can learn more about creating paths using UIBezierPath in Recipe 6.15.

When you create a path for use as a polygon body, the points in the path need to be defined in clockwise order.

Additionally, the path you provide isn't allowed to contain any curves—it can only contain straight lines. (You won't get any crashes if you use curves, but the resulting shape will behave strangely.)

If you want to more easily visualize the custom shapes you're creating for use with physics bodies, you can attach the same path that you've created to an SKShapeNode, as illustrated in Figure 7-1. See Recipe 6.12 for more information about this.

You can't change the shape of a body's collider after it's been created. If you want a sprite to have a different shape, you need to replace the sprite's SKPhysicsBody.

Figure 7-1. SKShapeNodes being used to visually represent custom collider shapes

7.5. Setting Velocities

Problem

You want to make an object start moving at a specific speed and in a specific direction.

Solution

To change the velocity of an object, you modify the `velocity` property:

```
// Start moving upward at 500 units per second (quite fast!)
sprite.physicsBody?.velocity = CGVector(dx: 0, dy: 500)
```

Discussion

The simplest way to change the velocity of a physics body is to directly set the `veloci` `ty` property. This is a `CGVector` that represents the velocity, in pixels per second, at which the body is moving.

Note that directly setting the velocity tends to have the best-looking results when you use the technique to set the initial velocity of an object. For example, if you want to create rockets that come out of a rocket launcher, those rockets should start out moving quickly. In this case, you'd create the rocket sprite, and then immediately set the velocity of its physics body to make it start moving.

If you want things to *change* their movement in a realistic way, consider using forces on your bodies (see Recipe 7.14). Alternatively, if you want precise frame-by-frame control over how your objects move, make the physics bodies static (see Recipe 7.3), and manually set the position of the objects or use actions (see Recipe 6.9).

7.6. Working with Mass, Size, and Density

Problem

You want to control how heavy your objects are.

Solution

Set the `density` or `mass` properties of your physics bodies to control how heavy they are:

```
// Change density, and the mass will be updated (based on size)
sprite.physicsBody?.density = 2.0

// Alternatively, set the mass property (which will change density)
sprite.physicsBody?.mass = 4.0
```

Discussion

An object's *mass* is how much matter the object is composed of. Note that this is different from how much the object *weighs*, which is the amount of force applied to an object by gravity, dependent on the object's mass and how strong gravity is.

Objects with more mass require more force to move around. If you apply the same force to an object with low mass and one with high mass, the object with lower mass will move farther.

The mass of an object is calculated based on the volume of the object (i.e., its size) and the object's *density*. The mass of an object is automatically calculated when you create the body, based on the size of the body and a default density of 1; however, you can change an object's mass and density at any time you like.

The initial mass of an object is calculated like this:

```
Mass = Area x Density
```

The default density of an object is 1.0. The area depends on the shape of the body:

- The area of a rectangle is width × height.
- The area of a circle is $\pi \times r^2$ (where r is the radius).
- The area of a polygon depends on its shape; search the Web for "irregular polygon area" for different kinds of formulae. A common strategy is to break the polygon into triangles, calculate the area for each one, and then add them together.

The actual units you use for density and mass don't matter—you can use pounds, kilograms, or grapnars (if you are from Venus). However, the values you choose should be consistent across the objects in your scene. For example, if you create two crates, both of the same size, and you set the mass of the first to 2 (kilograms) and the second to 4 (pounds), it won't be apparent to the user why one appears lighter than the other.

Because mass and density are linked, if you change an object's density, the mass will change (and vice versa).

7.7. Creating Walls in Your Scene

Problem

You want to create walls for your collision scene.

Solution

The most efficient way to create walls is to use edge colliders:

```
let wallsNode = SKNode()
wallsNode.position = CGPoint(x: self.frame.midX, y: self.frame.midY)

let rect = CGRectOffset(self.frame,
    -self.frame.width / 2.0, -self.frame.height / 2.0)
wallsNode.physicsBody = SKPhysicsBody(edgeLoopFromRect:rect)

scene.addChild(wallsNode)
```

Discussion

An *edge collider* is a collider that's just a single line, or a collection of connected lines. Edge colliders are different from other kinds of colliders in that they have no volume or mass, and are always treated as static colliders.

There are two different types of edge colliders: *edge loops* and *edge chains*. An edge chain is a linked collection of lines; an edge loop always links from the end point to the start point.

Edge colliders can have almost any shape you want. The easiest ways to create them are either to create a single line from one point to another:

```
let point1 = CGPoint(x: -50, y: 0)
let point2 = CGPoint(x: 50, y: 0)

let edgeBody = SKPhysicsBody(edgeFromPoint: point1, toPoint: point2)
```

or with a rectangle, using SKPhysicsBody(edgeLoopFromRect:), as seen in the preceding example.

In addition to lines and rectangles, you can create arbitrary shapes. These can be either edge chains or edge loops.

You create these shapes using a path, much like when you make polygon bodies (see Recipe 7.4). In this case, though, there's a difference: you don't have to close your paths, because edge chains don't have to form a closed polygon:

```
let path = UIBezierPath()
path.moveToPoint(CGPoint(x: -50, y:-10))
path.addLineToPoint(CGPoint(x: -25, y:10))
path.addLineToPoint(CGPoint(x: 0, y:-10))
path.addLineToPoint(CGPoint(x: 25, y:10))
path.addLineToPoint(CGPoint(x: 50, y:-10))

let wallNode = SKShapeNode()
wallNode.path = path.CGPath
wallNode.physicsBody = SKPhysicsBody(edgeChainFromPath: path.CGPath)
wallNode.position = CGPoint(x: self.frame.midX, y: self.frame.midY-50)
```

7.8. Controlling Gravity

Problem

You want to customize the gravity in your scene.

Solution

To change the gravity in your scene, you must first get access to your scene's `physics World`. Once you have that, you can change the physics world's `gravity` property:

```
// Half gravity
self.physicsWorld.gravity = CGVector(dx: 0.0, dy: -4.5)
```

Discussion

For the purposes of a physics simulation, *gravity* is a constant force that's applied to all bodies. (Gravity in the real universe is quite a bit more complex than that, but this simplification is more than adequate for most games.)

 A game that deals with gravity in a much more realistic way than "gravity equals down" is Kerbal Space Program (*http://www.kerbal spaceprogram.com*), in which players launch rockets and use orbital mechanics to travel to other planets. In this kind of game, the force of gravity depends on how close you are to various planets, each of which has a different mass.

By default, the gravity in a scene is set to (0, –9.81). That is to say, all bodies have a constant force that's pushing them down (i.e., toward the bottom of the screen), at a rate of 9.81 pixels per second per second. By changing this property, you can make gravity nonexistent:

```
// Zero gravity
self.physicsWorld.gravity = CGVector(dx: 0.0, dy: 0.0)
```

Or, you can reverse gravity:

```
// Reverse gravity
self.physicsWorld.gravity = CGVector(dx: 0.0, dy: 9.81)
// note the lack of a minus symbol
```

You can also make an individual physics body be unaffected by gravity by changing the body's `affectedByGravity` property:

```
sprite.physicsBody?.affectedByGravity = false
```

Note that a body that isn't affected by gravity still has mass, and still responds to other forces. A really heavy object that's floating in the air will still require quite a bit of force to move.

 If you want to make an object fixed in midair, and never be affected by physical forces, you want a *static* physics body, and should go look at Recipe 7.3.

7.9. Keeping Objects from Falling Over

Problem

You want to prevent certain objects, such as the player character, from rotating.

Solution

Change the `allowsRotation` property of your body:

```
sprite.physicsBody?.allowsRotation = true
```

Discussion

In many games with 2D physics, it's useful to have some objects that move around, but never rotate. For example, if you're making a platform game, you almost never want the character to actually rotate.

Locking the rotation of a body means that it won't ever rotate, no matter how many forces are applied to it. However, you can still change the angle of the body by manually setting the `zRotation` of the node, or by using an action (see Recipe 6.9).

7.10. Controlling Time in Your Physics Simulation

Problem

You want to pause or speed up the physics simulation.

Solution

Change the `speed` property of your scene's `SKPhysicsWorld` to control how quickly time passes in your scene's physics simulation:

```
self.physicsWorld.speed = 2.0 // double speed

self.physicsWorld.speed = 0.0 // paused
```

```
self.physicsWorld.speed = 1.0 // normal speed
```

Discussion

The speed property of your scene's SKPhysicsWorld controls the rate at which time passes in your physics simulation. For example, setting the speed to 2.0 makes things move twice as fast (note, however, that increasing the speed of the simulation can lead to some instability in your simulation).

You can also use this to create slow-motion effects: if you set the speed property to a value between 0 and 1, time will be slowed down, which you can use to highlight totally sweet stunts or explosions.

7.11. Detecting Collisions

Problem

You want to detect when objects collide.

Solution

First, make your SKScene subclass conform to the SKPhysicsContactDelegate protocol.

Next, implement the didBeginContact and didEndContact methods in your SKScene:

```
func didBeginContact(contact: SKPhysicsContact) {
    println("Contact started between \(contact.bodyA) and \(contact.bodyB)")
}

func didEndContact(contact: SKPhysicsContact) {
    println("Contact ended between \(contact.bodyA) and \(contact.bodyB)")
}
```

When you're setting up your scene's contents, set the contactDelegate property of your scene's physicsWorld to the scene:

```
self.physicsWorld.contactDelegate = self
```

Next, make every physics body for which you want to get notifications about collisions set its contactTestBitMask to a nonzero value, like 0x01. You'll probably want to store it in a variable, like so:

```
let myObjectBitMask : UInt32 = 0x00001
```

You can then apply it to your SKPhysicsBody objects:

```
physicsSprite.physicsBody?.contactTestBitMask = myObjectBitMask;
```

Now, every object collision that occurs will make your `didBeginContact` and `didEnd Contact` methods get called.

Discussion

If you want an object to be notified about objects coming into contact with each other, you make that object conform to the `SKPhysicsContactDelegate` protocol, and then set the scene's `physicsWorld` to use the object as its `contactDelegate`.

The contact delegate methods, `didBeginContact` and `didEndContact`, will only be called when two objects that have an intersecting `contactTestBitMask` come into contact with each other.

The contact test bitmask lets you define categories of objects. By default, it's set to zero, which means that objects aren't in any collision category.

The contact delegate methods receive an `SKPhysicsContact` object as their parameter, which contains information about which bodies collided, at which point they collided, and with how much force.

7.12. Finding Objects

Problem

You want to find physics objects in the scene.

Solution

Use the `enumerateBodiesInRect(_, usingBlock:)`, `enumerateBodiesAtPoint(_, usingBlock:)`, and `enumerateBodiesAlongRayStart(_, end:, usingBlock:)` methods to find `SKPhysicsBody` objects in your world:

```
let searchRect = CGRect(x: 10, y: 10, width: 200, height: 200)

self.physicsWorld.enumerateBodiesInRect(searchRect) {(body, stop) in
    println("Found a body: \(body)")
}

let searchPoint = CGPoint(x: 40, y: 100)

self.physicsWorld.enumerateBodiesAtPoint(searchPoint) { (body, stop) in
    println("Found a body: \(body)")
}

let searchRayStart = CGPoint(x: 0, y: 0)
let searchRayEnd = CGPoint(x: 320, y: 480)
```

```
self.physicsWorld.enumerateBodiesAlongRayStart(searchRayStart,
    end: searchRayEnd) { (body, point, normal, stop) in
    println("Found a body: \(body) (point: \(point), normal: \(normal))")
}
```

Discussion

You can use these methods to find SKPhysicsBody objects in a rectangle, at a certain point, or along a line. When you call them, you pass in the location you want to search, as well as a block; this block is called for each body that is found.

All of the results blocks used by these methods receive as parameters the body that was found and stop, which is a pointer to a Bool variable. If you set this variable to true, the search will stop. This means that if you're looking for a specific body, you can stop the search when you find it, which saves time:

```
// Stop when we've found two bodies
var count : Int = 0
self.physicsWorld.enumerateBodiesInRect(searchRect) { (body, stop) in
    count = count + 1

    if count >= 2 {
        stop.memory = true
    }
}
```

Note that when you call enumerateBodiesAlongRayStart(_, end:, usingBlock:), the results block takes *three* parameters: the block, a *normal*, and the stop variable. The normal is a vector that indicates the direction at which the line bounces off the body it hit. (This is useful for determining, for example, the directions in which sparks should fly when something hits a surface.)

If you're looking for a single body and don't care which one, you can use the bodyAt Point, bodyInRect, and bodyAlongRayStart(_, end:) methods, which just return the first body they find:

```
let firstBodyAtPoint = self.physicsWorld.bodyAtPoint(searchPoint)

let firstBodyInRect = self.physicsWorld.bodyInRect(searchRect)

let firstBodyAlongRay =
        self.physicsWorld.bodyAlongRayStart(searchRayStart, end:searchRayEnd)
```

These methods won't find nodes that don't have an SKPhysicsBody attached to them—they only check the physics simulation. If you're looking for nodes that have no physics body, use the nodeAtPoint, nodesAtPoint, childNodeWithName, or enumerateChild NodesWithName(_, usingBlock:) methods on your SKScene.

7.13. Working with Joints

Problem

You want to connect physics objects together.

Solution

Use one of the several SKPhysicsJoint classes available:

```
let anchor = SKSpriteNode(color:SKColor.whiteColor(),
    size:CGSize(width: 100, height: 100))
anchor.position = CGPointMake(self.frame.midX, self.frame.midY)
anchor.physicsBody = SKPhysicsBody(rectangleOfSize:anchor.size)
anchor.physicsBody?.dynamic = false

scene.addChild(anchor)

let attachment = SKSpriteNode(color:SKColor.yellowColor(),
    size:CGSize(width: 100, height: 100))
attachment.position = CGPointMake(self.frame.midX + 100,
    self.frame.midY - 100)
attachment.physicsBody = SKPhysicsBody(rectangleOfSize:attachment.size)

scene.addChild(attachment)

let pinJoint = SKPhysicsJointPin.jointWithBodyA(anchor.physicsBody,
    bodyB:attachment.physicsBody, anchor:anchor.position)

scene.physicsWorld.addJoint(pinJoint)
```

Discussion

A *joint* is an object that constrains the movement of one or more objects. Joints are pretty straightforward to work with: you create your joint object, configure it, and then give it to your scene's SKPhysicsWorld.

In this example, we're using a pin joint, which pins two bodies together at a point, and lets them rotate around that point. There are several different types of joints available:

- *Pin joints*, as we've just mentioned, let you pin two objects together. The objects can rotate around that pin point. Pin joints are sometimes called *hinge* joints in other physics systems.

- *Fixed joints* fuse two objects together. Once they're joined, they're not allowed to move relative to each other, and they're not allowed to rotate relative to each other. This is very useful for creating larger objects that you want to break apart later.

- *Slider joints* let you create objects that can move away from or closer to each other, but only along a certain line.
- *Limit joints* make it so that the two objects can move freely relative to each other, but aren't allowed to move past a certain radius. This makes them act as if they're tethered with a rope.

Once you've created your joint, you add it to the physics simulation by using the `add Joint` method:

```
scene.physicsWorld.addJoint(pinJoint)
```

You can remove a joint from an `SKPhysicsWorld` by using the `removeJoint` method. Once you remove a joint, the bodies that it affected are able to move freely once again:

```
scene.physicsWorld.removeJoint(pinJoint)
```

A body can have multiple joints acting on it at once. Try connecting several bodies together with joints, and see what you come up with!

7.14. Working with Forces

Problem

You want to apply a force to an object.

Solution

Use the `applyForce` or `applyTorque` methods:

```
node.physicsBody?.applyForce(CGVector(dx: 0, dy: 100))
node.physicsBody?.applyTorque(0.01)
```

Discussion

When you apply a force, you change the movement of a body. When you're using the Sprite Kit physics engine, there's a constant gravitational force being applied to all bodies in the scene, which makes them move downward.

You can apply your own forces to bodies using the `applyForce` method, which takes a `CGVector` that describes the amount of force you'd like to apply. Forces get applied immediately.

When you call `applyForce`, the force is evenly applied across the entire body. If you need to apply the force to a specific point on the body, you can use `applyForce(_, atPoint:)`:

```
// Apply a force just to the right of the center of the body
let position = CGPoint(x: 10, y: 0)
node.physicsBody?.applyForce(CGVector(dx: 0, dy: 100), atPoint: position)
```

The point that you provide to applyForce(_, atPoint:) is defined in scene coordinates.

In addition to force, which changes the position of a body, you can also apply *torque*, which is a change to the angular movement (i.e., the spin) of a body.

 The units that you use with applyForce and applyTorque don't really matter as long as they're consistent. Technically, they're measured in newtons and newton-meters, respectively.

7.15. Adding Thrusters to Objects

Problem

You want to make an object move continuously in a certain direction.

Solution

First, add this property to your SKScene subclass:

```
var lastTime = 0.0
```

Then, in your scene's update method, apply whatever forces and torque you need:

```
override func update(currentTime: NSTimeInterval) {

    if self.lastTime == 0 {
        self.lastTime = currentTime
    }


    let deltaTime = currentTime - self.lastTime

    if let node = self.childNodeWithName("Box") {

        node.physicsBody?.applyForce(CGVector(dx: 0 * deltaTime,
                                              dy: 10 * deltaTime))
        node.physicsBody?.applyTorque(CGFloat(0.5 * deltaTime))

    }
}
```

Discussion

The `update:` method is called on your `SKScene` subclass every frame, immediately before physics simulation and rendering. This is your opportunity to apply any continuous forces to your objects.

The `update` method receives one parameter: a float named `currentTime`. This variable contains the current system time, measured in seconds. To apply an even amount of force per second, you need to know how long each frame takes to render. You can calculate this by subtracting the system time at the last frame from the system time at the current frame (you can learn more about this in Recipe 1.4):

```
deltaTime = time at start of current frame - time at start of last frame
```

Once you have that, you can multiply forces by that number.

7.16. Creating Explosions

Problem

You want to apply an explosion force to some objects.

Solution

Add this method to your SKScene:

```
func applyExplosionAtPoint(point: CGPoint,
    radius:CGFloat, power:CGFloat) {

    // Work out which bodies are in range of the explosion
    // by creating a rectangle
    let explosionRect = CGRect(x: point.x - radius,
        y: point.y - radius,
        width: radius*2, height: radius*2)

    // For each body, apply an explosion force
    self.physicsWorld.enumerateBodiesInRect(explosionRect,
        usingBlock:{ (body, stop) in

        // Work out if the body has a node that we can use
        if let bodyPosition = body.node?.position {

            // Work out the direction that we should apply
            // the force in for this body
            let explosionOffset =
                CGVector(dx: bodyPosition.x - point.x,
                dy: bodyPosition.y - point.y)

            // Work out the distance from the explosion point
            let explosionDistance =
```

```
        sqrt(explosionOffset.dx * explosionOffset.dx +
             explosionOffset.dy * explosionOffset.dy)

    // Normalize the explosion force
    var explosionForce = explosionOffset
    explosionForce.dx /= explosionDistance
    explosionForce.dy /= explosionDistance

    // Multiply by explosion power
    explosionForce.dx *= power
    explosionForce.dy *= power

    // Finally, apply the force
    body.applyForce(explosionForce)
  }
})

}
```

When you want an explosion to happen, call this method like so:

```
// 'point' is a CGPoint in world space
self.applyExplosionAtPoint(point, radius:150, power:10)
```

Discussion

An explosion is simply a force that's applied to a group of nearby bodies, which pushes those bodies away from a point.

So, to make an explosion, you need to do the following:

1. Determine which bodies are affected by the explosion.
2. Decide in which direction each body should be sent.
3. Calculate how much force should be applied.
4. Apply that force to each body!

Simple, right?

You can determine which bodies are affected by the explosion by using the `enumerate BodiesInRect(_, usingBlock:)` method on your scene's `SKPhysicsWorld`. This calls a block for each body that it finds, which gives you your opportunity to calculate the forces for each body.

To calculate the amount of force you need to apply to each body, you do the following:

1. Subtract the body's position from the explosion's position. This is the *explosion offset*, calculated as follows:

```
let explosionOffset =
CGVector(dx: bodyPosition.x - point.x,
    dy: bodyPosition.y - point.y)
```

2. Determine the distance from the body's position by *normalizing* the explosion off-set. This means calculating the length (or *magnitude*) of the vector, and then dividing the vector by that magnitude.

To calculate the magnitude of the vector, you take the square root of the sums of the squares of the components of the offset vector:

```
let explosionDistance =
sqrt(explosionOffset.dx * explosionOffset.dx +
    explosionOffset.dy * explosionOffset.dy)
```

Once you have that, you divide the offset by this length, and then multiply it by the power. This ensures that all affected objects get the same total amount of power, regardless of their position:

```
let explosionDistance =
sqrt(explosionOffset.dx * explosionOffset.dx +
    explosionOffset.dy * explosionOffset.dy)
```

3. Finally, you apply this calculated force vector to the body:

```
body.applyForce(explosionForce)
```

7.17. Using Device Orientation to Control Gravity

Problem

You want the direction of gravity to change when the player rotates her device.

Solution

First, make your application only use the portrait orientation by selecting the project at the top of the Project Navigator, selecting the General tab, scrolling down to "Device Orientation," and turning off everything except Portrait. This will keep your app from rotating its interface as you rotate the device.

Next, open your SKScene subclass. Import the Core Motion module:

```
import CoreMotion
```

and add a new instance variable to your class:

```
let motionManager = CMMotionManager()
```

Finally, when your scene is being set up, add the following code:

```
motionManager.startDeviceMotionUpdatesToQueue(
    NSOperationQueue.mainQueue(), withHandler: { (motion, error) -> Void in
```

```
if error != nil {
    println("Error getting motion data: \(error)")
} else {

    let gravityMagnitude = 9.81
    let gravityVector = CGVector(
        dx: motion.gravity.x * gravityMagnitude,
        dy: motion.gravity.y * gravityMagnitude)

    self.physicsWorld.gravity = gravityVector
}
})
```

Discussion

When you create a `CMMotionManager` and call `startDeviceMotionUpdatesToQueue(_,`
`withHandler:)`, the motion system will call a block that you provide and give it information on how the player's device is moving.

To get the direction of gravity, you ask the `motion` object that gets passed in as a parameter for its `gravity` property. Gravity has three components: `x`, `y`, and `z`. These
correspond to how much gravity is pulling on the sides of the device, the top and bottom
edges of the device, and the front and back of the device.

In a 2D game, there are only two dimensions we care about: `x` and `y`. That means that
we can just discard the `z` component of gravity, and build a `CGVector` out of the `x` and
`y` information stored in the `motion` object.

However, the values contained in the `gravity` property are measured in *gravities*—that
is, if you lay your phone perfectly flat with the back of the phone pointed down, there
will be precisely one gravity of force on the z-axis. In Sprite Kit, however, gravity is
measured in meters per second (by default). So, you need to convert between the two
units.

The conversion is very easy: one gravity is equal to 9.81 meters per second. So, all you
need to do is multiply both the `x` and `y` components of the gravity vector by 9.81.

Finally, this updated gravity vector is given to the scene's `physicsWorld`, which in turn
affects the physics objects in the scene.

7.18. Dragging Objects Around

Problem

You want the player of your game to be able to drag physics objects on the screen.

Solution

First, create two new instance variables: an SKNode object called `dragNode`, and an SKPhsyicsJointPin called `dragJoint`.

In the code for your SKScene, add the following methods:

```
override func touchesBegan(touches: Set<NSObject>,
    withEvent event: UIEvent) {

    // We only care about one touch at a time
    if let touch = touches.first as? UITouch {

        // Work out what node got touched
        let touchPosition = touch.locationInNode(self)
        let touchedNode = self.nodeAtPoint(touchPosition)

        // Make sure that we're touching something that _can_ be dragged
        if touchedNode == dragNode || touchedNode.physicsBody == nil {
            return
        }

        // Create the invisible drag node, with a small static body
        let newDragNode = SKNode()
        newDragNode.position = touchPosition
        newDragNode.physicsBody =
            SKPhysicsBody(rectangleOfSize:CGSize(width: 10,
                                                 height: 10))
        newDragNode.physicsBody?.dynamic = false

        self.addChild(newDragNode)

        // Link this new node to the object that got touched
        let newDragJoint = SKPhysicsJointPin.jointWithBodyA(
            touchedNode.physicsBody,
            bodyB:newDragNode.physicsBody,
            anchor:touchPosition)

        self.physicsWorld.addJoint(newDragJoint)

        // Store the reference to the joint and the node
        self.dragNode = newDragNode
        self.dragJoint = newDragJoint

    }
}

override func touchesMoved(touches: Set<NSObject>,
    withEvent event: UIEvent) {

    if let touch = touches.first as? UITouch {
        // When the touch moves, move the static drag node.
```

```
            // The joint will drag the connected
            // object with it.
            let touchPosition = touch.locationInNode(self)

            dragNode?.position = touchPosition
        }
    }

    override func touchesEnded(touches: Set<NSObject>,
        withEvent event: UIEvent) {

        stopDragging()
    }

    override func touchesCancelled(touches: Set<NSObject>,
        withEvent event: UIEvent) {

        stopDragging()
    }

    func stopDragging() {
        // Remove the joint and the drag node.
        self.physicsWorld.removeJoint(dragJoint!)
        dragJoint = nil

        dragNode?.removeFromParent()
        dragNode = nil
    }
```

Discussion

The first thing that often comes into people's heads when they start thinking about how
to do this is something like this: "When a touch begins, store a reference to the object
that got touched. Then, when the touch moves, update the `position` property, and it'll
move with it!"

This has a couple of problems, though. First, if you're only setting the position of the
object that the user is dragging when the touch updates, gravity's going to be dragging
the object down. This will have the effect of making the object's position flicker quite
noticeably as it's moved around.

Second, if you're directly setting the position of an object, it becomes possible to make an object move through walls or through other objects, which may not be what you want.

A better solution, which is what we're doing in this recipe, is to create a static, invisible object, and connect it to the object that you want to actually let the user drag around. When the touch moves, you change the position of this static object, not the object you want dragged—as a result, the joint will move the object around. Because we're not overriding the physics system, the object being dragged around won't do impossible things like intersect with other objects. Additionally, by attaching the dragged body via a pin joint, the object will swing slightly as you move it, which looks really nice.

You'll notice that in both the `touchesEnded` and `touchesCancelled` methods, a new method called `stopDragging` is called. It's important to call `stopDragging` in both the ended and cancelled phases of the touch—a touch can get cancelled while the user's dragging the object around (such as when a gesture recognizer claims the touch), in which case you'll need to act as if the finger has been deliberately lifted up.

7.19. Creating a Car

Problem

You want to create a vehicle with wheels.

Solution

A vehicle is composed of at least two main parts: the body of the vehicle, and one or more wheels. In the case of a car (at least, a two-dimensional car) we can model this with a box and two wheels—in other words, a rectangular SKSpriteNode and two SKShapeNodes that are set up to draw circles (see Figure 7-2).

In addition to creating the nodes, we need to link the wheels to the body with two SKPhysicsJointPin objects:

```
func createWheel(wheelRadius: CGFloat) -> SKShapeNode {
    let wheelRect = CGRect(x: -wheelRadius, y: -wheelRadius,
        width: wheelRadius*2, height: wheelRadius*2)

    let wheelNode = SKShapeNode()
    wheelNode.path = UIBezierPath(ovalInRect: wheelRect).CGPath

    return wheelNode
}

func createCar() -> SKNode {

    // Create the car
```

```
let carNode = SKSpriteNode(color:SKColor.yellowColor(),
    size:CGSize(width: 150, height: 50))
carNode.physicsBody = SKPhysicsBody(rectangleOfSize:carNode.size)
carNode.position = CGPoint(x: self.frame.midX, y: self.frame.midY);
self.addChild(carNode)

// Create the left wheel
let leftWheelNode = self.createWheel(30)
leftWheelNode.physicsBody = SKPhysicsBody(circleOfRadius:30)
leftWheelNode.position = CGPoint(x: carNode.position.x-80,
    y: carNode.position.y)
self.addChild(leftWheelNode)

// Create the right wheel
let rightWheelNode = self.createWheel(30)
rightWheelNode.physicsBody = SKPhysicsBody(circleOfRadius:30)
rightWheelNode.position = CGPoint(x: carNode.position.x+80,
    y: carNode.position.y)
self.addChild(rightWheelNode)

// Attach the wheels to the body
let leftWheelPosition = leftWheelNode.position
let rightWheelPosition = rightWheelNode.position

let leftPinJoint = SKPhysicsJointPin.jointWithBodyA(carNode.physicsBody,
    bodyB:leftWheelNode.physicsBody, anchor:leftWheelPosition)
let rightPinJoint = SKPhysicsJointPin.jointWithBodyA(carNode.physicsBody,
    bodyB:rightWheelNode.physicsBody, anchor:rightWheelPosition)

self.physicsWorld.addJoint(leftPinJoint)
self.physicsWorld.addJoint(rightPinJoint)

return carNode
}
```

Discussion

When you create an SKPhysicsJointPin, you define the anchor point in scene coordinates, not relative to any other body. In this recipe, the pin anchors are set at the center of each wheel, which makes them rotate around their axes; if you set the anchor to be somewhere else, you'll end up with bumpy wheels (which may actually be what you want!).

Figure 7-2. The car object described in this recipe, composed of a rectangular main body, two circles for wheels, and two pin joints to connect the wheels to the main body

CHAPTER 8

3D Graphics

Using 3D graphics is the most popular approach for games these days. However, 3D is *complicated*. It's so complicated, in fact, that we're going to dedicate three whole chapters to it. The first chapter (this one) covers introductory 3D—setup, basic drawing, and understanding how 3D works overall. The next two chapters cover more intermediate and advanced topics in 3D rendering on the iPhone and iPad. After that, in Chapter 11, we cover SceneKit, Apple's newest framework for building games (and apps) in 3D.

When you work in 3D, you use a library called *OpenGL ES*. OpenGL ES is the "embedded" version of OpenGL, the industry-standard library for computer graphics. OpenGL is *everywhere*—you'll find it in desktop computers, in games consoles, in industrial hardware, and in mobile computers like iOS devices.

Because OpenGL is designed to be cross-platform, it doesn't have the same nice API as you might be used to from working with other tools on iOS. Apple's put quite a bit of effort into making things as easy as possible for developers, introducing a framework called *GLKit* that helps with the setup and integration of OpenGL in your game. However, you'll still need to get used to how OpenGL works.

You'll notice that this chapter, and the two chapters that follow it, are written in Objective-C rather than Swift. The reason for this is that GLKit, as it currently exists in iOS, doesn't play terribly well with Swift. This will change as the Swift language evolves, but in the meantime it's often easier to deal with GLKit in Objective-C.

If want to use GLKit with Swift, you'll typically write code that talks to GLKit in Objective-C, and then use a bridging header to make that Objective-C code available in Swift. See the section "Swift and Objective-C in the Same Project" (*http://bit.ly/swift_and_obj_c*) in *Using Swift with Cocoa and Objective-C* by Apple for more info.

Because it's not really possible to talk about 3D graphics features in isolation, this chapter is actually designed to be read in sequence. Whereas in other chapters you can basically jump straight to any recipe, we recommend that you start this one at the beginning and read through. As a precursor to the recipes, we'll begin with an introduction to 3D math.

8.1. Working with 3D Math

In addition to providing lots of useful support classes and functions for working with 3D graphics, GLKit also includes a number of types and functions that are helpful for working with 3D math.

The two most common kinds of mathematical constructs that you'll see when doing 3D math are *vectors* and *matrices*. We talked about two-dimensional vectors in "Vectors" on page 144; the 3D equivalent is a three-dimensional vector.

3D Vectors and GLKit

A 3D vector has three components. By convention, these are referred to as *x*, *y*, and *z*. In GLKit, a 2D vector is represented by the GLKVector2 structure, and 3D vectors are represented by GLKVector3 objects:

```
GLKVector2 myVector2D;
myVector2D.x = 1;
myVector2D.y = 2;

GLKVector3 myVector3D;
myVector2D.x = 1;
myVector2D.y = 2;
myVector2D.z = 4;
```

GLKit provides a number of useful functions for working with vectors:

GLKVector3Add *and* GLKVector2Add
    Add two vectors together.

GLKVector3Subtract *and* GLKVector2Subtract
    Subtract one vector from another.

GLKVector3Distance *and* GLKVector2Distance
    Get the distance from one vector to another.

GLKVector3Length *and* GLKVector2Length
    Get the length (or magnitude) of a vector.

GLKVector3Normalize *and* GLKVector2Normalize
    Get the normalized version of a vector (i.e., a vector with the same direction as the original but with a length of 1).

GLKVector3DotProduct *and* GLKVector2DotProduct
    Get the dot product between two vectors.

For more information on what these functions involve, see "Vectors" on page 144.

Matrices

A *matrix* is a grid of numbers (see Figure 8-1).

$$M = \begin{bmatrix} 1 & 2 & 3 \\ 4 & 5 & 7 \\ 0 & 1 & 2 \end{bmatrix}$$

Figure 8-1. A matrix

On their own, matrices are just a way to store numbers. However, matrices are especially useful when they're combined with vectors. This is because you can multiply a matrix with a vector, which results in a changed version of the original vector.

Additionally, if you multiply two matrices together, the result is a matrix that, if you multiply it with a vector, has the same result as if you had multiplied the vector with each matrix individually. This means that a single matrix can be used to represent a combination of operations.

Additionally, there's a single matrix that, if multiplied with a vector, returns a vector with no changes (i.e., it returns the original vector). This is referred to as the *identity matrix*, and it's a good starting point for building a matrix: you start with the identity matrix and then translate it, rotate it, and so on.

The three most useful things a matrix can do with a vector are:

Translation
    Moving the vector

Rotation
    Rotating the vector in 3D space

Scaling
    Increasing or decreasing the distance of the vector from the origin

Another common kind of matrix, called a *perspective projection transform matrix*, does the work of making objects get smaller as they move away from the origin point. You can multiply a vector with a perspective projection transform matrix, just like any other transform.

Conversely, if you use an *orthographic projection transform matrix*, objects remain the same size no matter how far away they get. In both of these cases, you define the height and width of the view area, and objects outside of the view area aren't visible.

In GLKit, the `GLKMatrix4` structure represents a 4-by-4 matrix, which you use with vectors to apply transforms. `GLKMatrix4Identity` is the identity matrix.

You can create matrices that represent specific transformations by using the `GLKMatrix4MakeTranslation`, `GLKMatrix4MakeRotation`, and `GLKMatrix4MakeScale` functions:

```
// Make a matrix that represents a translation of 1 unit on the y-axis
GLKMatrix4 translationMatrix = GLKMatrix4MakeTranslation(0, 1, 0)

// Make a matrix that represents a rotation of π radians around the x-axis
GLKMatrix4 rotationMatrix = GLKMatrix4MakeRotation(M_PI, 1, 0, 0);

// Make a matrix that represents a scaling of 0.9 on the x-axis,
// 1.2 on the y-axis, and 1 on the z-axis
GLKMatrix4 scaleMatrix = GLKMatrix4MakeScale(0.9, 1.2, 1);
```

Once you have a matrix, you can create additional matrices, and combine them together using `GLKMatrixMultiply`:

```
GLKMatrix4 translationMatrix = GLKMatrix4MakeTranslation(0, 1, 0)
GLKMatrix4 rotationMatrix = GLKMatrix4MakeRotation(M_PI, M_PI_2, 0);

GLKMatrix4 translateAndRotateMatrix = GLKMatrix4Multiply(translationMatrix,
                                                         rotationMatrix);
```

Once you're done constructing your matrices, you give them to GLKit when it needs a *model-view matrix*. Model-view matrices are discussed in Recipe 8.5.

Finally, you can create projection matrices using the `GLKMatrix4MakePerspective` and `GLKMatrix4MakeOrtho` functions.

When you create a perspective projection, you need to provide four pieces of information:

Field of view
How "wide" the viewable region should be, measured in radians. The field of view is the angle from the leftmost viewable point to the rightmost viewable point.

Aspect ratio
The width of the viewable area, as a ratio to its height. For example, if you want the viewable region to be twice as wide as the height, the aspect ratio is 2; if you want the viewable region to be one-third the height, the aspect ratio is 0.333.

Near clipping plane
The minimum distance from the camera at which objects are allowed to be.

Far clipping plane
  The maximum distance from the camera at which objects are allowed to be.

 Humans have a field of view of almost 180° (i.e., π radians), but using this setting can cause problems in a game because the screen takes up a much smaller section of the player's field of view. Play around with 90° to 70° (i.e., π/2, or 1.57 radians to 1.22 radians).

Creating an orthographic projection requires different information. You need to provide the following:

- The *left* coordinate of the viewable region, relative to the center (i.e., the coordinate (0,0) is the center of the viewable region; if you want objects 5 units to the left of the camera to be viewable, you set this to –5)
- The *right* coordinate of the viewable region
- The *bottom* coordinate
- The *top* coordinate
- The *near* coordinate (i.e., the minimum distance that objects can be from the camera)
- The *far* coordinate (the maximum distance that objects can be from the camera)

Here's how you create perspective and orthographic matrices:

```
// Make a perspective projection with a n/2 (i.e., 90°) field of view,
// a 1.5:1 aspect ratio (the viewable area is 1.5x as wide as it is high),
// a near clipping plane 0.1 units away, and a far clipping plane 200
// units away
GLKMatrix4 perspectiveMatrix = GLKMatrix4MakePerspective(M_PI_2, 1.5, 0.1, 1.0);

// Make an orthographic projection with left coordinate -5,
// right coordinate 5, bottom coordinate -5, top coordinate 5,
// near coordinate 0.1, and far coordinate 200

GLKMatrix4 orthographicMatrix = GLKMatrix4MakeOrtho(-5, 5, -5, 5, 0.1, 100);
```

With this math primer in mind, it's on to the recipes!

8.2. Creating a GLKit Context

Problem

You want to create an application that draws using OpenGL.

Solution

Note that while Xcode includes a template that sets up a lot of this for you, in this exercise we're going to go through each part of it step by step, so you can understand it better:

1. Create a new single-view application.

2. Import the GLKit framework and OpenGLES framework.

3. Open *ViewController.xib*.

4. Select the view, open the Identity Inspector, and set the view's class to GLKView.

5. Open *ViewController.h*, import *GLKit/GLKit.h*, and change ViewController's parent class from UIViewController to GLKViewController.

6. Add the following code to viewDidLoad:

   ```
   GLKView* view = (GLKView*)self.view;
   view.context = [[EAGLContext alloc] initWithAPI:kEAGLRenderingAPIOpenGLES2];
   ```

7. Then add the following method:

   ```
   - (void)glkView:(GLKView *)view drawInRect:(CGRect)rect {
       glClearColor(0.0, 0.5, 0.0, 1.0);
       glClear(GL_COLOR_BUFFER_BIT);
   }
   ```

Discussion

When you create a GLKit context, you're creating the space in which all of your 3D graphics will be drawn. GLKit contexts are contained inside GLKView objects, which are just UIView objects that know how to draw OpenGL content.

When the context gets created, you need to specify which version of the OpenGL ES API you want to use. There are three different versions that you can use:

- *OpenGL ES 1.0*, which supports very simple, fixed-function rendering
- *OpenGL ES 2.0*, which adds support for *pixel shaders* (small programs that let you customize a great deal of the rendering process)
- *OpenGL ES 3.0*, which adds a number of low-level features that improve rendering speed and flexibility

 The changes from OpenGL ES 1.0 to 2.0 were much more significant than the changes from 2.0 to 3.0. The new stuff in 3.0 isn't as relevant to people starting out using OpenGL ES, so what we're covering in this book is largely content that was added in 2.0.

OpenGL works by continuously redrawing the entire scene every time a frame needs to be shown. Every time this happens, your `GLKView` calls the `glkView:drawInRect:` method. In this example, the only thing that happens is that the content of the view is cleared:

```
glClearColor(0.0, 0.5, 0.0, 1.0);
glClear(GL_COLOR_BUFFER_BIT);
```

The first line of the code calls `glClearColor`, which effectively tells OpenGL that the clear color should be set to the RGBA value (0.0, 0.5, 0.0, 1.0)—that is, fully opaque, dark green.

The next line instructs OpenGL to actually clear the *color buffer*—that is, it fills the entire screen with the clear color that was set on the previous line (see Figure 8-2).

Figure 8-2. The final result of this recipe: a screen filled with solid color

8.3. Drawing a Square Using OpenGL

Problem

You want to draw a square on the screen using OpenGL.

Solution

Make *ViewController.m* contain this code:

```objc
#import "ViewController.h"

typedef struct {
    GLKVector3 position;
} Vertex;

const Vertex SquareVertices[] = {
    {-1, -1 , 0}, // bottom left
    {1, -1 , 0},  // bottom right
    {1, 1 , 0},   // top right
    {-1, 1 , 0},  // top left
};

const GLubyte SquareTriangles[] = {
    0, 1, 2, // BL->BR->TR
    2, 3, 0  // TR->TL->BL
};

@interface ViewController () {
    GLuint _vertexBuffer; // contains the collection of vertices used to
                          // describe the position of each corner
    GLuint _indexBuffer;  // indicates which vertices should be used in each
                          // triangle used to make up the square

    GLKBaseEffect* _squareEffect; // describes how the square is going to be
                                  // rendered
}

@end

@implementation ViewController

- (void)viewDidLoad
{
    [super viewDidLoad];
    // Do any additional setup after loading the view, typically from a nib

    GLKView* view = (GLKView*)self.view;
    view.context = [[EAGLContext alloc] initWithAPI:kEAGLRenderingAPIOpenGLES2];

    [EAGLContext setCurrentContext:view.context];

    // Create the vertex array buffer, in which OpenGL will store the vertices

    // Tell OpenGL to give us a buffer
    glGenBuffers(1, &_vertexBuffer);

    // Make this buffer be the active array buffer
```

```
    glBindBuffer(GL_ARRAY_BUFFER, _vertexBuffer);

    // Put this data into the active array buffer. It's as big as the
    // 'SquareVertices' array, so we can use the data from that array;
    // also, this data isn't going to change.
    glBufferData(GL_ARRAY_BUFFER, sizeof(SquareVertices), SquareVertices,
                GL_STATIC_DRAW);


    // Now do the same thing for the index buffer, which indicates which
    // vertices to use when drawing the triangles
    glGenBuffers(1, &_indexBuffer);
    glBindBuffer(GL_ELEMENT_ARRAY_BUFFER, _indexBuffer);
    glBufferData(GL_ELEMENT_ARRAY_BUFFER, sizeof(SquareTriangles),
        SquareTriangles, GL_STATIC_DRAW);

    // Prepare the GL effect, which tells OpenGL how to draw our triangle
    _squareEffect = [[GLKBaseEffect alloc] init];

    // First, we set up the projection matrix
    float aspectRatio = self.view.bounds.size.width /
                        self.view.bounds.size.height;
    float fieldOfViewDegrees = 60.0;
    GLKMatrix4 projectionMatrix = GLKMatrix4MakePerspective(
                                GLKMathDegreesToRadians(fieldOfViewDegrees),
                                aspectRatio, 0.1, 10.0);

    _squareEffect.transform.projectionMatrix = projectionMatrix;

    // Next, we describe how the square should be positioned (6 units away
    // from the camera)
    GLKMatrix4 modelViewMatrix = GLKMatrix4MakeTranslation(0.0f, 0.0f, -6.0f);
    _squareEffect.transform.modelviewMatrix = modelViewMatrix;

    // Tell the effect that it should color everything with a single color
    // (in this case, red)
    _squareEffect.useConstantColor = YES;
    _squareEffect.constantColor = GLKVector4Make(1.0, 0.0, 0.0, 1.0);

}


- (void)glkView:(GLKView *)view drawInRect:(CGRect)rect {

    // Erase the view by filling it with black
    glClearColor(0.0, 0.0, 0.0, 1.0);
    glClear(GL_COLOR_BUFFER_BIT);

    // Tell the effect that it should prepare OpenGL to draw using the
    // settings we've configured it with
    [_squareEffect prepareToDraw];

    // OpenGL already knows that the vertex array (GL_ARRAY_BUFFER) contains
```

```
    // vertex data. We now tell it how to find useful info in that array.

    // Tell OpenGL how the data is laid out for the position of each
    // vertex in the vertex array
    glEnableVertexAttribArray(GLKVertexAttribPosition);
    glVertexAttribPointer(GLKVertexAttribPosition, 3, GL_FLOAT, GL_FALSE, 0, 0);

    // Now that OpenGL knows where to find vertex positions, it can draw them
    int numberOfVertices = sizeof(SquareTriangles)/sizeof(SquareTriangles[0]);
    glDrawElements(GL_TRIANGLES, numberOfVertices, GL_UNSIGNED_BYTE, 0);

}

- (void)didReceiveMemoryWarning
{
    [super didReceiveMemoryWarning];
    // Dispose of any resources that can be re-created
}

@end
```

Discussion

Drawing triangles in OpenGL is easier than drawing squares or more complex polygons, because triangles are always coplanar—that is, all of the points in the shape are on the same plane.

So, to draw a square, what we do is draw two triangles that share an edge, as illustrated in Figure 8-3.

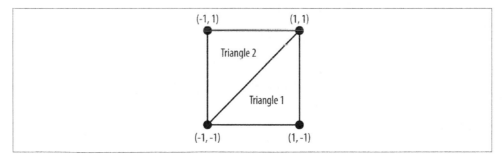

Figure 8-3. The vertices that define the triangles

This means that we need to tell OpenGL about two different things:

- Where each of these vertices is
- Which of these vertices are used in each triangle

To tell OpenGL about where the vertices are, we start by defining a structure for vertices and making an array. This will later be uploaded to OpenGL, so that it can be used:

```
typedef struct {
    GLKVector3 position;
} Vertex;

const Vertex SquareVertices[] = {
    {-1, -1 , 0}, // vertex 0: bottom left
    {1, -1 , 0},  // vertex 1: bottom right
    {1, 1 , 0},   // vertex 2: top right
    {-1, 1 , 0},  // vertex 3: top left
};
```

The positions used in each vertex are defined in arbitrary "units." These units can be anything you like: inches, centimeters, or whatever.

Once the vertices have been laid out, we need to define which triangles use which vertices. In OpenGL, we do this by numbering each vertex, and then describing triangles by giving OpenGL three numbers at a time:

```
const GLubyte SquareTriangles[] = {
    0, 1, 2, // BL->BR->TR
    2, 3, 0  // TR->TL->BL
};
```

In this case, the first triangle uses vertices 0, 1, and 2, and the second triangle uses vertices 2, 3, and 0. Note that both triangles use vertices 0 and 2. This means that they share an edge, which means that there won't be any gap between the two triangles.

This data needs to be passed to OpenGL before it can be used. Both the SquareVertices and SquareTriangles arrays need to be stored in a *buffer*, which is OpenGL's term for a chunk of information that it can use for rendering.

When you create a buffer, OpenGL gives you a number, which is the buffer's *name*. (A name is still a number, not text—it's just a weird OpenGL terminology thing.) When you want to work with a buffer, you use that buffer's name. In this code, we store the names as instance variables:

```
@interface ViewController () {
    GLuint _vertexBuffer; // contains the collection of vertices used to
                          // describe the position of each corner
    GLuint _indexBuffer;  // indicates which vertices should be used in each
                          // triangle used to make up the square

    GLKBaseEffect* _squareEffect; // describes how the square is going to be
                                  // rendered
}

@end
```

That last instance variable is a `GLKBaseEffect`, which is used to control the position of the square on the screen, as well as its color. We'll come back to this in a few moments.

The first part of the actual code that gets executed is in `viewDidLoad:`. First, we set up the `GLKView` with an OpenGL context. Because we're about to start issuing OpenGL commands, we also make that context the current context (if you don't do this, none of your OpenGL commands will do anything):

```
GLKView* view = (GLKView*)self.view;
view.context = [[EAGLContext alloc] initWithAPI:kEAGLRenderingAPIOpenGLES2];

[EAGLContext setCurrentContext:view.context];
```

Next, we create the buffers, starting with the vertex buffer. It's also bound to GL_AR RAY_BUFFER, which instructs OpenGL that whenever we're talking about "the GL_AR RAY_BUFFER," we mean _vertexBuffer. If you're making a game where you have more than one array buffer (which is common), you call `glBindBuffer` every time you want to start working with a different array buffer:

```
glGenBuffers(1, &_vertexBuffer);
glBindBuffer(GL_ARRAY_BUFFER, _vertexBuffer);
```

The vertex buffer is then filled with the vertex information:

```
glBufferData(GL_ARRAY_BUFFER, sizeof(SquareVertices),
    SquareVertices, GL_STATIC_DRAW);
```

The call to `glBufferData` basically says this: "Hey, OpenGL, I want you to put data into the currently bound GL_ARRAY_BUFFER. The size of the data is however big the Square Vertices array is, and the data should come from the SquareVertices array. Also, this data is unlikely to change, so you can optimize for that."

The same thing is then done for the index buffer, which you'll recall stores information on which vertices the two triangles will use:

```
glGenBuffers(1, &_indexBuffer);
glBindBuffer(GL_ELEMENT_ARRAY_BUFFER, _indexBuffer);
glBufferData(GL_ELEMENT_ARRAY_BUFFER, sizeof(SquareTriangles), SquareTriangles,
    GL_STATIC_DRAW);
```

Once this is done, all of the information has been passed to OpenGL. The next step is to configure how the object will be presented when OpenGL renders the scene.

GLKit provides *GLKit effects,* which are objects that contain information like color, lighting information, position, and orientation. This information can be configured ahead of time and is used at the moment of rendering. GLKit effects encapsulate a lot of the complexity that can go along with configuring how a rendered object gets drawn.

In this simple example, we want the square to be red and to be positioned in the middle of the screen.

The first step is to create the effect object, and then provide it with a projection matrix. The projection matrix controls the overall sizes of things on the screen, and effectively acts as the lens in front of the camera. In this case, we create a projection matrix that uses the aspect ratio of the screen and uses a field of view of 60 degrees:

```
_squareEffect = [[GLKBaseEffect alloc] init];

float aspectRatio = self.view.bounds.size.width /
                    self.view.bounds.size.height;
float fieldOfViewDegrees = 60.0;
GLKMatrix4 projectionMatrix = GLKMatrix4MakePerspective(
                    GLKMathDegreesToRadians(fieldOfViewDegrees),
                    aspectRatio, 0.1, 10.0);

_squareEffect.transform.projectionMatrix = projectionMatrix;
```

Once we've set up the projection matrix, we provide a model-view matrix. The model-view matrix controls the position of the object, relative to the camera:

```
GLKMatrix4 modelViewMatrix = GLKMatrix4MakeTranslation(0.0f, 0.0f, -6.0f);
_squareEffect.transform.modelviewMatrix = modelViewMatrix;
```

Finally, we tell the effect that whenever it's used to render anything, everything should be rendered with a constant color of red:

```
_squareEffect.useConstantColor = YES;
_squareEffect.constantColor = GLKVector4Make(1.0, 0.0, 0.0, 1.0);
```

The actual work of rendering is done in the glkView:drawInRect: method. The first thing that happens in this is that the view is cleared, by filling the screen with black:

```
glClearColor(0.0, 0.0, 0.0, 1.0);
glClear(GL_COLOR_BUFFER_BIT);
```

The GLKit effect is then told to "prepare to draw." This means that it configures OpenGL in such a way that anything you draw will use that effect's settings. If you have multiple GLKit effects, you call prepareToDraw on each one before you start drawing:

```
[_squareEffect prepareToDraw];
```

At this point, OpenGL knows that the `GL_ARRAY_BUFFER` contains per-vertex data, and that the `GL_ELEMENT_ARRAY_BUFFER` contains information on what data in the array buffer should be used for each triangle. This is because both of these buffers were bound during the `viewDidLoad` method.

In the next step, we tell OpenGL how to use the data in the `GL_ARRAY_BUFFER`. There's only one piece of information relevant in this app: the *position* of each vertex. (In more complex apps, there's often much more information that each vertex needs, such as color information, normals, and texture coordinates. We're keeping it simple.)

To tell OpenGL where the position information is in the vertex array, we first tell OpenGL that we're going to be working with positions, and then tell OpenGL where to find the position information in the vertex data:

```
glEnableVertexAttribArray(GLKVertexAttribPosition);
glVertexAttribPointer(GLKVertexAttribPosition, 3, GL_FLOAT, GL_FALSE, 0, 0);
```

The call to `glVertexAttribPointer` is interpreted by OpenGL like this: "OK, OpenGL, here's where you'll find the position information I just mentioned. There are three numbers, and they're all floating point. They're not normalized. Once you've read the three numbers, don't skip any information, because the next position will be right after that. Also, the position information starts right at the start of the array."

Finally, the triangles can actually be drawn:

```
int numberOfTriangles = sizeof(SquareTriangles)/sizeof(SquareTriangles[0]);
glDrawElements(GL_TRIANGLES, numberOfTriangles, GL_UNSIGNED_BYTE, 0);
```

First, we need to know how many vertices we're asking OpenGL to draw. We can figure this out by taking the size of the entire index array, and dividing that by the size of one element in that array. In our case, the array is made up of unsigned bytes, and there are six bytes in the array, so we're going to be asking OpenGL to render six vertices.

This call translates to: "OK, OpenGL! I want you to draw triangles (i.e., three vertices at a time). The number of triangles is 2. Each entry in the triangle list is an unsigned byte. Don't skip over any items in the element array."

OpenGL will then draw the two triangles on the screen, as shown in Figure 8-4.

Figure 8-4. A square being drawn by OpenGL

8.4. Loading a Texture

Problem

You want to display a texture on an OpenGL surface.

Solution

In this solution, we'll be loading a texture and applying it to the square that was drawn in the previous recipe.

First, in your vertex structure, you need to include texture coordinate information:

```
typedef struct {
    GLKVector3 position; // the location of each vertex in space
    GLKVector2 textureCoordinates; // the texture coordinates for each vertex
} Vertex;

const Vertex SquareVertices[] = {
    {{-1, -1 , 0}, {0,0}}, // bottom left
    {{1, -1 , 0}, {1,0}},  // bottom right
    {{1, 1 , 0}, {1,1}},   // top right
    {{-1, 1 , 0}, {0,1}},  // top left
};
```

Next, when preparing for rendering in `viewDidLoad`:

```
NSString* imagePath = [[NSBundle mainBundle]
pathForResource:@"Texture" ofType:@"png"];
NSError* error = nil;

GLKTextureInfo* texture = [GLKTextureLoader
textureWithContentsOfFile:imagePath options:nil error:&error];

if (error != nil) {
    NSLog(@"Problem loading texture: %@", error);
}

_squareEffect.texture2d0.name = texture.name;
```

If you're modifying the previous recipe, remove these lines:

```
_squareEffect.useConstantColor = YES;
_squareEffect.constantColor = GLKVector4Make(1.0, 0.0, 0.0, 1.0);
```

Finally, when rendering in `glkView:drawInRect:`, you indicate to OpenGL where to find texture coordinates in the vertex information:

```
glEnableVertexAttribArray(GLKVertexAttribTexCoord0);
glVertexAttribPointer(GLKVertexAttribTexCoord0, 2, GL_FLOAT, GL_FALSE,
    sizeof(Vertex), (void*)offsetof(Vertex, textureCoordinates));
```

When the square is rendered, you'll see your image appear on it.

Discussion

`GLKTextureLoader` allows you to take an image and upload it to the graphics chip that's built into your device. To get an image, you use the `pathForResource:ofType:` method on `NSBundle`, which gives you the location of the image that you specify.

Once you've got that location, you pass it to `GLKTextureLoader` using the `textureWith ContentsOfFile:options:error:` method. This sends the image to the graphics chip, and returns a `GLKTextureInfo` object. This object contains information about the texture, including its name.

In OpenGL, a texture's name is a number used to identify that specific texture. To use a texture, you provide its name to the `GLKEffect` that you're using to render your geometry.

In addition to loading a texture, you need to indicate to OpenGL which parts of the texture are attached to the geometry you're drawing. You do this by defining *texture coordinates*.

Texture coordinates indicate points in the texture. As illustrated in Figure 8-5, the position (0,0) refers to the lower-left corner of the texture, while the position (1,1) refers to the upper-right corner.

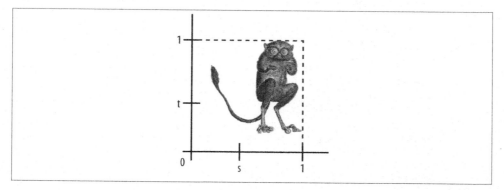

Figure 8-5. Texture coordinates

You give texture coordinates to OpenGL by using the `glEnableVertexAttribArray` and `glVertexAttribPointer` functions. The first function tells OpenGL that you want to enable the use of texture coordinates, and the second tells OpenGL where in the vertex data the texture coordinates will be found (see Figure 8-6).

Figure 8-6. A textured square drawn by OpenGL

8.5. Drawing a Cube

Problem

You want to draw a three-dimensional cube, and draw a texture on its faces.

Solution

This solution builds from Recipe 8.4.

A cube is made up of eight vertices, one for each of its corners. To draw the cube, therefore, you need to provide information for each vertex, including its position and texture coordinates.

Additionally, you'll need to tell OpenGL how to build the triangles that make up each of the cube's six faces. (Recall from Recipe 8.3 that you draw a square by drawing two triangles that share an edge.)

Note that in this example, we've renamed SquareVertices to CubeVertices and SquareTriangles to CubeTriangles:

```
const Vertex CubeVertices[] = {
    {{-1, -1, 1}, {0,0}}, // bottom left front
    {{1, -1, 1}, {1,0}},  // bottom right front
    {{1, 1, 1}, {1,1}},   // top right front
    {{-1, 1, 1}, {0,1}},  // top left front

    {{-1, -1, -1}, {1,0}}, // bottom left back
    {{1, -1, -1}, {0,0}},  // bottom right back
    {{1, 1, -1}, {0,1}},   // top right back
    {{-1, 1, -1}, {1,1}},  // top left back
};

const GLubyte CubeTriangles[] = {
    0, 1, 2, // front face 1
    2, 3, 0, // front face 2

    4, 5, 6, // back face 1
    6, 7, 4, // back face 2

    7, 4, 0, // left face 1
    0, 3, 7, // left face 2

    2, 1, 5,   // right face 1
    5, 6, 2,   // right face 2

    7, 3, 6, // top face 1
    6, 2, 3, // top face 2

    4, 0, 5, // bottom face 1
    5, 1, 0, // bottom face 2
};
```

The next step is a purely aesthetic one: the cube will be rotated, in order to illustrate that it is in fact a three-dimensional object.

Replace these lines:

```
GLKMatrix4 modelViewMatrix = GLKMatrix4MakeTranslation(0.0f, 0.0f, -6.0f);
_squareEffect.transform.modelviewMatrix = modelViewMatrix;
```

with the following:

```
GLKMatrix4 modelViewMatrix = GLKMatrix4MakeTranslation(0.0f, 0.0f, -6.0f);
modelViewMatrix = GLKMatrix4RotateX(modelViewMatrix,
                                    GLKMathDegreesToRadians(45));
modelViewMatrix = GLKMatrix4RotateY(modelViewMatrix,
                                    GLKMathDegreesToRadians(45));
_squareEffect.transform.modelviewMatrix = modelViewMatrix;
```

On its own, this is almost enough: as we saw in the previous recipe, the call to glDrawElements uses the size of the triangles array to determine how many triangles (and, consequently, how many vertices) it needs to use.

However, to draw our cube we need to add and enable a depth buffer.

Add this code immediately after the call to EAGLContext's setCurrentContext method:

```
view.drawableDepthFormat = GLKViewDrawableDepthFormat24;
glEnable(GL_DEPTH_TEST);
```

Finally, replace this line:

```
glClear(GL_COLOR_BUFFER_BIT);
```

with this:

```
glClear(GL_COLOR_BUFFER_BIT | GL_DEPTH_BUFFER_BIT);
```

The result is shown in Figure 8-7.

Discussion

A *depth buffer* is a region of memory that keeps track of how far away each pixel is from the camera. This makes it possible to draw, for example, a close object before drawing one farther away—without a depth buffer, you'd need to make sure that you drew your farthest objects before drawing closer ones, or you'd end up with distant objects over-lapping closer ones. If you want to learn more about this, check out the Wikipedia article on the Painter's Algorithm (*http://en.wikipedia.org/wiki/Painter's_algorithm*).

Depth buffers work like this: every time a pixel is drawn onto the screen, OpenGL calculates how far away that pixel is from the camera. When the pixel is right up against the camera, a 0 is written into the depth buffer, and when the pixel is very, very far away from the camera, a 1 is written into the depth buffer. Pixels that fall somewhere between get written in as numbers in between (0.1, 0.12, and so on).

Figure 8-7. A cube rendered in OpenGL

When `GL_DEPTH_TEST` is turned on, OpenGL checks the depth buffer to see if the pixel it's about to draw is farther away than the most recently drawn pixel. If the pixel is closer to the camera than the nearest existing pixel, that means that it's closer than the existing pixels, so it's drawn on the screen and the distance of the new pixel replaces the old one in the depth buffer. However, if it's farther away than any existing pixel, it's behind the old ones, and consequently it's not drawn.

Just like with the color buffer, you have to clear the depth buffer every time you begin a new frame; if you don't, you'll end up with rendering glitches, because OpenGL will start comparing the depth values of pixels against an out-of-date depth buffer.

8.6. Rotating a Cube

Problem

You want to animate movement in a scene, such as rotation.

Solution

This solution builds upon the previous recipe.

Add the following instance variable to the `ViewController` class:

```
float rotation;
```

Next, add the following method to the class:

```
- (void) update {

    // Find out how much time has passed since the last update
    NSTimeInterval timeInterval = self.timeSinceLastUpdate;

    // We want to rotate at 15 degrees per second, so multiply
    // this amount times the time since the last update and
    // update the "rotation" variable.
    float rotationSpeed = 15 * timeInterval;
    rotation += rotationSpeed;

    // Now construct a model view matrix that places the object 6 units away
    // from the camera and rotates it appropriately
    GLKMatrix4 modelViewMatrix = GLKMatrix4MakeTranslation(0.0f, 0.0f, -6.0f);

    modelViewMatrix = GLKMatrix4RotateX(modelViewMatrix,
                                        GLKMathDegreesToRadians(45));
    modelViewMatrix = GLKMatrix4RotateY(modelViewMatrix,
                                        GLKMathDegreesToRadians(rotation));

    // Apply this to the effect so that the drawing will use this positioning
    _squareEffect.transform.modelviewMatrix = modelViewMatrix;
}
```

When you run the application, your cube will be rotating.

Discussion

The update method on a `GLKViewController` is called once per frame, and this is your game's opportunity to update in-game content.

In this solution, we're creating a GLKMatrix4, which defines the position and orientation of the object. You create it using the GLKMatrix4MakeTranslation function, and then rotate it around the x- and y-axes. Finally, the matrix is given to the object's GLKEffect, which sets the position and orientation.

8.7. Moving the Camera in 3D Space

Problem

You want to be able to move the camera based on user input.

Solution

First, we'll define how quickly the camera moves. Add the following line of code at the top of *ViewController.m*:

```
const float dragSpeed = 1.0f / 120.0f;
```

Next, add the following instance variable to ViewController:

```
GLKVector3 _cameraPosition;
```

Then add this code to the end of viewDidLoad:

```
UIPanGestureRecognizer* pan =
[[UIPanGestureRecognizer alloc] initWithTarget:self action:@selector(dragged:)];
[self.view addGestureRecognizer:pan];

_cameraPosition.z = -6;
```

Add this method to ViewController:

```
- (void) dragged:(UIPanGestureRecognizer*)pan {
    if (pan.state == UIGestureRecognizerStateBegan ||
        pan.state == UIGestureRecognizerStateChanged) {
        CGPoint translation = [pan translationInView:pan.view];
        _cameraPosition.x += translation.x * dragSpeed;
        _cameraPosition.y -= translation.y * dragSpeed;

        [pan setTranslation:CGPointZero inView:pan.view];
    }
}
```

And finally, update this line in the update method:

```
GLKMatrix4 modelViewMatrix = GLKMatrix4MakeTranslation(0, 0, -6);
```

with this code:

```
GLKMatrix4 modelViewMatrix =
GLKMatrix4MakeTranslation(_cameraPosition.x, _cameraPosition.y,
                          _cameraPosition.z);
```

Discussion

The term *camera* in OpenGL is actually kind of a misnomer. In OpenGL, you don't create a camera object and move it around; instead, the camera is always positioned at (0,0,0), and you position objects in front of it. In practical terms, this just means that the matrices that define the position and orientation of your objects need to be *reversed* —that is, when you want your object to be positioned 6 units in front of the camera, you set the z-position of the object to be –6.

 In Recipe 9.5, you'll see how to create a movable camera in OpenGL.

CHAPTER 9

Intermediate 3D Graphics

Once you've got OpenGL drawing basic 3D content, you'll likely want to create more complicated scenes. In this chapter, you'll learn how to load meshes from files, how to compose complex objects by creating parent-child relationships between objects, how to position a camera in 3D space, and more.

This chapter builds on the basic 3D graphics concepts covered in Chapter 8, and makes use of the component-based layout shown in Recipe 1.3.

9.1. Loading a Mesh

Problem

You want to load meshes from files, so that you can store 3D objects in files.

Solution

First, create an empty text file called *MyMesh.json*. Put the following text in it:

```
{
    "vertices":[
        {
            "x":-1, "y":-1, "z":1
        },
        {
            "x":1, "y":-1, "z":1
        },
        {
            "x":-1, "y":1, "z":1
        },
        {
            "x":1, "y":1, "z":1
        },
```

```
    {
        "x":-1, "y":-1, "z":-1
    },
    {
        "x":1, "y":-1, "z":-1
    },
    {
        "x":-1, "y":1, "z":-1
    },
    {
        "x":1, "y":1, "z":-1
    }
],
"triangles":[
    [0,1,2],
    [2,3,1],
    [4,5,6],
    [6,7,5]
]
}
```

JSON is but one of many formats for storing 3D mesh data; many popular 3D modeling tools, such as the open source Blender (*http://www.blender.org/*), support it.

This mesh creates two parallel squares, as shown in Figure 9-1.

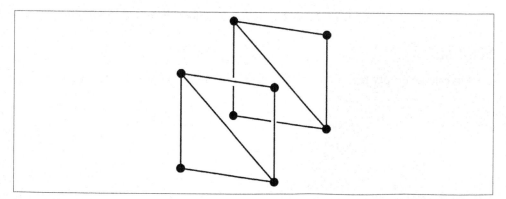

Figure 9-1. The mesh

Next, create a new subclass of NSObject, called Mesh. Put the following code in *Mesh.h*:

```
#import <GLKit/GLKit.h>

typedef struct {
    GLKVector3 position;
    GLKVector2 textureCoordinates;
    GLKVector3 normal;
} Vertex;

typedef struct {
    GLuint vertex1;
    GLuint vertex2;
    GLuint vertex3;
} Triangle;

@interface Mesh : NSObject

+ (Mesh*) meshWithContentsOfURL:(NSURL*)url error:(NSError**)error;

// The name of the OpenGL buffer containing vertex data
@property (readonly) GLuint vertexBuffer;

// The name of the OpenGL buffer containing the triangle list
@property (readonly) GLuint indexBuffer;

// A pointer to the loaded array of vector info
@property (readonly) Vertex* vertexData;

// The number of vertices
@property (readonly) NSUInteger vertexCount;

// A pointer to the triangle list data
@property (readonly) Triangle* triangleData;

// The number of triangles
@property (readonly) NSUInteger triangleCount;

@end
```

Next, put the following methods into *Mesh.m*. The first of these, meshWithContentsO
fURL:error:, attempts to load an NSDictionary from disk, and then tries to create a
new Mesh object with its contents:

```
+ (Mesh *)meshWithContentsOfURL:(NSURL *)url
error:(NSError *__autoreleasing *)error {

    // Load the JSON text into memory

    NSData* meshJSONData = [NSData dataWithContentsOfURL:url options:0
                            error:error];

    if (meshJSONData == nil)
        return nil;
```

```
// Convert the text into an NSDictionary,
// then check to see if it's actually a dictionary
NSDictionary* meshInfo =
    [NSJSONSerialization JSONObjectWithData:meshJSONData
        options:0
        error:error];

if ([meshInfo isKindOfClass:[NSDictionary class]] == NO)
    return nil;

// Finally, attempt to create a mesh with this dictionary
return [[Mesh alloc] initWithMeshDictionary:meshInfo];

}
```

The next method, initWithMeshDictionary:, checks the contents of the provided NSDictionary and loads the mesh information into memory. It then prepares OpenGL buffers so that the mesh information can be rendered:

```
- (id)initWithMeshDictionary:(NSDictionary*)dictionary
{
    self = [super init];
    if (self) {

        // Get the arrays of vertices and triangles, and ensure they're arrays
        NSArray* loadedVertexDictionary = dictionary[@"vertices"];
        NSArray* loadedTriangleDictionary = dictionary[@"triangles"];

        if ([loadedVertexDictionary isKindOfClass:[NSArray class]] == NO) {
            NSLog(@"Expected 'vertices' to be an array");
            return nil;
        }

        if ([loadedTriangleDictionary isKindOfClass:[NSArray class]] == NO) {
            NSLog(@"Expected 'triangles' to be an array");
            return nil;
        }

        // Calculate how many vertices and triangles we have
        _vertexCount = loadedVertexDictionary.count;
        _triangleCount = loadedTriangleDictionary.count;

        // Allocate memory to store the vertices and triangles in
        _vertexData = calloc(sizeof(Vertex), _vertexCount);
        _triangleData = calloc(sizeof(Triangle), _triangleCount);

        if (_vertexData == NULL || _triangleData == NULL) {
            NSLog(@"Couldn't allocate memory!");
            return nil;
        }
```

```
// For each vertex in the list, read information about it and store it
for (int vertex = 0; vertex < _vertexCount; vertex++) {

    NSDictionary* vertexInfo = loadedVertexDictionary[vertex];

    if ([vertexInfo isKindOfClass:[NSDictionary class]] == NO) {
        NSLog(@"Vertex %i is not a dictionary", vertex);
        return nil;
    }

    // Store the vertex data in memory, at the correct position:

    // Position:
    _vertexData[vertex].position.x = [vertexInfo[@"x"] floatValue];
    _vertexData[vertex].position.y = [vertexInfo[@"y"] floatValue];
    _vertexData[vertex].position.z = [vertexInfo[@"z"] floatValue];

    // Texture coordinates
    _vertexData[vertex].textureCoordinates.s =
        [vertexInfo[@"s"] floatValue];
    _vertexData[vertex].textureCoordinates.t =
        [vertexInfo[@"t"] floatValue];

    // Normal
    _vertexData[vertex].normal.x = [vertexInfo[@"nx"] floatValue];
    _vertexData[vertex].normal.y = [vertexInfo[@"ny"] floatValue];
    _vertexData[vertex].normal.z = [vertexInfo[@"nz"] floatValue];



}

// Next, for each triangle in the list, read information and store it
for (int triangle = 0; triangle < _triangleCount; triangle++) {
    NSArray* triangleInfo = loadedTriangleDictionary[triangle];

    if ([triangleInfo isKindOfClass:[NSArray class]] == NO) {
        NSLog(@"Triangle %i is not an array", triangle);
        return nil;
    }

    // Store the index of each referenced vertex
    _triangleData[triangle].vertex1 =
        [triangleInfo[0] unsignedIntegerValue];
    _triangleData[triangle].vertex2 =
        [triangleInfo[1] unsignedIntegerValue];
    _triangleData[triangle].vertex3 =
        [triangleInfo[2] unsignedIntegerValue];

    // Check to make sure that the vertices referred to exist

    if (_triangleData[triangle].vertex1 >= _vertexCount) {
```

```
                NSLog(@"Triangle %i refers to an unknown vertex %i", triangle,
                        _triangleData[triangle].vertex1);
                return nil;
            }

            if (_triangleData[triangle].vertex2 >= _vertexCount) {
                NSLog(@"Triangle %i refers to an unknown vertex %i", triangle,
                        _triangleData[triangle].vertex2);
                return nil;
            }

            if (_triangleData[triangle].vertex3 >= _vertexCount) {
                NSLog(@"Triangle %i refers to an unknown vertex %i", triangle,
                        _triangleData[triangle].vertex3);
                return nil;
            }
        }

        // We've now loaded all of the data into memory. Time to create
        // buffers and give them to OpenGL!

        glGenBuffers(1, &_vertexBuffer);
        glGenBuffers(1, &_indexBuffer);

        glBindBuffer(GL_ARRAY_BUFFER, _vertexBuffer);
        glBufferData(GL_ARRAY_BUFFER,
                        sizeof(Vertex) * _vertexCount,
                        _vertexData,
                        GL_STATIC_DRAW);

        glBindBuffer(GL_ELEMENT_ARRAY_BUFFER, _indexBuffer);
        glBufferData(GL_ELEMENT_ARRAY_BUFFER,
                        sizeof(Triangle) * _triangleCount,
                        _triangleData,
                        GL_STATIC_DRAW);


    }
    return self;
}
```

The final method, dealloc, releases the resources that are created in the init method:

```
- (void)dealloc {
    // We're going away, so we need to tell OpenGL to get rid of the
    // data we uploaded
    glDeleteBuffers(1, &_vertexBuffer);
    glDeleteBuffers(1, &_indexBuffer);

    // Now free the memory that we allocated earlier
    free(_vertexData);
    free(_triangleData);
}
```

Discussion

In this solution, we're creating a Mesh object, which represents a loaded mesh. One of the advantages of this approach is that you can load a mesh once, and then reuse it multiple times.

At minimum, a mesh is a collection of vertices combined with information that links up the vertices into polygons. This means that when you load a mesh, you need to get the positions of every vertex, as well as information describing which vertices make up which polygons.

The specific format that you use to store your mesh on disk can be anything you like. In this solution, we went with JSON because it's easy to read and write, and iOS has a built-in class designed for reading it. However, it's not the only format around, and not necessarily the best one for your uses. Other popular mesh formats include Wavefront OBJ, which is a text-based format, and Autodesk FBX, which is binary and supports a number of handy features like embedded animations and hierarchical meshes.

As we discussed in Recipe 8.3, to draw a mesh, you first need to load the information for its vertices and how the vertices are linked together into memory. The actual format for how this information is stored in memory is up to you because you describe to OpenGL where to find the specific types of information that it needs.

When you load a mesh and give it to OpenGL to draw, you first allocate a chunk of memory, fill it with information, and then create an OpenGL buffer. You then tell OpenGL to fill the buffer with the information you've loaded. This happens twice: once for the vertices, and again for the list of indices that describe how the vertices are linked into triangles.

In this solution, the format for vertices is a structure that looks like this:

```
typedef struct {
    GLKVector3 position;
    GLKVector2 textureCoordinates;
} Vertex;
```

However, a mesh is almost always going to contain more than one vertex, and it isn't possible to know how many vertices you're going to be dealing with at compile time. To deal with this, the memory that contains the vertices needs to be *allocated*, using the calloc function. This function takes two parameters—the size of each piece of memory you want to allocate and the number of pieces:

```
_vertexData = calloc(sizeof(Vertex), _vertexCount);
```

So, to create the memory space that contains the list of vertices, you need to know how big each vertex is, and how many vertices you need. To find out the size of any structure, you use the sizeof function, and to find out the number of vertices, you check the file that you're loading.

Once this memory has been allocated, you can work with it: for each vertex, you read information about it and fill in the data. The same process is done for the triangle list.

When you allocate memory using `calloc` (or any of its related methods, including `malloc` and `realloc`), you need to manually free it, using the `free` function. You do this in your `Mesh` object's `dealloc` method, which is called when the `Mesh` is in the process of being removed from memory.

 It's very important that any memory that you allocate using `calloc` or `malloc` gets freed with `free`. If you don't do this, you end up with a memory leak: memory that's been allocated but never freed and is never referred to again. Memory leaks waste memory, which is something you *really* don't want in the memory-constrained environment of iOS.

9.2. Parenting Objects

Problem

You want to attach objects to other objects, so that multiple animations can combine.

Solution

The code in this solution uses the component-based architecture discussed in Recipe 1.3, though the idea can also be applied to hierarchy-based architectures (see Recipe 1.2). In this solution, we'll be creating a `Transform` component.

Create a new class named `Transform`, and put the following contents in *Transform.h*:

```
@interface Transform : Component

@property (weak) Transform* parent;
@property (strong, readonly) NSSet* children;

- (void) addChild:(Transform*)child;
- (void) removeChild:(Transform*)child;

// Position relative to parent
@property (assign) GLKVector3 localPosition;

// Rotation angles relative to parent, in radians
@property (assign) GLKVector3 localRotation;

// Scale relative to parent
@property (assign) GLKVector3 localScale;

// The matrix that maps local coordinates to world coordinates
```

```
@property (readonly) GLKMatrix4 localToWorldMatrix;

// Vectors relative to us
@property (readonly) GLKVector3 up;
@property (readonly) GLKVector3 forward;
@property (readonly) GLKVector3 left;

// Position in world space
@property (readonly) GLKVector3 position;

// Rotation in world space
@property (readonly) GLKQuaternion rotation;

// Scale, taking into account parent object's scale
@property (readonly) GLKVector3 scale;

@end
```

And in *Transform.m*:

```
#import "Transform.h"

@interface Transform () {
    NSMutableSet* _children;
}

@end

@implementation Transform

@dynamic position;
@dynamic rotation;
@dynamic scale;

@dynamic up;
@dynamic left;
@dynamic forward;

- (id)init
{
    self = [super init];
    if (self) {
        // The list of children
        _children = [NSMutableSet set];

        // By default, we're scaled to 1 on all 3 axes
        _localScale = GLKVector3Make(1, 1, 1);
    }
    return self;
}

// Add a transform as a child of us
- (void)addChild:(Transform *)child {
```

```objc
    [_children addObject:child];
    child.parent = self;
}

// Remove a transform from the list of children
- (void)removeChild:(Transform *)child {
    [_children removeObject:child];
    child.parent = nil;
}

// Rotate a vector by our local axes
- (GLKVector3)rotateVector:(GLKVector3)vector {
    GLKMatrix4 matrix = GLKMatrix4Identity;
    matrix = GLKMatrix4RotateX(matrix, self.localRotation.x);
    matrix = GLKMatrix4RotateY(matrix, self.localRotation.y);
    matrix = GLKMatrix4RotateZ(matrix, self.localRotation.z);

    return GLKMatrix4MultiplyVector3(matrix, vector);
}

- (GLKVector3)up {
    return [self rotateVector:GLKVector3Make(0, 1, 0)];
}

- (GLKVector3)forward {
    return [self rotateVector:GLKVector3Make(0, 0, 1)];
}

- (GLKVector3)left {
    return [self rotateVector:GLKVector3Make(1, 0, 0)];
}

// Create a matrix that represents our position, rotation, and scale in
// world space
- (GLKMatrix4)localToWorldMatrix {

    // First, get the identity matrix
    GLKMatrix4 matrix = GLKMatrix4Identity;

    // Next, get the matrix of our parent
    if (self.parent)
        matrix = GLKMatrix4Multiply(matrix, self.parent.localToWorldMatrix);

    // Translate it
    matrix = GLKMatrix4TranslateWithVector3(matrix, self.localPosition);

    // Rotate it
    matrix = GLKMatrix4RotateX(matrix, self.localRotation.x);
    matrix = GLKMatrix4RotateY(matrix, self.localRotation.y);
    matrix = GLKMatrix4RotateZ(matrix, self.localRotation.z);

    // And scale it!
```

```
        matrix = GLKMatrix4ScaleWithVector3(matrix, self.localScale);

        return matrix;
}

// Get a quaternion that describes our orientation in world space
- (GLKQuaternion)rotation {

        // First, get the identity quaternion (i.e., no rotation)
        GLKQuaternion rotation = GLKQuaternionIdentity;

        // Now, multiply this rotation with its parent, if it has one
        if (self.parent)
            rotation = GLKQuaternionMultiply(rotation, self.parent.rotation);

        // Finally, rotate around our local axes
        GLKQuaternion xRotation = GLKQuaternionMakeWithAngleAndVector3Axis(
            self.localRotation.x, GLKVector3Make(1, 0, 0));
        GLKQuaternion yRotation = GLKQuaternionMakeWithAngleAndVector3Axis(
            self.localRotation.y, GLKVector3Make(0, 1, 0));
        GLKQuaternion zRotation = GLKQuaternionMakeWithAngleAndVector3Axis(
            self.localRotation.z, GLKVector3Make(0, 0, 1));

        rotation = GLKQuaternionMultiply(rotation, xRotation);
        rotation = GLKQuaternionMultiply(rotation, yRotation);
        rotation = GLKQuaternionMultiply(rotation, zRotation);

        return rotation;

}

// Get our position in world space
- (GLKVector3)position {
        GLKVector3 position = self.localPosition;

        if (self.parent)
            position = GLKVector3Add(position, self.parent.position);

        return position;
}

// Get our scale in world space
- (GLKVector3)scale {
        GLKVector3 scale = self.localScale;

        if (self.parent)
            scale = GLKVector3Multiply(scale, self.parent.scale);

        return scale;
}
```

To get the model-view matrix for an object at a given position, you just ask for its `localToWorldMatrix`, which you can then provide to a GLKBaseEffect's `transform.modelViewMatrix` property.

Discussion

It's often the case that you'll have an object (called the "child" object) that needs to be attached to another object (called the "parent"), such that when the parent moves, the child moves with it. You can make this happen by allowing objects to keep a reference to their parent and use the position, orientation, and scale of the parent when calculating their own position, orientation, and scale:

```
my world position = parent's position + my local position
my world rotation = parent's rotation + my local rotation
my world scale = parent's scale * my local scale
```

When you do this, you can have a long chain of parents: one can be the parent of another, which can be the parent of yet another, and so on.

The easiest way to represent this is by making each object calculate a matrix, which is a single value that represents the *transform* of an object (i.e., the position, rotation, and scale of the object). Matrices are useful, both because a single matrix represents all three operations and because matrices can be combined. So, if you get the transform matrix of the parent and multiply that by your own transform matrix, you end up with a matrix that combines the two.

It just so happens that a transform matrix is exactly what's needed when you render a mesh: the model-view matrix, which converts the coordinates of vertices in a mesh to world space, *is* a transform matrix.

9.3. Animating a Mesh

Problem

You want to animate objects by moving them over time.

Solution

The code in this solution uses the component-based architecture discussed in Recipe 1.3, though the idea can also be applied to hierarchy-based architectures (see Recipe 1.2). In this solution, we'll be creating an Animation component.

Add a new class called Animation, and put the following contents in *Animation.h*:

```
#import "Component.h"
#import <GLKit/GLKit.h>
```

```
// Animates a property on "object"; t is between 0 and 1
typedef void (^AnimationBlock)(GameObject* object, float t);

@interface Animation : Component

@property (assign) float duration;

- (void) startAnimating;
- (void) stopAnimating;

- (id) initWithAnimationBlock:(AnimationBlock)animationBlock;

@end
```

And in *Animation.m*:

```
#import "Animation.h"

@implementation Animation {
    AnimationBlock _animationBlock;

    float _timeElapsed;

    BOOL _playing;

}

- (void)startAnimating {
    _timeElapsed = 0;
    _playing = YES;
}

- (void)stopAnimating {
    _playing = NO;
}

- (void) update:(float)deltaTime {

    // Don't do anything if we're not playing
    if (_playing == NO)
        return;

    // Don't do anything if the duration is zero or less
    if (self.duration <= 0)
        return;

    // Increase the amount of time that this animation's been running for
    _timeElapsed += deltaTime;

    // Go back to the start when time elapsed > duration
    if (_timeElapsed > self.duration)
        _timeElapsed = 0;
```

```
        // Dividing the time elapsed by the duration returns a value between 0 and 1
        float t = _timeElapsed / self.duration;

        // Finally, call the animation block
        if (_animationBlock) {
            _animationBlock(self.gameObject, t);
        }
    }

    - (id)initWithAnimationBlock:(AnimationBlock)animationBlock
    {

        self = [super init];
        if (self) {
            _animationBlock = animationBlock;
            _duration = 2.5;
        }
        return self;
    }

    @end
```

To use the animation component, you create one and provide a block that performs an animation:

```
GameObject* myObject = ... // a GameObject

// Create an animation that rotates around the y-axis
Animation* rotate =
[[Animation alloc] initWithAnimationBlock:^(GameObject *object, float t) {

    // Rotate a full circle (2n radians)
    float angle = 2*M_PI*t;

    object.transform.localRotation = GLKVector3Make(0, angle, 0);
}];

// The animation takes 10 seconds to complete
rotate.duration = 10;

// Add the animation to the object
[myObject addComponent:rotate];

// Kick off the animation
[rotate startAnimating];
```

Discussion

An animation is a change in value over time. When you animate an object's position, you're changing the position from a starting point to the ending point.

An animation can take as long as you want to complete, but it's often very helpful to think of the animation's time scale as going from 0 (animation start) to 1 (animation end). This means that the animation's duration can be kept separate from the animation itself.

You can use this value as part of an *easing equation*, which smoothly animates a value over time.

If t is limited to the range of 0 to 1, you can write the equation for a linear progression from value v1 to value v2 like this:

```
result = v1 + (v2 - v1) * t;
```

Imagine that you want to animate the *x* coordinate of an object from 1 to 5. If you plot this position on a graph, where the y-axis is the position of the object and the x-axis is time going from 0 to 1, the coordinates look like Table 9-1.

Table 9-1. Plot points to animate x

Position	t
1	0.00
2	0.25
3	0.50
4	0.75
5	1.00

This equation moves smoothly from the first value to the second, and maintains the same speed the entire way.

There are other equations that you can use:

```
// Ease-in - starts slow, reaches full speed by the end
result = v1 + (v2 - v1) * pow(t,2);

// Ease-out - starts at full speed, slows down toward the end
result = v1 + (v1 - v2) * t * (t-2)
```

You can also create more complex animations by combining multiple animations, using parenting (see Recipe 9.2).

9.4. Batching Draw Calls

Problem

You have a number of objects, all of which have the same texture, and you want to improve rendering performance.

Solution

This solution uses the Mesh class discussed in Recipe 9.1.

If you have a large number of objects that can be rendered with the same GLKEffect (but with varying positions and orientations), create a new vertex buffer and, for each copy of the object, copy each vertex into the buffer.

For each vertex you copy in, multiply the vertex by the object's transform matrix (see Recipe 9.2). Next, create an index buffer and copy each triangle from each object into it. (Because they're triangles, they don't get transformed.)

When you render the contents of these buffers, all copies of the object will be rendered at the same time.

Discussion

The glDrawElements function is the slowest function involved in OpenGL. When you call it, you kick off a large number of complicated graphics operations: data is fetched from the buffers, vertices are transformed, shaders are run, and pixels are written into the frame buffer. The more frequently you call glDrawElements, the more work needs to happen, and as discussed in Recipe 15.1, the more work you do, the lower your frame rate's going to be.

To reduce the number of calls to glDrawElements and improve performance, it's better to group objects together and render them at the same time. If you have a hundred crates, instead of drawing a crate 100 times, you draw 100 crates once.

There are a couple of limitations when you use this technique, though:

- All objects have to use the same texture and lights, because they're all being drawn at the same time.
- More space in memory gets taken up, because you have to store a duplicate set of vertices for each copy of the object.
- If any of the objects are moving around, you have to dynamically create a new buffer and fill it with vertex data every frame, instead of creating a buffer once and reusing it.

9.5. Creating a Movable Camera Object

Problem

You want your camera to be an object that can be moved around the scene like other objects.

Solution

This solution builds on the component-based architecure discussed in Recipe 1.3 and uses the `Transform` component from Recipe 9.2.

Create a new subclass of `Component` called `Camera`, and put the following contents in *Camera.h*:

```
#import "Component.h"
#import <GLKit/GLKit.h>

@interface Camera : Component

// Return a matrix that maps world space to view space
- (GLKMatrix4) viewMatrix;

// Return a matrix that maps view space to eye space
- (GLKMatrix4) projectionMatrix;

// Field of view, in radians
@property (assign) float fieldOfView;

// Near clipping plane, in units
@property (assign) float nearClippingPlane;

// Far clipping plane, in units
@property (assign) float farClippingPlane;

// Clear screen contents and get ready to draw
- (void) prepareToDraw;

// The color to erase the screen with
@property (assign) GLKVector4 clearColor;

@end
```

And in *Camera.m*:

```
#import "Camera.h"
#import "Transform.h"
#import "GameObject.h"

@implementation Camera

// By default, start with a clear color of black (RBGA 1,1,1,0)
- (id)init
{
    self = [super init];
    if (self) {
        self.clearColor = GLKVector4Make(0.0, 0.0, 0.0, 1.0);
    }
    return self;
}
```

```
- (void) prepareToDraw {
    // Clear the contents of the screen
    glClearColor(self.clearColor.r, self.clearColor.g, self.clearColor.b,
                 self.clearColor.a);
    glClear(GL_COLOR_BUFFER_BIT | GL_DEPTH_BUFFER_BIT);
}

// Return a matrix that maps world space to view space
- (GLKMatrix4)viewMatrix {

    Transform* transform = self.gameObject.transform;

    // The camera's position is its transform's position in world space
    GLKVector3 position = transform.position;

    // The camera's target is right in front of it
    GLKVector3 target = GLKVector3Add(position, transform.forward);

    // The camera's up direction is the transform's up direction
    GLKVector3 up = transform.up;

    return GLKMatrix4MakeLookAt(position.x, position.y, position.z,
                                target.x, target.y, target.z,
                                up.x, up.y, up.z);

}

// Return a matrix that maps view space to eye space
- (GLKMatrix4)projectionMatrix {

    // We'll assume that the camera is always rendering into the entire screen
    // (i.e., it's never rendering to just a subsection of it).
    // This means the aspect ratio of the camera is the screen's aspect ratio.

    float aspectRatio = [UIScreen mainScreen].bounds.size.width /
                        [UIScreen mainScreen].bounds.size.height;

    return GLKMatrix4MakePerspective(self.fieldOfView, aspectRatio,
                                     self.nearClippingPlane,
                                     self.farClippingPlane);
}

@end
```

Discussion

The idea of a "camera" in OpenGL is kind of the reverse of how people normally think of viewing a scene. While it's easy to think of a camera that moves around in space, looking at objects, what's really going on in OpenGL is that objects get rearranged to be in front of the viewer. That is, when the camera "moves forward," what's really happening is that objects are moving closer to the camera.

When objects in your 3D scene are rendered, they get transformed through a variety of *coordinate spaces*. The first space that vertices begin in is *model space*, where all vertices are defined relative to the point of the model. Because we don't want all the meshes to be drawn on top of one another, they need to be transformed into *world space*, in which all vertices are defined relative to the origin point of the world.

Once they're in world space, they need to be rearranged such that they're in front of the camera. You accomplish this by calculating a view matrix, which you do by taking the position of the camera in world space, the position of a point it should be looking toward, and a vector defining which direction is "up" for the camera, and then calling `GLKMatrix4MakeLookAt`.

The view matrix rearranges vertices so that the camera's position is at the center of the coordinate space, and arranges things so that the camera's "up" and "forward" directions become the coordinate space's y- and z-axes.

So, when you "position" a camera, what you're really doing is preparing a matrix that arranges your vertices in a way that puts the camera in the center, with everything else arranged around it.

CHAPTER 10

Advanced 3D Graphics

OpenGL provides a huge amount of flexibility in how objects get rendered, and you can do all kinds of interesting things with light and material. In this chapter, we're going to look at *shaders*, which are small programs that give you complete control over how OpenGL should draw your 3D scene. We'll look at lighting, texturing, bump-mapping, and nonphotorealistic rendering.

This chapter builds on beginning and intermediate concepts covered in Chapters 8 and 9, respectively.

10.1. Understanding Shaders

Problem

You want to create shader programs, which control how objects are drawn onscreen, so that you can create different kinds of materials.

Solution

A shader is composed of three elements: a *vertex shader*, a *fragment shader*, and a *shader program* that links the vertex and fragment shaders together. To make a shader, you first write the vertex and fragment shaders, then load them in to OpenGL, and then tell OpenGL when you want to use them.

First, create the vertex shader. Create a file called *SimpleVertexShader.vsh*, and add it to your project:

```
uniform mat4 modelViewMatrix;
uniform mat4 projectionMatrix;

attribute vec3 position;
```

```
void main()
{

    // "position" is in model space. We need to convert it to camera space by
    // multiplying it by the modelViewProjection matrix.
    gl_Position = (projectionMatrix* modelViewMatrix) * vec4(position,1.0);
}
```

 When you drag and drop the file into your project, Xcode won't add it to the list of files that get copied into the app's resources. Instead, it will add it to the list of files that should be compiled. You don't want this.

To fix it, open the project build phases by clicking the project at the top of the Project Navigator and clicking Build Phases, and move the file from the Compile Sources to the Copy Bundle Resources list by dragging and dropping it.

Next, create the fragment shader by creating a file called *SimpleFragmentShader.fsh*, and putting the following code in it:

```
void main()
{
    // All pixels in this object will be pure red
    gl_FragColor = vec4(1.0, 0.0, 0.0, 1.0);
}
```

Finally, provide your shader code to OpenGL. You do this by first creating two shaders, using the glCreateShader function. You then give each shader its source code using the glShaderSource function, and then compile the shader with the glCompileShad er function. This needs to be done twice, once for each of the two shaders. Note that you'll need to keep the GLuint variable around in your Objective-C code (not the shader code):

```
// Keep this variable around as an instance variable
GLuint _shaderProgram;

// Compile the vertex shader
NSString* vertexSource = ... // an NSString containing the source code of your
                             // vertex shader. Load this string from a file.
GLUint _vertexShader = glCreateShader(GL_VERTEX_SHADER);
const char* vertexShaderSourceString =
[vertexSource cStringUsingEncoding:NSUTF8StringEncoding];
glShaderSource(_vertexShader, 1, &vertexShaderSourceString, NULL);
glCompileShader(_vertexShader);

// Compile the fragment shader
NSString* fragmentSource = ... // contains the fragment shader's source code
GLuint _fragmentShader = glCreateShader(GL_FRAGMENT_SHADER);
const char* fragmentShaderSourceString =
```

```
[fragmentSource cStringUsingEncoding:NSUTF8StringEncoding];

glShaderSource(_fragmentShader, 1, &fragmentShaderSourceString, NULL);
glCompileShader(_fragmentShader);
```

After you give the shader source to OpenGL, you then need to check to see if there were any errors. You do this by creating a variable called success and giving its address to the glGetShaderiv function, asking it for the shader's compile status. After the function returns, success will contain a 1 if it succeeded, and a 0 if it didn't. If a shader didn't succeed, you can get information on what went wrong using the glGetShaderInfo Log function:

```
// Check to see if both shaders compiled
int success;

// Check the vertex shader
glGetShaderiv(_vertexShader, GL_COMPILE_STATUS, &success);
if (success == 0) {
    char errorLog[1024];
    glGetShaderInfoLog(_vertexShader, sizeof(errorLog), NULL, errorLog);}
    NSLog(@"Error: %s");
    return;
}

glGetShaderiv(_fragmentShader, GL_COMPILE_STATUS, &success);
if (success == 0) {
    char errorLog[1024];
    glGetShaderInfoLog(_fragmentShader, sizeof(errorLog), NULL, errorLog);}
    NSLog(@"Error: %s");
    return;
}
```

Once the shaders have been checked, you then create the shader program, which links the shaders together. You do this with the glCreateProgram function, and then attach the two shaders with the glAttachShader function:

```
_shaderProgram = glCreateProgram();
glAttachShader(_shaderProgram, _vertexShader);
glAttachShader(_shaderProgram, _fragmentShader);
```

Next, you need to tell OpenGL how you want to pass information to the shader. You do this by creating a variable and setting it to 1, and then instructing OpenGL that you want to refer to a specific shader variable by this number. When you have multiple variables in a shader that you want to work with this way, you create another variable and set it to 2, and so on:

```
const MaterialAttributePosition = 1;

// Tell OpenGL that we want to refer to the "position" variable by the number 1
glBindAttribLocation(_shaderProgram, MaterialAttributePosition, "position");
```

Once the program is appropriately configured, you tell OpenGL to link the program. Once it's linked, you can check to see if there were any problems, in much the same way as when you compiled the individual shaders:

```
glLinkProgram(_shaderProgram);

int success;
glGetProgramiv(program, GL_LINK_STATUS, &success);
if (success == 0) {
    char errorLog[1024];
    glGetProgramInfoLog(program, sizeof(errorLog), NULL, errorLog);
    NSLog(@"Error: %s", errorLog);
    return;
}
```

This completes the setup process for the shader program. When you want to render using the program, you first tell OpenGL you want to use the program by calling `glUseProgram`, and pass information to the shader using the `glVertexAttribPointer` function. When `glDrawElements` is called, the shader will be used to draw the objects:

```
glUseProgram(_shaderProgram);

glEnableVertexAttribArray(MaterialAttributePosition);
glVertexAttribPointer(MaterialAttributePosition, 3, GL_FLOAT, GL_FALSE,
                      sizeof(Vertex), (void*)offsetof(Vertex, position));

glDrawElements(GL_TRIANGLES, (GLsizei)self.mesh.triangleCount * 3,
    GL_UNSIGNED_INT, 0);
```

Discussion

A shader program gives you a vast amount of control over how objects are rendered by OpenGL. Prior to OpenGL ES 2.0 (which became available in iOS 3 on the iPhone 3GS), the only way you could draw graphics was using the built-in functions available on the graphics chip. While these were useful, they didn't allow programmers to create their own custom rendering effects. Shaders let you do that.

Shaders are small programs that run on the graphics chip. Vertex shaders receive the vertex information provided by your code, and are responsible for transforming the vertices from object space into screen space.

Once each vertex has been transformed, the graphics chip determines which pixels on the screen need to have color drawn into them, which is a process called *rasterization*. Once rasterization is complete, the graphics chip then runs the shader program for each pixel to determine exactly what color needs to be shown.

Even though shaders appear to have very limited responsibilities, they have tremendous amounts of power. It's up to shaders to apply effects like lighting, cartoon effects, bump mapping, and more.

10.2. Working with Materials

Problem

You want to separate the appearance of an object from its geometry.

Solution

This solution makes use of the component architecture discussed in Recipe 1.3 and elaborated on in Chapter 9. In this solution, we're going to create a `Material` class, which loads shaders and keeps material information separate from mesh information.

Create a new class called `Material`, which is a subclass of `GLKBaseEffect`. Put the following code in *Material.h*:

```
enum MaterialAttributes {
    MaterialAttributePosition,
    MaterialAttributeNormal,
    MaterialAttributeColor,
    MaterialAttributeTextureCoordinates
};

@interface Material : GLKBaseEffect <GLKNamedEffect>

+ (Material*)effectWithVertexShaderNamed:(NSString*)vertexShaderName
fragmentShaderNamed:(NSString*)fragmentShaderName error:(NSError**)error;

- (void) prepareToDraw;

@end
```

Now, put the following code in *Material.m*. We're going to show one method at a time, because this file is kind of big. First, the instance variables. These store information about the shader, including where to find various variables. Not all of the variables will be used at the same time:

```
@interface Material () {
    // References to the shaders and the program
    GLuint _vertexShader;
    GLuint _fragmentShader;
    GLuint _shaderProgram;

    // Uniform locations:

    // Matrices, for converting points into different coordinate spaces
    GLuint _modelViewMatrixLocation;
    GLuint _projectionMatrixLocation;
    GLuint _normalMatrixLocation;

    // Textures, for getting texture info
```

```
    GLuint _texture0Location;
    GLuint _texture1Location;

    // Light information
    GLuint _lightPositionLocation;
    GLuint _lightColorLocation;
    GLuint _ambientLightColorLocation;
}

// Where to find the shader files
@property (strong) NSURL* vertexShaderURL;
@property (strong) NSURL* fragmentShaderURL;

@end
```

Next, add the methods that create the `Material` objects:

```
// Create a material by looking for a pair of named shaders
+ (Material*)effectWithVertexShaderNamed:(NSString*)vertexShaderName
fragmentShaderNamed:(NSString*)fragmentShaderName error:(NSError**)error {

    NSURL* fragmentShaderURL =
    [[NSBundle mainBundle] URLForResource:fragmentShaderName
                                            withExtension:@"fsh"];
    NSURL* vertexShaderURL =
    [[NSBundle mainBundle] URLForResource:vertexShaderName withExtension:@"vsh"];

    return [Material effectWithVertexShader:vertexShaderURL
    fragmentShader:fragmentShaderURL error:error];
}

// Create a material by loading shaders from the provided URLs.
// Return nil if the shaders can't be loaded.
+ (Material*)effectWithVertexShader:(NSURL *)vertexShaderURL
fragmentShader:(NSURL *)fragmentShaderURL error:(NSError**)error {

    Material* material = [[Material alloc] init];
    material.vertexShaderURL = vertexShaderURL;
    material.fragmentShaderURL = fragmentShaderURL;

    if ([material prepareShaderProgramWithError:error] == NO)
        return nil;

    return material;

}
```

Then, add the method that loads and prepares the shaders:

```
// Load and prepare the shaders. Returns YES if it succeeded, or NO otherwise.
- (BOOL)prepareShaderProgramWithError:(NSError**)error {

    // Load the source code for the vertex and fragment shaders
```

```objc
NSString* vertexShaderSource =
[NSString stringWithContentsOfURL:self.vertexShaderURL
encoding:NSUTF8StringEncoding error:error];
if (vertexShaderSource == nil)
    return NO;

NSString* fragmentShaderSource =
[NSString stringWithContentsOfURL:self.fragmentShaderURL
encoding:NSUTF8StringEncoding error:error];
if (fragmentShaderSource == nil)
    return NO;

// Create and compile the vertex shader
_vertexShader = glCreateShader(GL_VERTEX_SHADER);
const char* vertexShaderSourceString =
[vertexShaderSource cStringUsingEncoding:NSUTF8StringEncoding];

glShaderSource(_vertexShader, 1, &vertexShaderSourceString, NULL);
glCompileShader(_vertexShader);

if ([self shaderIsCompiled:_vertexShader error:error] == NO)
    return NO;

// Create and compile the fragment shader
_fragmentShader = glCreateShader(GL_FRAGMENT_SHADER);
const char* fragmentShaderSourceString =
[fragmentShaderSource cStringUsingEncoding:NSUTF8StringEncoding];

glShaderSource(_fragmentShader, 1, &fragmentShaderSourceString, NULL);
glCompileShader(_fragmentShader);

if ([self shaderIsCompiled:_fragmentShader error:error] == NO)
    return NO;

// Both of the shaders are now compiled, so we can link them together and
// form a program
_shaderProgram = glCreateProgram();
glAttachShader(_shaderProgram, _vertexShader);
glAttachShader(_shaderProgram, _fragmentShader);

// First, we tell OpenGL what index numbers we want to use to refer to
// the various attributes. This allows us to tell OpenGL about where
// to find vertex attribute data.
glBindAttribLocation(_shaderProgram, MaterialAttributePosition, "position");
glBindAttribLocation(_shaderProgram, MaterialAttributeColor, "color");
glBindAttribLocation(_shaderProgram, MaterialAttributeNormal, "normal");
glBindAttribLocation(_shaderProgram, MaterialAttributeTextureCoordinates,
                     "texcoords");

// Now that we've told OpenGL how we want to refer to each attribute,
// we link the program
glLinkProgram(_shaderProgram);
```

```
if ([self programIsLinked:_shaderProgram error:error] == NO)
    return NO;

// Get the locations of the uniforms
_modelViewMatrixLocation =
glGetUniformLocation(_shaderProgram, "modelViewMatrix");
_projectionMatrixLocation =
glGetUniformLocation(_shaderProgram, "projectionMatrix");
_normalMatrixLocation = glGetUniformLocation(_shaderProgram, "normalMatrix");

_texture0Location = glGetUniformLocation(_shaderProgram, "texture0");
_texture1Location = glGetUniformLocation(_shaderProgram, "texture1");

_lightPositionLocation =
glGetUniformLocation(_shaderProgram, "lightPosition");
_lightColorLocation = glGetUniformLocation(_shaderProgram, "lightColor");
_ambientLightColorLocation =
glGetUniformLocation(_shaderProgram, "ambientLightColor");

return YES;

}
```

This method calls a pair of error-checking methods, which check to see if the shaders and program have been correctly prepared. Add them next:

```
// Return YES if the shader compiled correctly, NO if it didn't
// (and put an NSError in "error")
- (BOOL)shaderIsCompiled:(GLuint)shader error:(NSError**)error {

    // Ask OpenGL if the shader compiled correctly
    int success;
    glGetShaderiv(shader, GL_COMPILE_STATUS, &success);

    // If not, find out why and send back an NSError object
    if (success == 0) {

        if (error != nil) {
            char errorLog[1024];
            glGetShaderInfoLog(shader, sizeof(errorLog), NULL, errorLog);
            NSString* errorString = [NSString stringWithCString:errorLog
                                     encoding:NSUTF8StringEncoding];

            *error = [NSError errorWithDomain:@"Material"
            code:NSFileReadCorruptFileError userInfo:@{@"Log":errorString}];
        }

        return NO;
    }

    return YES;
}
```

```
// Return YES if the program linked successfully, NO if it didn't
// (and put an NSError in "error")
- (BOOL) programIsLinked:(GLuint)program error:(NSError**)error {

    // Ask OpenGL if the program has been successfully linked
    int success;
    glGetProgramiv(program, GL_LINK_STATUS, &success);

    // If not, find out why and send back an NSError
    if (success == 0) {
        if (error != nil) {
            char errorLog[1024];
            glGetProgramInfoLog(program, sizeof(errorLog), NULL, errorLog);
            NSString* errorString = [NSString stringWithCString:errorLog
                                    encoding:NSUTF8StringEncoding];

            *error = [NSError errorWithDomain:@"Material"
            code:NSFileReadCorruptFileError
            userInfo:@{NSUnderlyingErrorKey:errorString}];
        }
        return NO;
    }

    return YES;
}
```

The next step is to write the `prepareToDraw` method, which is called immediately before drawing takes place and tells OpenGL that the next drawing operation should use the shaders controlled by this `Material`:

```
// Called when the shader is about to be used
- (void)prepareToDraw {
    // Select the program
    glUseProgram(_shaderProgram);

    // Give the model-view matrix to the shader
    glUniformMatrix4fv(_modelViewMatrixLocation, 1, GL_FALSE,
    self.transform.modelviewMatrix.m);

    // Also give the projection matrix
    glUniformMatrix4fv(_projectionMatrixLocation, 1, GL_FALSE,
    self.transform.projectionMatrix.m);

    // Provide the normal matrix to the shader, too
    glUniformMatrix3fv(_normalMatrixLocation, 1, GL_FALSE,
    self.transform.normalMatrix.m);

    // If texture 0 is enabled, tell the shader where to find it
    if (self.texture2d0.enabled) {
        // "OpenGL, I'm now talking about texture 0."
        glActiveTexture(GL_TEXTURE0);
```

```
    // "Make texture 0 use the texture data that's referred to by
    // self.texture2d0.name."
    glBindTexture(GL_TEXTURE_2D, self.texture2d0.name);
    // "Finally, tell the shader that the uniform variable "texture0"
    // refers to texture 0.
    glUniform1i(_texture0Location, 0);
}

// Likewise with texture 1
if (self.texture2d1.enabled) {
    glActiveTexture(GL_TEXTURE1);
    glBindTexture(GL_TEXTURE_2D, self.texture2d1.name);
    glUniform1i(_texture1Location, 1);
}

// Pass light information into the shader, if it's enabled
if (self.light0.enabled) {
    glUniform3fv(_lightPositionLocation, 1, self.light0.position.v);
    glUniform4fv(_lightColorLocation, 1, self.light0.diffuseColor.v);
    glUniform4fv(_ambientLightColorLocation, 1,
                 self.lightModelAmbientColor.v);
}

// With this set, fragments with an alpha of less than 1 will be
// semitransparent
glEnable(GL_BLEND);
glBlendFunc(GL_SRC_ALPHA, GL_ONE_MINUS_SRC_ALPHA);
glBlendEquation(GL_FUNC_ADD);

}
```

Finally, add the `dealloc` method, which deletes the shaders and the shader program
when the `Material` object is being freed:

```
// Delete the program and shaders, to free up resources
- (void)dealloc {
    glDeleteProgram(_shaderProgram);
    glDeleteShader(_fragmentShader);
    glDeleteShader(_vertexShader);
}
```

To use a `Material` object, you first create one using the `effectWithVertexShader
Named:fragmentShaderNamed:error:` method, by passing in the names of the shaders
you want to use:

```
NSError* error = nil;
Material* material = [Material effectWithVertexShaderNamed:@"MyVertexShader"
fragmentShaderNamed:@"MyFragmentShader" error:&error];

if (material == nil) {
    NSLog(@"Couldn't create the material: %@", error);
    return nil;
}
```

When you're about to draw using the `Material`, you provide vertex attributes in the same way as when you're using a `GLKBaseEffect`, with a single difference—you use `MaterialAttributePosition` instead of `GLKVertexAttribPosition`, and so on for the other attributes:

```
[material prepareToDraw];

glEnableVertexAttribArray(MaterialAttributePosition);
glVertexAttribPointer(MaterialAttributePosition, 3, GL_FLOAT, GL_FALSE,
                      sizeof(Vertex), (void*)offsetof(Vertex, position));

glDrawElements(GL_TRIANGLES, (GLsizei)self.mesh.triangleCount * 3,
                      GL_UNSIGNED_INT, 0);
```

 Material is basically just a fancy word for a collection of properties and shaders.

Discussion

A `Material` object is useful for acting as a container for your shaders. As a subclass of `GLKBaseEffect`, your `Material` class is easily able to store material information like light color and where to find transforms.

The `Material` class presented here actually has *fewer* features than `GLKBaseEffect`, but it gives you more control. `GLKBaseEffect` works by dynamically creating shaders based on the parameters you supply, which means that you can't take the base effect and add stuff on top. If you want to do more advanced rendering, you have to do it yourself—which means, among other things, writing your own shaders.

10.3. Texturing with Shaders

Problem

You want to apply textures to your objects using shaders you've written.

Solution

Write a fragment shader that looks like this:

```
varying lowp vec4 vertex_color;
varying lowp vec2 vertex_texcoords;

uniform sampler2D texture0;
```

```
void main()
{
    gl_FragColor = texture2D(texture0, vertex_texcoords) * vertex_color;
}
```

Discussion

A `sampler2D` is an object that lets you get access to texture information provided by your app. When you call the `texture2D` function and pass in the sampler and the texture coordinates you want to sample, you get back a four-dimensional vector that contains the red, green, blue, and alpha components at that point in the texture.

By multiplying this color with the vertex color, you can then tint the texture.

Finally, the result is assigned to `gl_FragColor`, which means that OpenGL uses that color for the pixel.

10.4. Lighting a Scene

Problem

You want your objects to appear lit by light sources.

Solution

In this solution, we'll cover *point lights*, which are lights that exist at a single point in space and radiate light in all directions.

To work with lights, your mesh needs to have *normals*. A normal is a vector that indicates the direction that a vertex is facing, which is necessary for calculating the angle at which light is going to bounce off the surface.

If you're using the `Mesh` class described in Recipe 9.1, you can add normals (`"nx":0, "ny":0, "nz":1` in the following example) to your mesh by adding further info to your vertices:

```
{
    "x":-1, "y":-1, "z":1,
    "r":1, "g":0, "b":0,
    "s":0, "t":1,
    "nx":0, "ny":0, "nz":1
},
```

Next, use this vertex shader:

```
uniform mediump mat4 modelViewMatrix;
uniform mediump mat4 projectionMatrix;
uniform mediump mat3 normalMatrix;
```

```
attribute vec3 position;
attribute vec4 color;
attribute vec3 normal;
attribute vec2 texcoords;

varying mediump vec4 vertex_position;
varying mediump vec4 vertex_color;
varying mediump vec2 vertex_texcoords;
varying mediump vec4 vertex_normal;


void main()
{

    // "position" is in model space. We need to convert it to camera space by
    // multiplying it by the modelViewProjection matrix.
    gl_Position = (projectionMatrix* modelViewMatrix) * vec4(position,1.0);

    // Pass the color and position of the vertex in world space to the
    // fragment shader
    vertex_color = color;
    vertex_position = modelViewMatrix * vec4(position, 1.0);

    // Also pass the normal and the texture coordinates to the fragment shader
    vertex_normal = vec4(normal, 0.0);
    vertex_texcoords = texcoords;

}
```

Finally, use this fragment shader:

```
uniform mediump mat4 modelViewMatrix;
uniform mediump mat3 normalMatrix;

varying mediump vec4 vertex_color;
varying mediump vec2 vertex_texcoords;
varying mediump vec4 vertex_normal;
varying mediump vec4 vertex_position;

uniform sampler2D texture0;

uniform lowp vec3 lightPosition;
uniform lowp vec4 lightColor;
uniform lowp vec4 ambientLightColor;

void main()
{

    // Get the normal supplied by the vertex shader
    mediump vec3 normal = vec3(normalize(vertex_normal));

    // Convert the normal from object space to world space
    normal = normalMatrix * normal;
```

```
// Get the position of this fragment
mediump vec3 modelViewVertex = vec3(modelViewMatrix * vertex_position);

// Determine the direction of the fragment from the point on the surface
mediump vec3 lightVector = normalize(lightPosition - modelViewVertex);

// Calculate how much light is reflected
mediump float diffuse = clamp(dot(normal, lightVector), 0.0, 1.0);

// Combine everything together!
gl_FragColor = texture2D(texture0, vertex_texcoords) * vertex_color *
diffuse * lightColor  + ambientLightColor;

}
```

Discussion

To calculate how much light is bouncing off the surface and into the camera, you first need to know the direction in which the surface is oriented. You do this using *normals*, which are vectors that indicate the direction of the vertices that make up the surface.

Next, you need to know the angle from the camera to the light source. For this you need to know where the light source is in world space, and where each point that light is bouncing off of is in world space. You determine this by having the vertex shader convert the position of each vertex into world space by multiplying the position by the model-view matrix.

Once this is done, the vertex shader passes the normal information and vertex colors to the fragment shader. The fragment shader then does the following things:

1. It ensures that the normal has length 1 by normalizing it, which is important for the following calculations.

2. It converts the normal into world space by multiplying it with the normal matrix, which has been supplied by the Material.

3. It converts the position of the fragment into world space by multiplying the vertex position, which was provided by the vertex shader, with the model-view matrix.

4. It then determines the vector that represents the light source's position relative to the fragment's position.

5. Once that's done, it takes the dot product between the normal and the light vector. The result is how much light is bouncing off the surface and into the camera.

6. Finally, all of the information is combined together. The texture color, vertex color, light color, and how much light is hitting the surface are all multiplied together, and the ambient light is added.

10.5. Using Normal Mapping

Problem

You want to use normal mapping to make your objects appear to have lots of detail.

Solution

First, create a normal map. They are textures that represent the bumpiness of your object. You can make normal maps using a number of third-party tools; one that we find pretty handy is CrazyBump (*http://crazybump.com*).

Once you have your normal map, you provide a vertex shader:

```
uniform mediump mat4 modelViewMatrix;
uniform mediump mat4 projectionMatrix;
uniform mediump mat3 normalMatrix;

attribute vec3 position;
attribute vec4 color;
attribute vec3 normal;
attribute vec2 texcoords;

varying mediump vec4 vertex_color;
varying mediump vec2 vertex_texcoords;
varying mediump vec4 vertex_normal;

varying mediump vec4 vertex_position;

void main()
{
    // "position" is in model space. We need to convert it to camera space by
    // multiplying it by the modelViewProjection matrix.
    gl_Position = (projectionMatrix* modelViewMatrix) * vec4(position,1.0);

    // Next, we pass the color, position, normal, and texture coordinates
    // to the fragment shader by putting them in varying variables.
    vertex_color = color;
    vertex_position = modelViewMatrix * vec4(position, 1.0);

    vertex_normal = vec4(normal, 0.0);
    vertex_texcoords = texcoords;

}
```

and a fragment shader:

```
uniform mediump mat4 modelViewMatrix;
uniform mediump mat3 normalMatrix;

varying mediump vec4 vertex_color;
varying mediump vec2 vertex_texcoords;
varying mediump vec4 vertex_normal;
varying mediump vec4 vertex_position;

uniform sampler2D texture0; // diffuse map
uniform sampler2D texture1; // normal map

uniform lowp vec3 lightPosition;
uniform lowp vec4 lightColor;
uniform lowp vec4 ambientLightColor;

void main()
{

    // When normal mapping, normals don't come from the vertices, but rather
    // from the normal map

    mediump vec3 normal =
    normalize(texture2D(texture1, vertex_texcoords).rgb * 2.0 - 1.0);

    // Convert the normal from object space to world space.
    normal = normalMatrix * normal;

    // Get the position of this fragment.
    mediump vec3 modelViewVertex = vec3(modelViewMatrix * vertex_position);

    // Determine the direction of the fragment to the point on the surface
    mediump vec3 lightVector = normalize(lightPosition - modelViewVertex);

    // Calculate how much light is reflected
    mediump float diffuse = clamp(dot(normal, lightVector), 0.0, 1.0);

    // Combine everything together!
    gl_FragColor = texture2D(texture0, vertex_texcoords) * vertex_color *
    diffuse * lightColor + ambientLightColor;

}
```

When you create the `Material` using this shader, you need to provide two textures. The first is the *diffuse map*, which provides the base color of the surface. The second is the *normal map*, which is not shown to the player but is used to calculate light reflections.

Discussion

In Recipe 10.4, the normals came from the vertices. However, this generally means that there's not a lot of detail that the light can bounce off of, and the resulting surfaces look fairly flat.

When you use a normal map, the normals come from a texture, not from individual vertices. This means that you have a lot of control over how light bounces off the surface, and consequently can make the surface appear to have more detail.

The actual algorithm for lighting a normal-mapped surface is the same as that for lighting a non-normal-mapped surface. The only difference is that the normals come from the texture, instead of being passed in by the vertex shader.

Note that normal mapping doesn't actually make your object bumpier; it just reflects light *as if it were* bumpier. If you look at a normal-mapped surface side-on, it will be completely flat.

10.6. Making Objects Transparent

Problem

You want your objects to be transparent, so that objects behind them can be partly visible.

Solution

Before drawing an object, use the `glBlendFunc` function to control how the object you're about to draw is blended with the scene:

```
glEnable(GL_BLEND);
glBlendFunc(GL_SRC_ALPHA, GL_ONE_MINUS_SRC_ALPHA);
```

Discussion

When the fragment shader produces the color value of a pixel, that color is blended with whatever's already been drawn. By default, the output color replaces whatever was previously drawn, but this doesn't have to be the case.

When you call glEnable(GL_BLEND), OpenGL will blend the output color with the scene based on instructions that you provide. The specific way that the blending takes place is up to you, and you control it using the glBlendFunc function.

glBlendFunc takes two parameters. The first is how the source color is changed as part of the blend operation, and the second is how the destination color is changed. In this context, "source color" means the color that's emitted by the fragment shader, and "destination color" means the color that was already in the scene when the drawing took place.

By default, the blending function is this:

```
glBlendFunc(GL_ONE, GL_ZERO);
```

This means that the blending works like this:

```
Result Color = Source Color * 1 + Destination Color * 0;
```

In this case, because the destination is being multiplied by zero, it contributes nothing to the result color, and the source color completely replaces it.

A common blending method in games is to use the alpha value of the color to determine transparency: that is, 0 alpha means invisible, and 1 alpha means completely opaque. To make this happen, use glBlendFunc(GL_SRC_ALPHA, GL_ONE_MINUS_SRC_ALPHA), which has this effect:

```
Result Color = Source Color * Source Alpha +
               Destination Color * (1 - Source Alpha)
```

Doing this means that the higher the alpha value for the source color is, the more it will contribute to the final color.

Another common blending mode is "additive" blending, which creates a glowing appearance. You can create this effect by calling glBlendFunc(GL_ONE, GL_ONE), which adds the two colors together:

```
Result Color = Source Color * 1 + Destination Color * 1
```

 Additive blending is referred to as *linear dodge* in graphics programs like Adobe Photoshop.

10.7. Adding Specular Highlights

Problem

You want to have shiny specular highlights on your objects.

Solution

You can use the same vertex shader as shown in Recipe 10.4. However, to get specular highlights, you need a different fragment shader:

```
uniform mediump mat4 modelViewMatrix;
uniform mediump mat3 normalMatrix;

varying mediump vec4 vertex_color;
varying mediump vec2 vertex_texcoords;
varying mediump vec4 vertex_normal;
varying mediump vec4 vertex_position;

uniform sampler2D texture0; // diffuse map
uniform sampler2D texture1; // normal map

uniform lowp vec3 lightPosition;
uniform lowp vec4 lightColor;
uniform lowp vec4 ambientLightColor;

void main()
{

    mediump float shininess = 2.0;

    // With normal mapping, normals don't come from the vertices, but rather
    // from the normal map

    mediump vec3 normal =
    normalize(texture2D(texture1, vertex_texcoords).rgb * 2.0 - 1.0);
```

```
// Convert the normal from object space to world space
normal = normalMatrix * normal;

// Get the position of this fragment
mediump vec3 modelViewVertex = vec3(modelViewMatrix * vertex_position);

// Determine the direction of the fragment to the point on the surface
mediump vec3 lightVector = normalize(lightPosition - modelViewVertex);

// Calculate how much light is reflected
mediump float diffuse = clamp(dot(normal, lightVector), 0.0, 1.0);

// Determine the specular term
mediump float specular = max(pow(dot(normal, lightVector), shininess), 0.0);

// Combine everything together!
gl_FragColor = texture2D(texture0, vertex_texcoords) * vertex_color *
(diffuse * lightColor) + (lightColor * specular) + ambientLightColor;

}
```

Discussion

Specular highlights are bright spots that appear on very shiny objects. Specular highlights get added on top of the existing diffuse and ambient light, which makes them look bright.

In the real world, no object is uniformly shiny. If you want something to look slightly old and tarnished, use specular mapping: create a texture in which white is completely shiny and black is not shiny at all. In your shader, sample this texture (in the same way as when you sample a texture for color or for normals) and multiply the result by the specular term. The result will be an object that is shiny in some places and dull in others, as shown in Figure 10-1.

If you want to learn more about lighting, we recommend starting with the Wikipedia article on Phong shading (*http://en.wikipedia.org/wiki/Phong_shading*).

Figure 10-1. Using specular highlights to create shiny objects

10.8. Adding Toon Shading

Problem

You want to create a cartoon effect by making your object's lighting look flat.

Solution

Add the following code to your fragment shader:

```
diffuse = ... //  diffuse is calculated as per Recipe 10.4

// Group the lighting into three bands: one with diffuse lighting at 1.0,
// another at 0.75, and another at 0.5. Because there's no smooth
// transition between each band, hard lines will be visible between them.

if (diffuse > 0.75)
    diffuse = 1.0;
else if (diffuse > 0.5)
    diffuse = 0.75;
else
    diffuse = 0.5;

// Use diffuse in the shading process as per normal.
```

Discussion

Toon shading is an example of nonphotorealistic rendering, in that the colors that are calculated by the fragment shader are not the same as those that you would see in real life.

For a cartoon-like effect, the colors emitted should have hard edges, and fade smoothly from one area to another. You can achieve this in a fragment shader by reducing the possible values of lights to a small number. In this solution's example, the diffuse light is kept either at 0.5, 0.75, or 1.0. As a result, the final rendered color has hard, bold edges (see Figure 10-2).

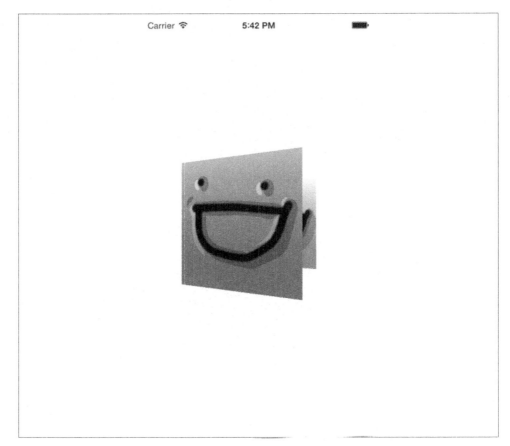

Figure 10-2. Toon shading

CHAPTER 11

Scene Kit

Scene Kit is a simple framework for creating, configuring, and rendering a 3D scene in real time. Scene Kit's designed for all kinds of 3D rendering situations, ranging from visualization of data to games. If you want to make a 3D game but don't want to spend ages learning how to deal with low-level OpenGL or Metal code, Scene Kit's a great way to get started.

11.1. Setting Up for Scene Kit

Problem

You want to set up your game to use Scene Kit for rendering graphics.

Solution

Open your application's storyboard, and locate the view controller that you want to use to present the 3D content in your game.

Select the view, and go to the Identity inspector. Change the class to SCNView.

Next, go to your view controller's source code. At the top of the file, you need to import the SceneKit module:

```
import SceneKit
```

The simplest way to ensure that Scene Kit is working properly is to make your SCNView show a background color. In the implementation of viewDidLoad, add the following code:

```
let sceneView = self.view as! SCNView
sceneView.backgroundColor = UIColor(white: 0.6, alpha: 1.0)
```

Discussion

An SCNView is responsible for drawing 3D content in your game. While you don't often work directly with the view, it's a necessary first step to make sure that you've got a view and that it's working. Once you have it, you can move on to bigger and brighter things.

11.2. Creating a Scene Kit Scene

Problem

You want to manage your 3D objects by grouping them into scenes.

Solution

Once you have an SCNView to render content, you need to create an SCNScene, and tell the SCNView to present it, like so:

```
let scene = SCNScene()
sceneView.scene = scene
```

Discussion

In Scene Kit, your 3D content is grouped into collections called *scenes*. Each scene contains a number of *nodes*, which contain the 3D objects that you want to show the user.

It's good practice to divide up your game into multiple scenes. For example, a simple game might have a main menu scene, a settings scene, a credits scene, and a scene for each of the game's levels.

 In a game that uses Scene Kit, you can often have just a single view controller, and manage all of the game's contents using scenes.

11.3. Showing a 3D Object

Problem

You want to render a 3D object on the screen.

Solution

First, define a geometry object, which describes to Scene Kit what the visual shape of the object is:

```
let capsule = SCNCapsule(capRadius: 2.5, height: 6)
```

Then, create an SCNNode with that geometry, position it, and add it to the scene:

```
let capsuleNode = SCNNode(geometry: capsule)
capsuleNode.position = SCNVector3(x: 0, y: 0, z: 0)
scene.rootNode.addChildNode(capsuleNode)
```

Discussion

Nodes are invisible objects that simply occupy a position in space. On their own, they do nothing at all; to make them influence the scene that the user sees, you attach various objects to them, including geometry, cameras, lights, and more. We'll be looking at these kinds of objects in other recipes in this chapter.

Nodes can also have *other nodes* attached to them. This allows you to pair objects together: if you move a node, all of the nodes attached to it will move with it. This allows you to create quite complex scenes while still being able to manage them in a simple way.

The scene contains a node called the *root node*. If you want an object to be in the scene, you need to add it to the scene by calling addChildNode on the scene's root node.

11.4. Working with Scene Kit Cameras

Problem

You want to control how the player views your 3D scene using a camera.

Solution

First, create an SCNCamera object and configure it:

```
let camera = SCNCamera()
camera.xFov = 45
camera.yFov = 45
```

Next, attach it to a node, position it, and add that node to the scene:

```
let cameraNode = SCNNode()
cameraNode.camera = camera

cameraNode.position = SCNVector3(x: 0, y: 0, z: 20)

scene.rootNode.addChildNode(cameraNode)
```

Discussion

A camera object controls how Scene Kit renders the contents of the scene. There are two main kinds of cameras: *perspective* cameras and *orthographic* cameras.

When you're using a perspective camera, objects get smaller as they move away from the camera, just like in real life. With an orthographic camera, objects don't get smaller when they move away from the camera.

Perspective cameras are used when you want to present a scene as though the user is moving around in 3D space. An orthographic camera is better for when you aren't going for a realistic look in your game, such as in a side-scrolling or isometric game.

11.5. Creating Lights

Problem

You want to set up and control the lighting of your scene.

Solution

To use lights, you create a light object and attach it to an SCNNode.

To start, it's often best to create an *ambient light* object, which applies an even light from all directions:

```
let ambientLight = SCNLight()
ambientLight.type = SCNLightTypeAmbient
ambientLight.color = UIColor(white: 0.25, alpha: 1.0)

let ambientLightNode = SCNNode()
ambientLightNode.light = ambientLight

scene.rootNode.addChildNode(ambientLightNode)
```

Next, add a *point light* (also called an *omni light*), which emits light in all directions from a single point:

```
let omniLight = SCNLight()
omniLight.type = SCNLightTypeOmni
omniLight.color = UIColor(white: 1.0, alpha: 1.0)

let omniLightNode = SCNNode()
omniLightNode.light = omniLight
omniLightNode.position = SCNVector3(x: -5, y: 8, z: 5)

scene.rootNode.addChildNode(omniLightNode)
```

Discussion

There are four different types of light:

Omni lights
> Omni lights emit light from a single point, in all directions.

Directional lights
> Directional lights emit light in a single direction, and have no position. The sun is generally approximated through the use of a directional light.

Spot lights
> Spot lights emit light from a single position, in a single direction. You can also control the angle at which light is emitted, to make the light cone smaller or wider.

Ambient lights
> Ambient lights have no position or direction, and apply light from all directions.

11.6. Animating Objects

Problem

You want your objects to move around the scene.

Solution

To animate objects in Scene Kit, you use the animation classes from Core Animation. To create an animation, you first define what property you want to animate. Use that to create an animation object, such as a CABasicAnimation:

```
// This animation changes the 'position' property
let moveUpDownAnimation = CABasicAnimation(keyPath: "position")

// Move 5 units on the y-axis (i.e., up)
moveUpDownAnimation.byValue =
    NSValue(SCNVector3: SCNVector3(x: 0, y: 3, z: 0))
// Accelerate and decelerate at the ends, instead of
// mechanically bouncing
moveUpDownAnimation.timingFunction =
    CAMediaTimingFunction(name: kCAMediaTimingFunctionEaseInEaseOut)

// Animation automatically moves back at the end
moveUpDownAnimation.autoreverses = true

// Animation repeats an infinite number of times (i.e., loops forever)
moveUpDownAnimation.repeatCount = Float.infinity

// The animation takes 2 seconds to run
moveUpDownAnimation.duration = 2.0
```

Once you have created the animation, you then apply it to the node that should animate:

```
capsuleNode.addAnimation(moveUpDownAnimation, forKey: "updown")
```

Discussion

You use the same class (CAAnimation and its subclasses) for animating Scene Kit content as you do UIKit content. This means that you can use both CABasicAnimation and CAKeyframeAnimation to control your animations, and you have the same level of control over the animations as you do for animating CALayers.

Only certain properties can be animated. To work out whether you can animate a property, look at the documentation for SCNNode and SCNMaterial; the properties that you can animate have *Animatable* in their description.

11.7. Working with Text Nodes

Problem

You want to render 3D text in your scene.

Solution

3D text is a kind of geometry, which you attach to a node. To create a 3D text geometry object, use the SCNText class, and attach it to a node:

```
let text = SCNText(string: "Text!", extrusionDepth: 0.2)

// text will be 2 units (meters) high
text.font = UIFont.systemFontOfSize(2)
let textNode = SCNNode(geometry: text)
// Positioned slightly to the left, and above the
// capsule (which is 10 units high)
textNode.position = SCNVector3(x: -2, y: 6, z: 0)

// Add the text node to the capsule node (not the scene's root node!)
capsuleNode.addChildNode(textNode)
```

Discussion

When you create an SCNText object, you provide it with a UIFont, in order to specify what font to use and its size. Keep in mind that the font size you provide is in Scene Kit units, not screen points.

11.8. Customizing Materials

Problem

You want to control the way your objects react to light.

Solution

To control the appearance of your objects, you create a *material*. Materials in Scene Kit are represented by the SCNMaterial class:

```
// Make the material green and shiny
let greenMaterial = SCNMaterial()
greenMaterial.diffuse.contents = UIColor.greenColor()
greenMaterial.specular.contents = UIColor.whiteColor()
greenMaterial.shininess = 1.0
```

Once you have a material, you apply it to a geometry object, which should be attached to a node:

```
// 'capsule' is an SCNGeometry
capsule.materials = [greenMaterial]
```

Discussion

Materials are composed of a number of elements that control the color of the surface. The most important ones are:

diffuse
: This property controls the *base* color of the material.

specular
: This property applies a shiny effect to the material, and controls the brightness and color of this effect.

emissive
: This property makes the material appear to glow, regardless of what light is reflecting off it.

transparent
: This property controls which areas of the material are transparent, and the amount of transparency for them.

normal
: This property controls the slope of the material, which affects how light bounces off it.

You can set `diffuse` and `specular` to be a color, an image, a `CALayer`, a path to a file (as a string or URL), a Sprite Kit scene, or an `SKTexture`. If you set a material's property to a color, it can be animated.

11.9. Texturing Objects

Problem

You want your objects to have a texture applied to them.

Solution

To apply a texture to an object, you first need to get that texture from somewhere. Usually, you'll be loading this texture from a file:

```
let loadedTexture = SKTexture(imageNamed: "Ball")
```

Once you have your image, set it to the `diffuse` component of the material you want to use:

```
let textureMaterial = SCNMaterial()
textureMaterial.diffuse.contents = loadedTexture

text.materials = [textureMaterial]
```

Discussion

In addition to loading images from files, you can also use Sprite Kit's ability to generate noise textures:

```
let noiseTexture = SKTexture(noiseWithSmoothness: 0.25,
    size: CGSize(width: 512, height: 512), grayscale: true)
```

11.10. Normal Mapping

Problem

You want to give your objects a bumpy texture.

Solution

To make the surface of your objects appear roughened, apply a *normal map* to your material. You can load a normal map from a texture, or you can generate one using Sprite Kit:

```
let noiseNormalMapTexture =
    noiseTexture.textureByGeneratingNormalMapWithSmoothness(0.1,
        contrast: 1.0)
```

Once you have your normal map texture, apply it to the `normal` property of your geometry's material:

```
greenMaterial.normal.contents = noiseNormalMapTexture
```

Discussion

When determining the color of an object that's receiving light, the 3D renderer works out how bright each pixel of the object is based on the direction of the light and the angle at which the light hits the object. This angle is called the *normal*. Under ordinary circumstances, the normal of any location on an object is perpendicular to the surface; that is, if you lay your phone flat on a table, the normal of the phone's top surface is pointing straight up.

When you apply a *normal map* to a material, you override the normal and tell the 3D renderer to make light bounce in a slightly different way. Because your eye uses variations in shading to get information about the surface it's looking at, the surface will appear to be roughened. The end result is that when you add a single texture to your material, the object will appear to have a lot more geometric detail, and can often look a lot better.

11.11. Constraining Objects

Problem

You want the position or rotation of objects to be tied to other objects.

Solution

First, create an object that should be constrained:

```
let pointer = SCNPyramid(width: 0.5, height: 0.9, length: 4.0)
let pointerNode = SCNNode(geometry: pointer)
pointerNode.position = SCNVector3(x: -5, y: 0, z: 0)

scene.rootNode.addChildNode(pointerNode)
```

Next, create a constraint object and add it to the object you want to constrain:

```
let lookAtConstraint = SCNLookAtConstraint(target: capsuleNode)

// When enabled, the constraint will try to rotate
// around only a single axis
lookAtConstraint.gimbalLockEnabled = true
pointerNode.constraints = [lookAtConstraint]
```

Discussion

A *constraint* is an object that indicates to Scene Kit that some part of an object's position or rotation should be based on other objects. For example, you can constrain a shadow square so that its *x* and *z* positions are always the same as the player's, which would mean that the shadow would be positioned underneath the object, but wouldn't move upward if the player jumped.

There are several different constraints you can use:

- *Look-at* constraints make one object point toward another object.
- *Transform* constraints allow you to attach a code block that updates the position and rotation of an object every frame.
- *Inverse kinematics (IK)* constraints allow you to chain together a collection of objects—such as a hand, forearm, and upper arm—that can reach toward a point while obeying the limits of how far each joint can rotate.

11.12. Loading COLLADA Files

Problem

You have an object that you've designed using 3D editing software, and you want to add it to your Scene Kit scene.

Solution

You can load 3D objects using the COLLADA file format. To use COLLADA, you first load the file from disk:

```
let critterDataURL =
    NSBundle.mainBundle().URLForResource("Critter",
        withExtension: "dae")
let critterData = SCNSceneSource(URL: critterDataURL!, options: nil)
```

Once it's loaded, you can retrieve objects from it, such as nodes and geometry objects:

```
// Find the node called 'Critter'; if it exists, add it
let critterNode = critterData?.entryWithIdentifier("Critter",
    withClass: SCNNode.self) as? SCNNode
if critterNode != nil {
    critterNode?.position = SCNVector3(x: 5, y: 0, z: 0)
    scene.rootNode.addChildNode(critterNode!)
}
```

Discussion

Most 3D editing tools can export into the COLLADA format, including 3D Studio Max, Maya, and Blender. COLLADA files don't contain just a single object—they're entire libraries, and they can contain a bunch of stuff. You can define an entire scene, with node hierarchies, materials, and lights, in your 3D editor and load them into the scene.

In addition, if you click on a COLLADA file in the Project Inspector, you can view the contents of the file directly inside Xcode.

11.13. Using 3D Physics

Problem

You want your 3D objects to have physical behiavor.

Solution

To add physics to your objects, you need to provide two pieces of information: the collision *shape*, and the object's *physics body*.

First, you define the shape:

```
var critterPhysicsShape : SCNPhysicsShape?
if let geometry = critterNode?.geometry {
    critterPhysicsShape =
        SCNPhysicsShape(geometry: geometry,
            options: nil)
}
```

Next, you create a physics body and provide it with a shape:

```
let critterPhysicsBody =
    SCNPhysicsBody(type: SCNPhysicsBodyType.Dynamic,
        shape: critterPhysicsShape)
```

Finally, you add the body to a node. Once a node has a physics body, it will begin to react to collisions and to physical forces like gravity:

```
critterNode?.physicsBody = critterPhysicsBody
```

Discussion

When you create a physics shape, you need to provide it with a geometry object that Scene Kit can use to build the shape from. Different geometries will result in different shapes. Keep in mind that Scene Kit will simplify the collision shape in order to make the physics system run smoothly, so the collision shape will be slightly different from the geometry that you see on screen.

When you create the body, you specify whether it is static, dynamic, or kinematic. Dynamic bodies respond to gravity, and can move around the scene. Static bodies are fixed in place, and while things can collide with them, they are themselves unaffected by collisions. Kinematic bodies are halfway between the two: they aren't affected by physical bodies or collisions, but they can move (when their node's position is changed) and can generate collisions when they do.

11.14. Adding Reflections

Problem

You want to add a reflective floor to your scene.

Solution

Use an SCNFloor object:

```
let floor = SCNFloor()
let floorNode = SCNNode(geometry: floor)
floorNode.position = SCNVector3(x: 0, y: -5, z: 0)
scene.rootNode.addChildNode(floorNode)
```

Discussion

A floor is a great way to visually ground the scene, and give a sense of where objects are in 3D space.

You can also add physics to your SCNFloor object, to provide a surface for objects to fall onto:

```
let floorPhysicsBody =
    SCNPhysicsBody(type: SCNPhysicsBodyType.Static,
        shape: SCNPhysicsShape(geometry: floor, options: nil))
floorNode.physicsBody = floorPhysicsBody
```

11.15. Hit-Testing the Scene

Problem

You want to tap on the screen, and receive information about what object is under the user's finger.

Solution

Use the SCNView's hitTest function:

```
// locationToQuery is a CGPoint in view-space

// Find the object that was tapped
let sceneView = self.view as! SCNView
let hits = sceneView.hitTest(locationToQuery,
    options: nil) as! [SCNHitTestResult]

for hit in hits {
    println("Found a node: \(hit.node)")
}
```

Discussion

Hit tests return every object at a point. This can return a lot of nodes; pass the dictionary [SCNHitTestFirstFoundOnlyKey: true] for the options parameter to return only the first one.

CHAPTER 12

Artificial Intelligence and Behavior

Games are often at their best when they're a challenge to the player. There are a number of ways to make your game challenging, including creating complex puzzles; however, one of the most satisfying challenges that a player can enjoy is defeating something that's trying to outthink or outmaneuver her.

In this chapter, you'll learn how to create movement behavior, how to pursue and flee from targets, how to find the shortest path between two locations, and how to design an AI system that thinks ahead.

12.1. Making Vector Math Nicer in Swift

Problem

You have a collection of CGPoint values, and you want to be able to use the +, -, * and / operators with them. You also want to treat CGPoints like vectors, and get information like their length or a normalized version of that vector.

Solution

Use Swift's operator overloading feature to add support for working with two CGPoints, and for working with a CGPoint and a scalar (like a CGFloat):

```
/* Adding points together */
func + (left: CGPoint, right : CGPoint) -> CGPoint {
    return CGPoint(x: left.x + right.x, y: left.y + right.y)
}

func - (left: CGPoint, right : CGPoint) -> CGPoint {
    return CGPoint(x: left.x - right.x, y: left.y - right.y)
}
```

```swift
func += (inout left: CGPoint, right: CGPoint) {
    left = left + right
}

func -= (inout left: CGPoint, right: CGPoint) {
    left = left + right
}

/* Working with scalars */

func + (left: CGPoint, right: CGFloat) -> CGPoint {
    return CGPoint(x: left.x + right, y: left.y + right)
}

func - (left: CGPoint, right: CGFloat) -> CGPoint {
    return left + (-right)
}

func * (left: CGPoint, right: CGFloat) -> CGPoint {
    return CGPoint(x: left.x * right, y: left.y * right)
}

func / (left: CGPoint, right: CGFloat) -> CGPoint {
    return CGPoint(x: left.x / right, y: left.y / right)
}

func += (inout left: CGPoint, right: CGFloat) {
    left = left + right
}

func -= (inout left: CGPoint, right: CGFloat) {
    left = left - right
}

func *= (inout left: CGPoint, right: CGFloat) {
    left = left * right
}

func /= (inout left: CGPoint, right: CGFloat) {
    left = left / right
}
```

Additionally, you can extend the CGPoint type to add properties like length and normalized:

```swift
extension CGPoint {
    var length :  CGFloat {
        return sqrt(self.x * self.x + self.y * self.y)
    }

    var normalized : CGPoint {
        return self / length
    }
```

```
func rotatedBy(radians : CGFloat) -> CGPoint {
    var rotatedPoint = CGPoint(x: 0, y: 0)
    rotatedPoint.x = self.x * cos(radians) - self.y * sin(radians)
    rotatedPoint.y = self.y * cos(radians) + self.x * sin(radians)

    return rotatedPoint
}

func dot(other : CGPoint) -> CGFloat {
    return self.x * other.x + self.y * other.y
}

init (angleRadians : CGFloat) {
    self.x = sin(angleRadians)
    self.y = cos(angleRadians)
}

}
```

Discussion

When you override an operator, you're defining exactly what it means for an operator to be applied to a value. It's extremely convenient to be able to type vector1 += vec tor2 instead of vector1.x += vector2.x; vector1.y += vector2.y, and operator overloading lets you do just that.

Note that the first parameters of += and related operators are an inout parameter. This is because += assigns the value of the operator and stores the result in the lefthand operand, rather than returning a brand new value (like + and its related operators do).

 The rest of the recipes in this chapter make use of these operators and helper functions. If you just copy another recipe's code without also including a file that includes this recipe's code in your project, you'll get errors.

12.2. Making an Object Move Toward a Position

Problem

You want an object to move toward another object.

Solution

Subtract the target position from the object's current position, normalize the result, and then multiply it by the speed at which you want to move toward the target. Then, add the result to the current position:

```
// Work out the direction to this position
var offset = self.position - targetPosition

// Reduce this vector to be the same length as our movement speed
offset = offset.normalized
offset *= CGFloat(self.movementSpeed) * deltaTime

// Add this to our current position
let newPosition = self.position + offset

self.position = newPosition;
```

Discussion

To move toward an object, you need to know the direction of your destination. To get this, you take your destination's position minus your current position, which results in a vector.

Let's say that you're located at [0, 5], and you want to move toward [1, 8] at a rate of 1 unit per second. The destination position minus your current location is:

```
My Location     = [0, 5]
Target Location = [1, 8]

Offset          = Target Location - My Location
                = [1, 8] - [0, 5]
                = [1, 3]
```

However, the length (or magnitude) of this vector will vary depending on how far away the destination is. If you want to move toward the destination at a fixed speed, you need to ensure that the length of the vector is 1, and then multiply the result by the speed at which you want to move.

Remember, when you normalize a vector, you get a vector that points in the same direction but has a length of 1. If you multiply this normalized vector with another number, such as your speed, you get a vector with that length.

So, to calculate how far you need to move, you take your offset, normalize it, and multiply the result by your movement speed.

To get smooth movement, you're likely going to run this code every time a new frame is drawn. Every time this happens, it's useful to know how many seconds have elapsed between the last frame and the current frame (see Recipe 1.4).

To calculate how far an object should move, given a speed in units per second and an amount of time measured in seconds, you just use the time-honored equation:

```
Speed = Distance ÷ Time
```

Rearranging, you get:

```
Distance = Speed × Time
```

You can now substitute, assuming a delta time of 1/30 of a second (i.e., 0.033 seconds):

```
Movement speed = 5
Delta time     = 0.033
Distance       = Movement Speed * Delta Time
               = 5 * 0.333
               = 1.666
```

Having worked out how much farther you must travel, and the direction in which you need to travel, you normalize the direction vector and multiply it by distance:

```
Normalized offset = Normalize(Offset) * Distance
                  = [0.124, 0.992]
Muliplied offset  = Normalized offset * Distance
                  = [0.206, 1.652]
```

You can then add this multiplied offset to your current position to get your new position. Then, you do the whole thing over again on the next frame.

This method of moving from a current location to another over time is fundamental to all movement behaviors, because everything else relies on being able to move.

12.3. Making Things Follow a Path

Problem

You want to make an object follow a path from point to point, turning to face the next destination.

Solution

When you have a path, keep a list of points. Move to the target (see Recipe 12.2). When you reach it, remove the first item from the list; then move to the new first item in the list.

Here's an example that uses Sprite Kit (discussed in Chapter 6):

```
func moveAlongPath(points: [CGPoint]) {

    // If we've been given an empty path, do nothing
    if points.count == 0 {
        return
```

```
    }

    // Go through the list, and add an SKAction that moves from the previous
    // point to the current point
    var currentPoint = self.position
    var actions : [SKAction] = []

    for point in points {
        // Work out how long the movement should take, based on how
        // far away this point is and our movement speed
        let distance = (currentPoint - point).length
        let time = distance / CGFloat(self.movementSpeed)

        // Create a move-to action
        let moveToPoint = SKAction.moveTo(point, duration: NSTimeInterval(time))
        actions.append(moveToPoint)

        // Use this current point as the 'previous point' for the next step
        currentPoint = point
    }

    // Run all of these actions in sequence
    let sequence = SKAction.sequence(actions)
    self.runAction(sequence)
}
```

Discussion

To calculate a path from one point to another, use a path algorithm (see Recipe 12.9).

12.4. Making an Object Intercept a Moving Target

Problem

You want an object to move toward another object, intercepting it.

Solution

Calculate where the target is going to move to based on its velocity, and use the "move to" algorithm from Recipe 12.2 to head toward that position:

```
let toTarget = target.position - self.position

let lookAheadTime = toTarget.length / CGFloat(self.movementSpeed
    + target.movementSpeed)

let destination = target.position
    + (CGFloat(target.movementSpeed) * lookAheadTime)

self.moveToPosition(destination, deltaTime:deltaTime)
```

Figure 12-1 illustrates the result.

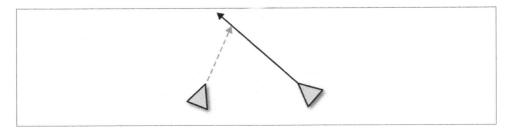

Figure 12-1. Intercepting a moving object

Discussion

When you want to intercept a moving object, your goal should be to move to where the target is going to be, rather than where it is right now. If you just move to where the target currently is, you'll end up always chasing it.

Instead, what you want to do is calculate where the target is going to be when you arrive by taking the target's current position and its speed, determining how fast you can get there, and then seeking toward that.

12.5. Making an Object Flee When It's in Trouble

Problem

You want an object to flee from something that's chasing it.

Solution

Use the "move to" method, but use the reverse of the force it gives you:

```
var offset = target.position - self.position

// Reduce this vector to be the same length as our movement speed
offset = offset.normalized

// Note the minus sign - we're multiplying by the reverse of our
// movement speed, which means we're moving away from it
offset *= CGFloat(-self.movementSpeed) * deltaTime

// Add this to our current position
let newPosition = self.position + offset

self.position = newPosition
```

Discussion

Moving away from a point is very similar to moving toward a point. All you need to do is use the inverse of your current movement speed. This will give you a vector that's pointing in the opposite direction of the point you want to move away from.

12.6. Making an Object Decide on a Target

Problem

You want to determine which of several targets is the best target for an object to pursue.

Solution

The general algorithm for deciding on the best target looks like this:

1. Set bestScoreSoFar to the worst possible score (either zero or infinity, depending on what you're looking for).

2. Set bestTargetSoFar to nothing.

3. Loop over each possible target:

   a. Check the score of the possible target.

   b. If the score is better than bestScoreSoFar:

      i. Set bestTargetSoFar to the possible target.

      ii. Set bestScoreSoFar to the possible target's score.

4. After the loop is done, bestTargetSoFar will either be the best target, or it will be nothing.

This algorithm is shown in code form in the following example. The bestScoreSoFar variable is called nearestTargetDistance; it stores the distance to the closest target found so far, and begins as the highest possible distance (i.e., infinity). You then loop through the array of possible targets, resetting it every time you find a new target nearer than the previous ones:

```
var nearestNodeDistance = CGFloat.infinity
var nearestNode : Critter? = nil

// Find the nearest critter
scene?.enumerateChildNodesWithName("Critter") { (node, stop) -> Void in
    if let otherCritter = node as? Critter {

        if otherCritter == self {
            return
        }
```

```
        let distanceToTarget = (otherCritter.position - self.position).length

        if distanceToTarget < nearestNodeDistance {
            nearestNode = otherCritter
            nearestNodeDistance = distanceToTarget
        }

    }
}

self.target = nearestNode
```

Discussion

It's worth keeping in mind that there's no general solution to this problem because it can vary a lot depending on what your definition of "best" is. You should think about what the best target is in your game. Is it:

- Closest?
- Most dangerous?
- Weakest?
- Worth the most points?

Additionally, it depends on what information you can access regarding the nearby targets. Something that's worth keeping in mind is that doing a search like this can take some time if there are many potential targets. Try to minimize the number of loops that you end up doing.

12.7. Making an Object Steer Toward a Point

Problem

You want an object to steer toward a certain point, while maintaining a constant speed.

Solution

You can steer toward an object by figuring out the angle between the direction in which you're currently heading and the direction to the destination. Once you have this, you can limit this angle to your maximum turn rate:

```
// Work out the vector from our position to the target
let toTarget = target - self.position

// Work out our forward direction)
let forward = CGPoint(x: 0, y: 1).rotatedBy(self.zRotation)
```

```
// Get the angle needed to turn toward this position
var angle = toTarget.dot(forward)
angle /= acos(toTarget.length * forward.length)

// Clamp the angle to our turning speed
angle = min(angle, CGFloat(self.turningSpeed))
angle = max(angle, CGFloat(-self.turningSpeed))

// Apply the rotation
self.zRotation += angle * deltaTime
```

Discussion

You can calculate the angle between two vectors by taking the dot product of the two vectors, dividing it by the lengths of both, and then taking the arc cosine of the result.

To gradually turn over time, you then limit the result to your maximum turning rate (to stop your object from turning instantaneously), and then multiply *that* by how long you want the turning action to take, in seconds.

12.8. Making an Object Know Where to Take Cover

Problem

You want to find a location where an object can move to, where it can't be seen by another object.

Solution

First, draw up a list of nearby points that your object (the "prey") can move to.

Then, draw lines from the position of the other object (the "predator") to each of these points. Check to see if any of these lines intersect an object. If they do, this is a potential cover point.

Then, devise paths from your object to each of these potential cover points (see Recipe 12.9). Pick the point that has the shortest path, and start moving toward it (see Recipe 12.3).

If you're using Sprite Kit with physics bodies, you can use the bodyAlongRayStart(_, end) method to find out whether you can draw an uninterrupted line from your current position to the potential cover position:

```
func findPotentialCover(steps : Int, distance : CGFloat) -> [CGPoint] {

    // Start with an empty list
    var coverPoints : [CGPoint] = []
```

```
// Step around the circle 'steps' times
for coverPoint in 0..<steps {

    // Work out the angle at which we're considering
    let angle = Float(M_PI * 2.0) * (Float(coverPoint) / Float(steps))

    // Use that to create a point to check for cover
    let potentialPoint = CGPoint(angleRadians: CGFloat(angle)) * distance

    // Check to see if there's something between there and here
    if self.scene?.physicsWorld.bodyAlongRayStart(self.position,
        end: potentialPoint) != nil {
        // There's something between where we are and where we're
        // considering, so add this to the list
        coverPoints.append(potentialPoint)
    }
}

// Return the list of points that we found
return coverPoints
}
```

Discussion

A useful addition to this algorithm is to make some cover "better" than others. For example, chest-high cover in a shooting game may be worth less than full cover, and cover that's closer to other, nearby cover may be worth more than an isolated piece of cover.

In these cases, your algorithm needs to take into account both the distance to the cover and the "score" for the cover.

12.9. Calculating a Path for an Object to Take

Problem

You want to determine a path from one point to another, avoiding obstacles.

Solution

There are several path-calculation algorithms for you to choose from; one of the most popular is called A* (pronounced "A star").

To use the A* algorithm, you give it the list of all of the possible waypoints at which an object can be ahead of time, and determine which points can be directly reached from other points. Later, you run the algorithm to find a path from one waypoint to another.

You can create a single data type that represents a collection of traversable points, and use Swift's ability to extend types to write a pretty compact implementation of the A* algorithm:

```
// Add support for storing CGPoints inside dictionaries, so that
// our code can be nice and elegant
extension CGPoint : Hashable {
    public var hashValue : Int {
        // Derive the hash by using hash values of
        // the x and y components
        return self.x.hashValue << 32 ^ self.y.hashValue
    }

    // Also add a convenience function that calculates
    // how far away this point is from another
    public func distanceTo(other : CGPoint) -> CGFloat {
        return (self - other).length
    }
}

struct NavigationGrid {

    // The points that this structure knows about
    var points : [CGPoint]

    // For each point in self.points, a list of points
    // that are one 'hop' away
    var neighbors : [CGPoint : [CGPoint]]

    // When starting up, store the points we're given,
    // plus a list of neighbors for each node
    init (points:[CGPoint], maximumDistance: CGFloat) {

        self.points = points
        self.neighbors = [:]

        // Make a list of neighbors for each node and store that
        for point in self.points {

            // Start with an empty list
            self.neighbors[point] = []

            // Check all other points..
            for otherPoint in self.points {

                // (..except this current one)
                if point == otherPoint {
                    continue
                }

                // Add this point as a neighbor if it's within range
                if point.distanceTo(otherPoint) <= maximumDistance {
```

```
                    self.neighbors[point]?.append(otherPoint)
                }
            }
        }

    }

    // Find the nearest point in our collection of points
    func nearestPointToPoint(point : CGPoint) -> CGPoint {
        var nearestPointSoFar : CGPoint = self.points[0]
        var nearestDistanceSoFar = CGFloat.infinity

        for node in self.points {
            let distance = node.distanceTo(point)
            if distance < nearestDistanceSoFar {
                nearestDistanceSoFar = distance
                nearestPointSoFar = node
            }
        }

        return nearestPointSoFar
    }

    func pathTo(start: CGPoint, end:CGPoint) -> [CGPoint]? {

        // g-score of a node: the known length of the path
        // that reaches this node
        var gScores : [CGPoint : CGFloat] = [:]

        // f-score of a node: how important it is that we
        // check this node (= g-score + distance from this
        // point to goal); lower value means higher priority
        var fScores : [CGPoint : CGFloat] = [:]

        // Find the points in our collection that are closest
        // to where we've been asked to search from and to
        let startPoint = self.nearestPointToPoint(start)
        let goalPoint = self.nearestPointToPoint(end)

        // Closed nodes are nodes that we've checked
        var closedNodes = Set<CGPoint>()

        // Open nodes are nodes that we should check; the node
        // with the lowest f-score will be checked next
        var openNodes = Set<CGPoint>()

        // We begin the search at the start point
        openNodes.insert(startPoint)

        // Stores how we got from one node to another; used
        // to generate the final list of points once search
        // reaches the goal
```

```
var cameFromMap : [CGPoint : CGPoint] = [:]

// Keep searching for as long as we have points to check
while openNodes.count > 0 {

    // Find the point with the lowest f-score
    // We do this by turning the set into an array,
    // then sorting it based on the f-score of each
    // item in the array, then taking the first item
    // in the resulting array
    let currentNode = Array(openNodes).sorted{
        (first, second) -> Bool in
        return fScores[first] < fScores[second]
    }.first!

    // If we are now looking at the goal point, we're
    // done! Call reconstructPath to work backward
    // from the goal point, following the came-from
    // map to get back to the start.
    if currentNode == goalPoint {
        return [start] + reconstructPath(cameFromMap,
            currentNode: currentNode) + [end]
    }

    // Move this point from the open set to the closed set
    openNodes.remove(currentNode)
    closedNodes.insert(currentNode)

    let nodeNeighbors = self.neighbors[currentNode] ?? []

    // Examine each neighbor for this point
    for neighbor in nodeNeighbors {

        // Work out the scores for this node if it's
        // used in the path
        let tentativeGScore =
            (gScores[currentNode] ?? 0.0)
            + currentNode.distanceTo(neighbor)

        let tentativeFScore = tentativeGScore
            + currentNode.distanceTo(goalPoint)

        // If this neighbor is in the closed set,
        // and using it would result in a worse
        // path, don't use it
        if closedNodes.contains(neighbor)
            && tentativeFScore >=
                (fScores[neighbor] ?? 0.0) {
                continue
        }

        // If this neighbor is in the open set, OR
```

```
                    // using it would result in a better path,
                    // consider using it (by adding it to the
                    // open set, so we possibly consider it next
                    // iteration)
                    if openNodes.contains(neighbor)
                        || tentativeFScore <
                            (fScores[neighbor] ?? CGFloat.infinity) {

                            // Mark this neighbor on the path
                            // (indicating how we got to it)
                            cameFromMap[neighbor] = currentNode

                            // Give this neighbor its score
                            fScores[neighbor] = tentativeFScore
                            gScores[neighbor] = tentativeGScore

                            // Add this neighbor to the open set -
                            // depending on its f-score, it might
                            // be the next node we check!
                            openNodes.insert(neighbor)
                    }
                }
            }

            // If we've run through the entire open set and
            // still haven't found a path to the goal, it's
            // unreachable; return nil to indicate that we
            // found no path
            return nil

    }

    // Given a node and the came-from map, start working
    // backward until we reach the only node that has no
    // came-from node (which is the start node)
    func reconstructPath(cameFromMap: [CGPoint:CGPoint],
        currentNode:CGPoint) -> [CGPoint] {

        if let nextNode = cameFromMap[currentNode] {
            return reconstructPath(cameFromMap,
                currentNode: nextNode) + [currentNode]
        } else {
            return [currentNode]
        }
    }


}
```

Discussion

The A* algorithm is a reasonably efficient algorithm for computing a path from one point to another. It works by incrementally building up a path; every time it looks at a new point, it checks to see if the total distance traveled is lower than that traveled using any of the other potential points, and if that's the case, it adds it to the path. If it ever gets stuck, it backtracks and tries again. If it can't find *any* path from the start to the destination, it returns an empty path.

12.10. Finding the Next Best Move for a Puzzle Game

Problem

In a turn-based game, you want to determine the next best move to make.

Solution

The exact details here will vary from game to game, so in this solution, we'll talk about the general approach to this kind of problem.

Let's assume that the entire state of your game—the location of units, the number of points, the various states of every game object—is being kept in memory.

Starting from this current state, you figure out all possible moves that the next player can make. For each possible move, create a copy of the state where this move has been made.

Next, determine a score for each of the states that you've made. The method for determining the score will vary depending on the kind of game; some examples include:

- Number of enemy units destroyed minus number of my units destroyed
- Amount of money I have minus amount of money the enemy has
- Total number of points I have, ignoring how many points the enemy has

Once you have a score for each possible next state, take the top-scoring state, and have your computer player make that next move.

Discussion

The algorithm in this solution is often referred to as a *brute force* approach. This can get very complicated for complex games. Strategy games may need to worry about economy, unit movement, and so on—if each unit has 3 possible actions, and you have 10 units, you could end up in more than 59,000 possible states. To address this problem, you need to reduce the number of states that you calculate.

It helps to break up the problem into simpler, less-precise states for your AI to consider. Consider a strategy game in which you can, in general terms, spend points on attacking other players, researching technologies, or building defenses. Each turn, your AI just needs to calculate an estimate for the benefit that each general strategy will bring. Once it's decided on that, you can then have dedicated attacking, researching, or defense-building AI modules take care of the details.

12.11. Determining If an Object Can See Another Object

Problem

You want to find out if an object (the *hunter*) can see another object (the *prey*), given the direction the hunter is facing, the hunter's field of view, and the positions of both the hunter and the prey.

Solution

First, you need to define how far the hunter can see, as well as the field of view of the hunter. You also need to know what direction the hunter is currently facing. Finally, you need the positions of both the hunter and the prey.

The first test is to calculate how far away the prey is from the hunter. If the prey is farther away than `distance` units, the hunter won't be able to see it at all:

```
// Target is an SKNode,
// fieldOfView is a CGFloat,
// distance is a CGFloat

if (target.position - self.position).length > distance {
    return false
}
```

If the prey is within seeing distance, you then need to determine if the prey is standing within the hunter's field of view:

```
let facingDirection = CGPoint(x:0, y:1).rotatedBy(self.zRotation)

let vectorToTarget = (target.position - self.position).normalized
let angleToTarget = acos(facingDirection.dot(vectorToTarget))

return abs(angleToTarget) < fieldOfView / 2.0
```

Discussion

Figuring out if one object can see another is a common problem. If you're making a stealth game, for example, where the player needs to sneak behind guards but is in trouble if she's ever seen, you need to be able to determine what objects the guard can actually see. Objects that are within the field of view are visible, whereas those that are outside of it are not, as shown in Figure 12-2.

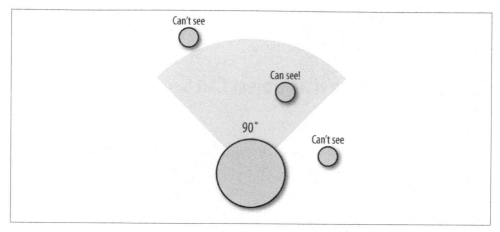

Figure 12-2. An example of how the field of view works

Calculating the distance between objects is very straightforward—you just need to have their positions, and use the `length` function to calculate how far each point is from the other. If the prey is too far away from the hunter, it isn't visible.

Figuring out whether or not the prey is within the angle of view of the hunter requires more math. What you need to do is to determine the angle between the direction the hunter is facing and the direction that the hunter would need to face in order to be directly facing the prey.

To do this, you create two vectors. The first is the vector representing the direction the hunter is facing:

```
let facingDirection = CGPoint(x:0, y:1).rotatedBy(self.zRotation)
```

The second vector represents the direction from the hunter to the prey, which you calculate by subtracting the hunter's position from the prey's position, and then normalizing:

```
let vectorToTarget = (target.position - self.position).normalized
```

Once you have these vectors, you can figure out the angle between them by first taking the dot product of the two vectors, and then taking the arc cosine of the result:

```
let angleToTarget = acos(facingDirection.dot(vectorToTarget))
```

You now know the angle from the hunter to the prey. If this angle is less than half of the field-of-view angle, the hunter can see the prey; otherwise, the prey is outside the hunter's field of view.

12.12. Using AI to Enhance Your Game Design

Problem

You want to make sure your game uses AI and behavior effectively to create a fun and engaging experience.

Solution

The fun in games comes from a number of places (see *http://8kindsoffun.com* for a discussion). In our opinion, one of the most important kinds of fun is challenge. Games that provoke a challenge for the player are often the most enjoyable.

Judicious and careful use of AI and behavior in your games can help them stand a cut above the rest in a sea of iOS games. You want to create an increasingly difficult series of challenges for your players, slowly getting more complex and introducing more pieces the longer they play.

Revealing the different components of gameplay as they play is an important way to stagger the difficulty, and it's important that any AI or behavior you implement isn't using tools that the player doesn't have access to.

Reveal the pieces of your game slowly and surely, and make sure the AI is only one step, if at all, ahead of the player.

Discussion

It's hard to make a game genuinely challenging without killing the fun factor by making it too difficult. The best way to do this is to slowly peel back the layers of your game, providing individual components one by one until the player has access to the full arsenal of things he can do in your game. The AI or behavior code of your game should get access to this arsenal at approximately the same rate as the player, or it will feel too difficult and stop being fun.

CHAPTER 13

Networking and Social Media

Nobody games alone. At least, not anymore.

While single-player games remain one of the most interesting forms of interactive media, it's increasingly rare to find a game that never communicates with the outside world. *Angry Birds*, for example, is by all definitions a single-player game; however, with only a couple of taps, you can send your most recent score to Twitter and Facebook. We'll be looking at how you can implement this functionality inside your own game.

In addition to this relatively low-impact form of engaging other people with the player's game, you can also have multiple people share the same game through networking. This is a complex topic, so we're going to spend quite a bit of time looking at the various ways you can achieve it, as well as ways in which it can get challenging and how to address them.

We'll also be looking at *Game Center*, the built-in social network that Apple provides. Game Center allows you to let users share high scores and achievements, as well as challenge their friends and play turn-based games. Before we get to the recipes, we'll take a quick look at it to familiarize you with how it works.

13.1. Using Game Center

Many of the powerful networking capabilities exposed to your app come from Game Center, Apple's game-based social network. Game Center handles a number of capabilities that you often want to have as a game developer, but that it would be very tedious to develop yourself. These include:

- Player profiles
- High score tables
- Match-making

- Turn-based gameplay

You get all of these for free when you add Game Center to your game, and all you need to do is write code that hooks into the service. To get started, you first need to turn on Game Center support for your app in Xcode, and sign your player into Game Center when the game starts.

Turning on Game Center support is easy. First, you'll need to have a working iOS Developer account, because Game Center relies on it. Then:

1. In Xcode, select your project in the Project Navigator.

2. Ensure that your app's bundle ID is what you want it be. You're about to attach Game Center services to it, and though it won't ever be shown to the user, it's very annoying if you want to change it later.

3. Open the Capabilities tab.

4. Open the Game Center section, and turn the switch to On (see Figure 13-1).

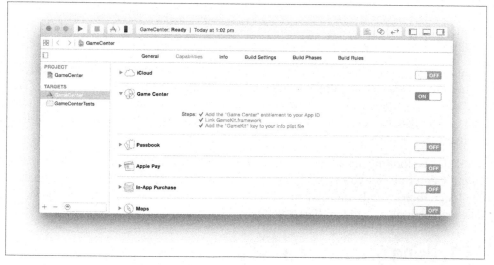

Figure 13-1. Enabling Game Center

Xcode will then walk you through the process of configuring your app to have access to Game Center.

When a player wants to use Game Center, that player needs to have a profile. This means that when you want to develop a game that uses Game Center, you also need to have a profile. When an app is running on the iOS Simulator, or is running on a device and is signed with a Developer certificate, it doesn't get access to the "real" Game Center service. Instead, it gets access to the *sandbox* version of the Game Center service, which is functionally identical to but shares no data with the real one. This means that you can play around with your game without the risk of it appearing in public. It also means that you need to get a profile on the sandbox version of the Game Center service.

Here's how to get a profile on the sandbox. You'll first need to create a new, empty Apple ID by going to *http://appleid.apple.com*. Then:

1. Open the iOS Simulator.

2. Open the Game Center application (see Figure 13-2).

3. Sign in to your new Apple ID. You'll be prompted to set up the new account.

You now need to register this product in iTunes Connect, so that Apple provisions resources like leaderboards. Once you've done this, your app will be able to access Game Center resources if the user is signed in:

1. Go to iTunes Connect by visiting *http://itunesconnect.apple.com*, and sign in to your Developer account:

   a. If you haven't already registered the app in iTunes Connect, add it. You'll need to provide the name of the app, the language it uses, the version number, and the SKU, which is the internal product code that Apple will use in sales reports (see Figure 13-3).

   You'll also need to select the bundle ID; the process of enabling Game Center in your app will mean that it's already registered in the Developer Center, and you can select it from the list. If it doesn't appear, go to the Developer Center at *http://developer.apple.com/ios* and make sure that your app's bundle ID is registered.

   b. If you *have* already registered the app in iTunes Connect, just click it in the list.

2. Go to the Game Center tab (see Figure 13-4).

3. Click either Single Game (if you're making a single game) or Group of Games (if you want to share leaderboards across multiple apps), as shown in Figure 13-5.

4. iTunes Connect will now show that Game Center is enabled for this game (see Figure 13-6).

Figure 13-2. The Game Center application in the iOS Simulator

Figure 13-3. Registering the game in iTunes Connect

Figure 13-4. Select the Game Center tab

Figure 13-5. Select either the Single Game or Group of Games button

Game Centre Test

Game Center

Game Center has been enabled for your app. Click below if you want to disable it.

Enabled

To share leaderboards and achievements of this app with other apps you have provided, move this app to a Game Center group.

Move to Group

Figure 13-6. iTunes Connect indicating that the game is enabled for use in Game Center

Don't sign in to your existing Apple ID. Existing Apple IDs are likely to have already been activated in the real, public Game Center, which means they won't work in the sandbox, and you'll get an error saying that your game is not recognized by Game Center.

iOS devices don't use the Game Center sandbox by default, whereas the iOS Simulator always does. If you want to test your game on a physical device while using a sandbox account, you can switch over to using the sandbox by following these steps:

1. Open the Settings application.
2. Scroll down to Game Center.
3. Scroll down to the Developer section.
4. Turn on the Sandbox checkbox.

Note that this section won't appear unless you've installed at least one app on your device via Xcode. If you have a brand-new device, it won't be visible.

Once this is done, a player profile is created in the sandbox, which you can use in your game.

To actually use Game Center, your game needs to ask Game Center if it has permission to access the player's profile. You do this by *authenticating* the player, by first getting the *local player* and then providing it with an authentication handler:

```
func authenticatePlayer() {
    if let localPlayer = GKLocalPlayer.localPlayer() {
        // Assigning a block to the localPlayer's
        // authenticateHandler kicks off the process
        // of authenticating the user with Game Center.
        localPlayer.authenticateHandler = {
            (viewController, error) in
```

```
        if viewController != nil {
            // We need to present a view controller
            // to finish the authentication process
            self.presentViewController(viewController,
                animated: true, completion: nil)

        } else if localPlayer.authenticated {
            // We're authenticated, and can now use Game Center features
            println("Authenticated!")
            self.playerAuthenticated()

        } else if let theError = error {
            // We're not authenticated.
            println("Error! \(error)")
            self.playerFailedToAuthenticate(theError)
        }
    }
}
```

Here's how this works. When you provide the GKLocalPlayer object with an authentication handler, Game Center immediately tries to authenticate the player so that the game can get access to the Game Center features. Whether this succeeds or not, the authentication handler is called.

The handler receives two parameters: a view controller and an error. If Game Center needs the user to provide additional information in order to complete the authentication, your app needs to present the view controller and let the user provide whatever information Game Center needs. If the view controller parameter is nil, you check to see if the GKLocalPlayer has been authenticated. If it has, great! If not, you can find out why by looking at the provided NSError parameter.

 There are many reasons why the player may not get authenticated. These include network conditions, the player not having a Game Center account, the player *declining* to sign up for one, the player being underage, or parental restrictions.

Regardless of the reason, your game needs to be designed to handle not being able to access Game Center. If your game displays errors or refuses to work without the user signing in, you'll have trouble getting it approved by Apple when you submit it to the store.

If an application tries to authenticate with Game Center and no user is currently signed in, the view controller that your authentication handler will be given is the sign-in view controller. When you present that view controller, you're presenting the screen that asks for the user's username and password. After the user is done with the sign-in screen, your authentication handler will be called again: if the user signed in, the localPlayer's authenticated property will now be true. If the user declined to sign in (or failed to sign in to his or her account for some reason), the error parameter that's passed to the block will be non-nil, and you can inspect it to find out what happened.

13.2. Getting Information About the Logged-in Player

Problem

You want to find out information about the currently logged-in player, such as the user's nickname and avatar.

Solution

Use the GKLocalPlayer class to get information about the player:

```
let player = GKLocalPlayer.localPlayer()
self.usernameLabel.text = player.alias

player.loadPhotoForSize(GKPhotoSizeSmall, withCompletionHandler: {
    (image, error) -> Void in

    if let theError = error {
        println("Can't load image: \(error)")
    } else if let theImage = image {
        self.imageView.image = image
    }
})
```

Discussion

Showing information about the player is a good way to indicate that she's a part of the game. You can get the display name and player ID from a GKPlayer object. GKLocal Player is a special object that represents the currently signed-in user.

If you want to load the player's photo, you have to do a special call. Note that not all users have a photo.

13.3. Getting Information About Other Players

Problem

You want to get information about the player's friends, such as their names and avatars.

Solution

Use the GKLocalPlayer class's loadFriendPlayersWithCompletionHandler method:

```
GKLocalPlayer.localPlayer().loadFriendPlayersWithCompletionHandler {
    (friends, error) -> Void in
    // Log out info about each friend
    for friend in friends as! [GKPlayer] {
        println("Friend: \(friend.displayName)")
    }

    // Store friends in a property
    self.friends = friends as! [GKPlayer]

}
```

Discussion

Using the `loadFriendPlayersWithCompletionHandler` method, you get the list of players that the local player is friends with. This list is an array of `GKPlayer` objects, which you can use to get their display name and image from.

13.4. Making Leaderboards and Challenges with Game Center

Problem

You want to show high scores and high-ranking players, and let players challenge their friends to beat their scores.

Solution

First, ensure that your game is set up in iTunes Connect for Game Center (by following the steps in Recipe 13.1). Once that's done, go to the Game Center tab in iTunes Connect.

Next, click Add Leaderboard. You'll be asked if you want to create a *single* leaderboard, or if you want to create a *combined* leaderboard that combines the results from two separate boards. Click Single Leaderboard.

 You'll only be able to create a combined leaderboard if you already have two or more single leaderboards.

You'll be prompted to provide information about the leaderboard, including:

- The name of the leaderboard (shown only to you, inside iTunes Connect, and not shown to the player)
- The ID of the leaderboard, used by your code
- How to format the leaderboard scores (whether to show them as integers, decimal numbers, currency, or times)
- Whether to sort them by best score or by most recent score
- Whether to sort them with low scores first or high scores first
- Optionally, a specified range that scores can be within (Game Center will ignore any scores outside this range)

You then need to provide at least one language in which the leaderboard will be shown. To do this, click Add Language in the Leaderboard Localization section, and choose a language (see Figure 13-7). For each language you provide, you need to provide information on how your leaderboard is shown to the player, and how your scores are being described (see Figure 13-8).

Figure 13-7. Adding a language to the leaderboard

To submit a high score, you need to create a GKScore object and provide it with the score information. When it's created, it's automatically filled out with other important information, such as the player ID of the player who's reporting the score, the date that the score was created, and other data.

When you create the score, you need to provide the ID of the leaderboard. This is the same ID as the one you gave to iTunes Connect when creating the leaderboard. This tells Game Center where the score should end up.

Figure 13-8. The information you need to provide for each language

Once that's done, you report the score to Game Center using the reportScores(_, withCompletionHandler:) method. This method takes an array of GKScore objects, which means you can submit multiple scores at the same time:

```
// Use your own leaderboard ID here
let leaderboardID = "main_leaderboard"

// Get the score from your game
let scoreValue : Int = getScore()

let score = GKScore(leaderboardIdentifier: leaderboardID)
score.value = Int64(scoreValue)

GKScore.reportScores([score], withCompletionHandler: { (error) -> Void in
    if error != nil {
        println("Failed to report score: \(error)")
    } else {
        println("Successfully logged score!")
    }
})
```

To get the scores, you use the GKLeaderboard class. This class lets you get the list of leaderboards that have been defined in iTunes Connect, and from there, get the list of scores in the leaderboard:

```
GKLeaderboard.loadLeaderboardsWithCompletionHandler {
    (leaderboards, error) -> Void in

    // Log an error if we can't load leaderboards
    if error != nil {
        println("Can't load leaderboards: \(error)")
        return
```

```
        }

        // For each leaderboard, load scores for it
        for leaderboard in leaderboards as! [GKLeaderboard] {

            leaderboard.loadScoresWithCompletionHandler {
                (scores, error) -> Void in
                if error != nil {
                    println("Can't load scores for " +
                        "leaderboard \(leaderboard.title): \(error)")
                } else {
                    // Log these scores to the console
                    println("Leaderboard \"\(leaderboard.title)\":")
                    for score in scores as! [GKScore] {
                        println("\(score.player.alias) \(score.player.playerID)" +
                            " - \(score.value)")
                    }
                }
            }
        }
    }
}
```

When you have a `GKScore`, you can issue a challenge to one or more of the player's friends. They'll receive a challenge notification, which will prompt them to try and beat the challenge. If a friend submits a score to the leaderboard that's better than this challenge, your player will receive a notification saying that the challenge has been beaten.

You issue a challenge by presenting a view controller to the players with the specified `GKPlayer` objects (listed in an array):

```
let leaderboardID = "main_leaderboard"
let playersToChallenge : [GKPlayer] = getPlayersToChallenge()
let message = "Try and beat this!"

// Get the score from your game
let scoreValue : Int = getScore()

let score = GKScore(leaderboardIdentifier: leaderboardID)
score.value = Int64(scoreValue)

let challengeComposeViewController =
    score.challengeComposeControllerWithMessage(message,
        players: playersToChallenge) {
            (viewController, didChallenge, playersChallenged) -> Void in

            if didChallenge {
                println("\(playersChallenged.count) players challenged")
            }

            self.dismissViewControllerAnimated(true, completion: nil)
    }
```

```
self.presentViewController(challengeComposeViewController,
    animated: true, completion: nil)
```

You can't issue a challenge to players who aren't your friends. You also can't issue a challenge to yourself.

Discussion

Leaderboards and challenges are a great way to encourage the player to try to best other players, and to keep track of their progress in your game. There's a huge degree of flexibility available to you when you create them.

If you want to quickly show a user interface that displays the scores, you can use the GKGameCenterViewController class. This is a view controller that shows Game Center information for the current player, including that player's scores and challenges.

To use it, you first need to make your view controller conform to the GKGameCenter ControllerDelegate protocol. Then, when you want to show the view controller, you create it and present it to the player:

```
let gameCenterViewController = GKGameCenterViewController()
gameCenterViewController.gameCenterDelegate = self
self.presentViewController(gameCenterViewController,
    animated: true, completion: nil)
```

You then implement the gameCenterViewControllerDidFinish method, which is called when the player decides to close the Game Center view controller. All this method has to do is dismiss the view controller:

```
func gameCenterViewControllerDidFinish(
    gameCenterViewController: GKGameCenterViewController!) {
    self.dismissViewControllerAnimated(true, completion: nil)
}
```

13.5. Finding People to Play with Using Game Center

Problem

You want your players to find people to play games with over the Internet.

Solution

To find people to play with, you first create a GKMatchRequest:

```
let matchRequest = GKMatchRequest()

matchRequest.maxPlayers = 2 // setting max and min players to 2
matchRequest.minPlayers = 2 // means we need precisely 2 players
```

You then create a GKMatchmakerViewController and give it the GKMatchRequest:

```
let matchmakerViewController =
        GKMatchmakerViewController(matchRequest: matchRequest)
matchmakerViewController.matchmakerDelegate = self
self.presentViewController(matchmakerViewController,
    animated: true, completion: nil)
```

You also need to conform to the GKMatchmakerViewControllerDelegate protocol, and implement three important methods:

```
func matchmakerViewController(viewController: GKMatchmakerViewController!,
    didFindMatch match: GKMatch!) {
    // We have a match, and can send data to other players using the GKMatch
    // object
    self.dismissViewControllerAnimated(true, completion: nil)
}

func matchmakerViewController(viewController: GKMatchmakerViewController!,
    didFailWithError error: NSError!) {
    // We failed to get a match
    self.dismissViewControllerAnimated(true, completion: nil)
}

func matchmakerViewControllerWasCancelled(
    viewController: GKMatchmakerViewController!) {
    // The user cancelled the match-maker
    self.dismissViewControllerAnimated(true, completion: nil)
}
```

The really important one is matchmakerViewController(_, didFindMatch:). This gives you a GKMatch object, which is what you use to communicate with other players.

 You'll note that in all three cases, it's up to you to dismiss the view controller.

Discussion

GKMatchRequest objects let you define what kinds of players you're looking for in a match. If you set the playerGroup property on a GKMatchRequest to any value other than 0, the player will only be matched with other people who have the same value for playerGroup.

Matches can be *peer-to-peer* or *hosted*; peer-to-peer means that players pass information between themselves directly, whereas hosted games go through a server that you run.

Many games work best in a client/server model, in which one player (the server) acts as the owner of the game, and all clients communicate with it. This simplifies the problem of keeping the clients in sync, because each client just needs to stay in sync with the server. However, it puts additional load on the server; this has to communicate with every client, which means that the server has to be the player with the best ability to perform these additional duties.

You can configure Game Center to automatically select the best player to act as the server, using the `chooseBestHostPlayerWithCompletionHandler` method. This method runs checks on all players to find out which one has the best connection, and then calls a block and passes it the player ID of the player who should be host (or `nil` if the best host couldn't be found). If the player ID returned is *your* player ID, you're the server, and you should start sending updates to other players and receiving input from them. If the player ID is not your player ID, you're the client, and you should start sending commands to the server and receiving game updates. If the player ID is `nil`, there was a problem, and each copy of the game running on the different players' devices should let its player know that network conditions probably aren't good enough to run a game.

13.6. Creating, Destroying, and Synchronizing Objects on the Network

Problem

You want to create and remove objects in the game, and ensure that everyone sees when an object changes state.

Solution

To synchronize objects across the network, you need to be able to get information from them that represents their current state. The "current state" of an object is all of the important information that defines its situation: its position, its health, where it's facing, and more. Because all games are different, the specific information that makes up game state in your game may vary.

In any case, you need to get the information from the object wrapped in an `NSData` object. For example, if you have an object whose entire state is a vector defining its position, you can create an `NSData` object for it. First, you need to create a data structure that lets you store the position of the object, as well as an identifying reference number:

```
struct DataBlock {
    var objectID : Int
```

```
    var position : (x: Float, y: Float)
}
```

Once you've done that, you can create an instance of this structure, fill it with the necessary data, and then create an NSData using it:

```
// Store data in a block
var data = DataBlock(objectID: networkedObject.objectID,
    position: (x: Float(networkedObject.position.x),
        Float(networkedObject.position.y)))

// Convert it to an NSData
let dataToSend = NSData(bytes: &data, length: sizeof(DataBlock))

// Send the data
// match is a GKMatch, which you can get using the match-maker
var error : NSError?
match.sendDataToAllPlayers(dataToSend,
    withDataMode: GKMatchSendDataMode.Unreliable, error: &error)

if error != nil {
    println("Error sending data: \(error)")
}
```

You can then send this data over the network. When it's received, you get the data, find the object that it's referring to, and apply the change. If it's an object that doesn't exist yet, you create it:

```
func dataReceived(data : NSData) {

    // Start with an empty datablock
    var objectInfo = DataBlock(objectID: 0, position: (x: 0, y: 0))

    // Fill it with data
    data.getBytes(&objectInfo, length: sizeof(DataBlock))

    // Get the object, and put the new data into it
    let object = findObjectWithID(objectInfo.objectID)

    object?.position = CGPoint(x: CGFloat(objectInfo.position.x),
                               y: CGFloat(objectInfo.position.y))
}
```

Removing an object is similar, but instead of sending an NSData object that contains information about the object, you send a packet that instructs clients to remove the object from the game.

Only the server should be in charge of creating, updating, and removing objects. Clients should send instructions to the server, telling it what changes they'd like to make, but it's up to the server to actually make those changes and send back the results of the changes to clients. This prevents clients from falling out of sync with each other, because the server is continuously telling them the "official" version of the game state. (For more on the client/server model of gameplay, see Recipe 13.5.)

Discussion

It's important that all players in a game have the same approximate game state at all times. If this ever stops being the case, the players aren't able to interact in any meaningful way because what they're all seeing will be different.

When you send data that contains instructions to create or remove objects, you want it to be reliable because it's important that all players have the same objects in their game. Updates can usually be sent as unreliably (see Recipe 13.7).

If you're using a component-based model, you'll need all components to be able to provide information to be sent over the network, so that every aspect of your object can be represented.

Don't forget that not every detail of an object needs to be exactly replicated on all players. Information like the position of a monster is important, but the position of sparks coming off it is not. If your game can work without that information being synchronized over the network, then don't synchronize it.

In this example, you'll notice that we do some casting from CGFloat to Float and back. The reason for this is that the precise size of a CGFloat depends on which platform your code is running on—if it's a 64-bit platform, CGFloats are Doubles, whereas on a 32-bit platform it's a Float. Because the device you're sending data to might be a different platform than the one you're sending from, it pays to ensure that you know the size of what you're sending by forcing it to be a certain size.

This also applies to integers, and is the reason why you have types like UInt32 and Int64 in addition to generic Int. When sending data to other devices, be specific about what you're sending.

13.7. Interpolating Object State

Problem

You want to minimize the amount of network traffic in your game, but ensure that everyone has a smooth experience.

Solution

When a packet is received from the server, note the time when it arrived, and subtract that from the time the *last* packet arrived. Store this value somewhere:

```
timeOfSecondMostRecentPacket = timeOfMostRecentPacket
timeOfMostRecentPacket = NSDate.timeIntervalSinceReferenceDate()
interpolationTime = 0.0
```

When a data packet arrives that updates the position of an object, first note the *current* location of the object (i.e., its position before the update is applied). Then, over the course of smoothingTime, move the object from its original position to that in the most recently received update:

```
// Update interpolation time to include the time taken to render
// this frame
self.interpolationTime += deltaTime

// Work out how far we should interpolate between the second most
// recent known location and the most recent location
// Note that if we don't get info for a while, this value will go over
// 1.0, meaning that we'll be extrapolating
let interpolationPoint = interpolationTime /
    (timeOfMostRecentPacket - timeOfSecondMostRecentPacket)

// secondMostRecentKnownPosition and mostRecentKnownPosition
// should be updated every time we get new data
let origin = object.secondMostRecentKnownPosition
let destination = object.mostRecentKnownPosition

// Interpolate from the two known positions to get our current position
object.position = interpolatePoint(origin,
    withPoint: destination, amount: interpolationPoint)
```

If an update packet arrives *during* this process (which is possible), restart the process using the object's current position and the *new* position.

Discussion

To save bandwidth, your server should send at a rate much lower than the screen refresh rate. While the screen is likely updating at 60 frames per second (at least, it should be!), the network should only be sending updates 10 to 15 times per second.

However, if you're only sending position updates at a rate of 10 frames per second, your network game will appear jerky, because objects will be moving around the screen at a low rate of updates.

What's better is *interpolation*: when an update comes in, smoothly move the object from its current location to the location that you just received. This has the effect of always making the player be a few milliseconds behind the server, but makes the whole game-play experience feel better.

13.8. Handling When a Player Disconnects and Rejoins

Problem

You want to gracefully handle when players drop out of your GKMatch, and when they rejoin.

Solution

Conform to the GKMatchDelegate protocol, and when your match begins, set the GKMatch object's to that object.

When a player's connection state changes, the delegate provided to your GKMatch receives the match(_, player:, didChangeState:) message:

```
func match(match: GKMatch!, player: GKPlayer!,
    didChangeConnectionState state: GKPlayerConnectionState) {
    if state == GKPlayerConnectionState.StateDisconnected {
        // The player has disconnected; update the game's UI
    }
}
```

If a player drops from a GKMatch, the delegate gets sent the match(_, shouldReinvite Player:) message. If this returns YES, Game Center will try to reconnect the player so that player rejoins the match:

```
func match(match: GKMatch!,
    shouldReinviteDisconnectedPlayer player: GKPlayer!) -> Bool {
    return true
}
```

Note that this happens *only* if there are exactly two players in the match. If there are more, the player who dropped from the GKMatch is gone forever, and you'll have to tell him to create a new match.

Discussion

Players can leave the game in one of two ways: they can deliberately decide to leave the game, or they can drop out due to a crash, networking conditions, or something else outside their control. Losing a player is generally annoying to other players, but it can be even more annoying if your game doesn't indicate the distinction between a player losing her connection and a player quitting the game. If your game lets your player know the difference, it feels nicer.

Making your game send an "I'm going away" packet immediately before quitting allows other players to understand the difference between a conscious decision to leave the game and a dropout.

13.9. Making Turn-Based Gameplay Work with Game Kit

Problem

You want to use Game Center to coordinate turn-based gameplay.

Solution

First, generate a match request by creating a `GKMatchRequest`. You create the `GKMatchRequest` in the exact same way as if you were making a non-turn-based game, and you can learn more about how you do that in Recipe 13.5.

Next, you should make your class conform to the `GKTurnBasedMatchmakerViewControllerDelegate` protocol, which contains some necessary methods used for determining which turn-based match the player wants to play.

Once you have your `GKMatchRequest`, you create a view controller, `GKTurnBasedMatchmakerViewController`, and provide your match request to it:

```
let matchRequest = GKMatchRequest()
matchRequest.minPlayers = 2
matchRequest.maxPlayers = 2

let matchmaker = GKTurnBasedMatchmakerViewController(matchRequest: matchRequest)
matchmaker.turnBasedMatchmakerDelegate = self
self.presentViewController(matchmaker, animated: true, completion: nil)
```

Next, you need to implement methods from the `GKTurnBasedMatchmakerViewControllerDelegate` protocol:

```
func turnBasedMatchmakerViewController(
    viewController: GKTurnBasedMatchmakerViewController!,
        didFailWithError error: NSError!) {
    // We failed to find a match
    self.dismissViewControllerAnimated(true, completion: nil)
}

func turnBasedMatchmakerViewController(
    viewController: GKTurnBasedMatchmakerViewController!,
        didFindMatch match: GKTurnBasedMatch!) {
    // We now have a match
    self.dismissViewControllerAnimated(true, completion: nil)

    // The match has now begun.
```

```
            if match.currentParticipant.player.playerID ==
                GKLocalPlayer.localPlayer().playerID {
                // We are the current player.
            } else {
                // Someone else is the current player.
            }

        }

        func turnBasedMatchmakerViewControllerWasCancelled(
            viewController: GKTurnBasedMatchmakerViewController!) {
            // The user closed the matchmaker without creating a match
            self.dismissViewControllerAnimated(true, completion: nil)
        }

        func turnBasedMatchmakerViewController(
            viewController: GKTurnBasedMatchmakerViewController!,
                playerQuitForMatch match: GKTurnBasedMatch!) {
            // We're quitting this game.

            self.dismissViewControllerAnimated(true, completion: nil)

            let matchData = match.matchData
            // Do something with the match data to reflect the fact that we're
            // quitting (e.g., give all of our buildings to someone else,
            // or remove them from the game)

            match.participantQuitInTurnWithOutcome(GKTurnBasedMatchOutcome.Quit,
                nextParticipants: nil, turnTimeout: 2000.0, matchData: matchData)
                { (error) in
                // We've now finished telling Game Center that we've quit
            }
        }
```

You should also conform to the GKLocalPlayerListener protcol, and implement methods that tell your code about when other players have changed the game state:

```
    func player(player: GKPlayer!,
        receivedTurnEventForMatch match: GKTurnBasedMatch!, didBecomeActive: Bool) {
        // The turn-based match has updated. We may now be the current player.
    }

    func player(player: GKPlayer!, matchEnded match: GKTurnBasedMatch!) {
        // The match has now ended.

        // List out the outcome for each player (if they came first, second,
        // third, etc., or quit)
        for participant in match.participants as! [GKTurnBasedParticipant] {
            println("\(participant.player.alias)'s outcome: " +
                "\(participant.matchOutcome)")
        }

    }
```

When it's the current player's turn, you show the interface that lets her make her turn—move objects around, make decisions, and otherwise do the actions that make up her turn. When that's done, you save the entire game state, for *all* players, in an NSData object, and provide it to the GKTurnBasedMatch by calling endTurnWithParticipants:

```
func endTurn(match: GKTurnBasedMatch, gameData:NSData,
    nextParticipants:[GKTurnBasedParticipant]) {

    // nextParticipants is the array of the players
    // in the match, in order of who should go next. You can get the list
    // of participants using match.participants. Game Center will tell the
    // first participant in the array that it's his turn; if he doesn't
    // take it within 600 seconds (10 minutes), it will be the next player's
    // turn, and so on. (If the last participant in the array
    // doesn't complete his turn within 10 minutes, it remains her
    // turn.)

    match.endTurnWithNextParticipants(nextParticipants, turnTimeout: 2000.0,
        matchData: gameData) { (error)  in
        // We're done telling Game Center about the state of the game
    }
}
```

You can also end the entire match by doing this:

```
func endMatch(match: GKTurnBasedMatch, finalGameData:NSData) {
    match.endMatchInTurnWithMatchData(finalGameData, completionHandler: {
        (error) in
        // We're done telling Game Center that the match is over
    })
}
```

Additionally, the current player can update the game state *without* ending his turn. If he does this, all other players get notified of the new game state:

```
func updateTurn(match: GKTurnBasedMatch, gameData: NSData) {
    match.saveCurrentTurnWithMatchData(gameData, completionHandler: { (error) in
        // The game data has been saved, but it's still our turn
    })

}
```

This can be used if the player decides to do something that's visible to all other players; for example, if the player decides to buy a house in a game like *Monopoly*, all other players should be notified of this so that they can adjust their strategy. However, buying a house doesn't end the player's turn.

You can also retrieve all GKTurnBasedMatches that the currently signed-in player is engaged in, like so:

```
GKTurnBasedMatch.loadMatchesWithCompletionHandler { (matches, error) -> Void in
    for match in matches as! [GKTurnBasedMatch] {
```

```
        // Show information about this match
    }
}
```

Discussion

Turn-based games are hosted by Game Center. In a turn-based game, the entire state of the game is wrapped up in an NSData object that's maintained by Game Center. When it's a given player's turn, your game retrieves the game state from the Game Center server and lets the player decide what she'd like to do with her turn. When the player's done, your game produces an NSData object that represents the *new* game state, which takes into account the decisions the player has made. It then sends it to Game Center, along with information on which player should play next.

It's possible for a player to be involved in multiple turn-based games at the same time. This means that even when it isn't the player's turn in a particular match, she can still play your game. When you present a GKTurnBasedMatchmakerViewController, the view controller that's displayed shows all *current* games that the player can play. When the player selects a match, your code receives the GKTurnBasedMatch object that represents the current state of the game.

If the player creates a new match, Game Center finds participants for the match based on the GKMatchRequest that you pass in, and tells its delegate about the GKTurnBased Match object. Alternatively, if the player selects a match that she's currently playing in, the view controller gives its delegate the appropriate GKTurnBasedMatch.

It's important to let the player know when it's her turn. When your code gets notified that it's the player's turn in any of the matches that she's playing in, your code should let the player know as soon as possible.

13.10. Sharing Text and Images to Social Media Sites

Problem

You want to allow your users to send tweets or post to Facebook from your games, so that they can share their high scores and characters.

Solution

Use a UIActivityViewController to share content:

```
// Get a string from somewhere
let textToShare : String = self.textField.text
// Put it in an array
let activityItems = [textToShare]
```

```
// Create an activity view controller and present it
let activityViewController =
    UIActivityViewController(activityItems: activityItems,
        applicationActivities: nil)
self.presentViewController(activityViewController,
    animated: true, completion: nil)
```

When you create a `UIActivityViewController`, you provide an array of objects that you want to share. These objects can be strings, URLs, images, or arbitrary `NSData` objects.

 In addition to data objects, you can also include objects that conform to the `UIActivityItemSource` protocol. This protocol defines methods for more precisely controlling whether a certain sharing service should be used, and also to provide control over what data should be sent *after* the user has selected a sharing service.

Discussion

Allowing your users to push content or high scores from your game out to their social networks is a great way to spread the word about what you've built. iOS makes it easy to attach content and links to social network posts, as you can see.

13.11. Storing Saved Games in Game Center

Problem

You want your player's saved games to appear on all of his devices.

Solution

You can store saved games in Game Center by first converting them into an `NSData` object (see Recipe 5.1 for an example of how to do this), and then giving them to Game Center.

To save a game, you provide the `NSData` object and the name of the saved game to the `GKLocalPlayer` object:

```
let localPlayer = GKLocalPlayer.localPlayer()

let saveData : NSData = getSaveData()

localPlayer.saveGameData(getSaveData(), withName: "My Save") {
    (savedGame, error) -> Void in
    if error != nil {
        println("Error saving: \(error)")
```

```
        }
    }
```

The saved game data will be uploaded to Game Center, and synchronized with all other devices that are signed into the same Game Center account and have the game installed.

When the player wants to load his games, you ask the GKLocalPlayer. You provide a completion handler, which receives an array of GKSavedGame objects. These objects contain the NSData that was stored, as well as the name of the saved game and the name of the device on which the game was saved:

```
localPlayer.fetchSavedGamesWithCompletionHandler {
    (savedGames, error) -> Void in
    if error != nil {
        println("Failed to find games: \(error)")
        return
    }

    println("Found \(savedGames).count games")
    for save in savedGames as! [GKSavedGame] {
        // List each game
        println("- \(save.name): (from \(save.deviceName), " +
            "modified \(save.modificationDate))")

        // Call save.loadDataWithCompletionHandler to get the data itself
    }

}
```

When you want to delete a saved game, simply call deleteSavedGamesWithName(_, completionHandler:):

```
localPlayer.deleteSavedGamesWithName("My Save") { (error) -> Void in
    if error != nil {
        println("Error removing save: \(error)")
    }
}
```

Discussion

Due to a variety of issues, it's possible that a conflict can occur—for example, if you're on a plane, your devices are likely to be offline. If you save a game on an iPad, and then also save the same game on an iPhone, both of the devices will try to upload their game.

The next time you retrieve the list of saved games, you'll see multiple games with the same name. It's up to your game to decide how to resolve this conflict. Common techniques include using the most recently saved game, though it's generally best to simply ask the user what to do. When you've decided on which game is correct, you pass the array of conflicting GKSavedGames to the GKLocalPlayer's resolveConflictingSavedG ames method, along with the NSData that you want to use. This will resolve the conflict on all devices.

13.12. Implementing iOS Networking Effectively

Problem

You want to make effective and compelling use of the networking features of iOS in your game.

Solution

There's one very simple rule you can follow to make a great iOS game with networking: use as much of the provided game-network infrastructure as possible!

By tying your game to the features that are provided by iOS, such as Game Center, you're ensuring that your game will work properly alongside future versions of iOS, and that players will already know how to work many of the network-based components of your game through their exposure to other games.

Discussion

By adhering to Apple's recommended standards and techniques for building networked games, you'll create experiences that users already know how to use and understand. Don't be tempted to deviate! Your users will suffer because of it.

13.13. Implementing Social Networks Effectively

Problem

You want to make sure that your game makes effective use of the social features of iOS.

Solution

The solution here is simple: don't go overboard with social. It's very tempting to encourage users to tweet and post status updates about your game at every turn. After all, you have near-unfettered access to their social networking accounts, so why not encourage them to post constantly?

Here's a tip: you should use these great powers only sparingly. Users don't want to spam their friends, and they probably don't want to talk about a game they're not enjoying—and you don't want them to do these things either! Offer the ability to tweet and post status updates at junctures in your game when your users are likely to be at their happiest.

Did they just win a level? Offer them the ability to tweet it. Did they just lose? Don't offer them the ability to tweet it.

Discussion

While it's tempting to put links to social media everywhere, it really only works best when it's exposed to happy, fulfilled users. Users who are bored or have just lost a game are likely to tweet (at best) meaningless spam or (at worst) critical comments about your game. Don't encourage them—choose your moments carefully.

CHAPTER 14

Game Controllers and External Screens

iOS devices can interact with a wide range of other devices. Some of these devices, such as external screens and game controllers, are particularly useful when you're building games!

iOS has supported multiple screens for several versions now, but as of iOS 7 it also supports game controllers, which are handheld devices that provide physical buttons for your players to use. Game controllers have both advantages and disadvantages when compared with touchscreens. Because a game controller has physical buttons, the player's hands can feel where the controls are, which makes it a lot easier to keep attention focused on the action in the game. Additionally, game controllers can have *analog inputs*: a controller can measure how hard a button is being held down, and the game can respond accordingly. However, game controllers have fixed buttons that can't change their position, or look and feel, which means that you can't change your controls on the fly.

Game controllers that work with iOS devices must obey a set of design constraints specified by Apple; these constraints mean that you can rely on game controllers built by different manufacturers to all behave in a consistent way and provide the same set of controls for your games. In a move that is both as empowering for gamers as it is infuriating for developers, Apple requires that *all* iOS games must be playable without a controller at all, even if they support a controller. A controller must never be required by an iOS game. This means that you'll end up developing two user interfaces: one with touchscreen controls, and one with game-controller controls.

To make matters more complex, there are several different *profiles* of game controller. The simplest (and usually cheapest) is the *standard* game controller (see Figure 14-1), which features two shoulder buttons, four face buttons, a pause button, and a d-pad. The next step up is the *extended* gamepad (see Figure 14-2), which includes everything in the standard profile, and adds two thumbsticks and two triggers. Your game doesn't need to make use of every single button that's available, but it helps.

Figure 14-1. The basic game controller

Figure 14-2. The extended game controller (note the thumbsticks and additional shoulder buttons)

In addition to game controllers, iOS games can make use of external screens. These can be directly connected to your device via a cable, or they can be wirelessly connected via AirPlay. Using external screens, you can do a number of things: for example, you can make your game appear on a larger screen than the one that's built in, or even turn the iPhone into a game controller and put the game itself on a television screen (effectively turning the device into a portable games console).

Like controllers, external screens should never be required by your game. External screens are useful for displaying supplementary components of your game, or providing the main game view while the iOS device itself is used as a controller and secondary view.

In this chapter, you'll learn how to connect to and use game controllers, how to use multiple screens via cables and wireless AirPlay, and how to design and build games that play well on the iPhone/iPod touch and iPad, or both.

14.1. Detecting Controllers

Problem

You want to determine whether the user is using a game controller. You also want to know when the user connects and disconnects the controller.

Solution

Game controllers are represented by instances of the `GCController` class. Each `GCController` lets you get information about the controller itself and the state all of its buttons and controls.

To access the `GCController` class, you first need to import the GameController framework:

```
import GameController
```

To get a `GCGameController`, you ask the `GCController` class for the `controllers` property, which is the list of all currently connected controllers:

```
for controller in GCController.controllers() as! [GCController] {
    NSLog("Found a controller: \(controller)")
}
```

The `controllers` array updates whenever controllers are connected or disconnected. If the user plugs in a controller or disconnects one, the system sends a `GCController DidConnectNotification` or a `GCControllerDidDisconnectNotification`, respectively. You can register to receive these notifications like this:

```
NSNotificationCenter.defaultCenter().addObserver(self,
    selector: "controllerConnected:",
    name: GCControllerDidConnectNotification, object: nil)

NSNotificationCenter.defaultCenter().addObserver(self,
    selector: "controllerDisconnected:",
    name: GCControllerDidDisconnectNotification, object: nil)
```

When a controller is connected, you can find out whether it's a standard gamepad or an extended gamepad by using the `gamepad` and `extendedGamepad` properties:

```
if controller.extendedGamepad != nil {
    // It's an extended gamepad
    NSLog("This is an extended gamepad")
} else if controller.gamepad != nil {
    // It's a standard gamepad
    NSLog("This is a standard gamepad")
} else {
    // It's something else entirely, and probably can't be used by your game
    NSLog("I don't know what kind of gamepad this is")
}
```

You can also check to find out whether the controller is physically attached to the device, by checking the `attachedToDevice` property:

```
if controller.attachedToDevice {
    NSLog("This gamepad is physically attached")
} else {
    NSLog("This gamepad is wireless")
}
```

Discussion

The `GCController` class updates automatically when a controller is plugged in to the device. However, your user might have a wireless controller that uses Bluetooth to connect to the iPhone, and it might not be connected when your game launches.

Your player can leave the game and enter the Settings application to connect the device, but you might prefer to let the player connect the controller while still in your game. To do this, you use the `startWirelessControllerDiscoveryWithCompletionHandler:` method. When you call this, the system starts looking for nearby game controllers, and sends you a `GCControllerDidConnectNotification` for each one that it finds. Once the search process is complete, regardless of whether or not any controllers were found, the method calls a completion handler block:

```
// Once called, you'll receive
// GCControllerDidConnectNotification and
// GCControllerDidDisconnectNotification for
// wireless devices
GCController.startWirelessControllerDiscoveryWithCompletionHandler {
    () -> Void in
```

```
        NSLog("Finished searching for wireless controllers")
    }
```

It's important to note that the system won't show any built-in UI when you're searching for wireless controllers. It's up to you to show the UI that indicates to the player that you're searching for controllers.

Once a wireless controller is connected, your game treats it just like a wired one—there's no difference in the way you talk to it.

Once you have a GCController, you can set the playerIndex property. When you set this property, an LED on the controller lights up to let the player know which player he is. This property is actually remembered by the controller and is the same across *all games*, so that the player can move from game to game and not have to relearn which player number he is in multiplayer games:

```
controller.playerIndex = 0
```

14.2. Getting Input from a Game Controller

Problem

You would like people to be able to control your game using their external controllers.

Solution

Each controller provides access to its buttons through various properties:

```
// Pressed (true/false)
let isButtonAPressed = controller.gamepad.buttonA.pressed

// Pressed amount (0.0 .. 1.0)
let buttonAPressAmount = controller.gamepad.buttonA.value
```

You use the same technique to get information about the gamepad's directional pads. The d-pad and the thumbsticks are both represented as GCControllerDirectionPad classes, which lets you treat them as a pair of axes (i.e., the x-axis and the y-axis), or as four separate buttons (up, down, left, and right):

```
let horizontalAxis = controller.gamepad.dpad.xAxis

// Alternatively, just ask if the left button is pressed
let isLeftDirectionPressed = controller.gamepad.dpad.left.pressed
```

Discussion

There are two different types of inputs available in a game controller:

- A *button input* tells you whether a button is being pressed, as a Boolean YES or NO. Alternatively, you can find out *how much* a button is being pressed down, as a floating-point value that goes from 0 (not pressed down at all) to 1 (completely pressed down).

- An *axis input* provides two-dimensional information on how far left, right, up, and down the d-pad or thumbstick is being pressed by the user.

The face and shoulder buttons are all represented as GCControllerButtonInput objects, which let you get their value either as a simple BOOL or as a float. The d-pad and the thumbsticks are both represented as GCControllerAxisInput objects.

Both button inputs and axis inputs also let you provide *value changed handlers*, which are blocks that the system calls when an input changes value. You can use these to make your game run code when the user interacts with the controller, as opposed to continuously polling the controller to see its current state.

For example, if you want to get a notification every time the A button on the controller is interacted with, you can do this:

```
controller.gamepad.buttonA.valueChangedHandler
    = { (input: GCControllerButtonInput!, value:Float, pressed:Bool) in

        NSLog("Button A pressed: \(pressed)")

}
```

This applies to both button inputs and axis inputs, so you can attach handlers to the thumbsticks and d-pad as well. Note that the value changed handler will be called multiple times while a button is pressed, because the value property will change continuously as the button is being pressed down and released.

In addition to adding handlers to the inputs, you can also add a handler block to the controller's pause button:

```
controller.controllerPausedHandler =
    { (controller: GCController!) in

    NSLog("Pause button pressed")

}
```

 The controller itself doesn't store any information about whether or not the game is paused—it's up to your game to keep track of the pause state. All the controller will do is tell you when the button is pressed.

14.3. Showing Content via AirPlay

Problem

You would like to use AirPlay to wirelessly display elements of your game on a high-definition screen via an Apple TV.

Solution

Use an `MPVolumeView` to provide a picker, which lets the user select an AirPlay device.

Because you can only add an `MPVolumeView` through code, positioning it isn't quite as simple as adding it in the Interface Builder. Instead, use code like the following:

```
let volumeView = MPVolumeView()
volumeView.showsRouteButton = true
volumeView.showsVolumeSlider = false

volumeView.sizeToFit()

self.volumeControlContainerView.addSubview(volumeView)
```

This creates a button that, when tapped, lets the user select an AirPlay device to connect to the existing device. When the user selects a screen, a `UIScreenDidConnectNotification` is sent, and your game can use the AirPlay device using the `UIScreen` class (see Recipe 14.4).

> The `MPVolumeView` will only show the AirPlay picker if there are AirPlay devices available. If no AirPlay device is nearby, nothing will appear.
>
> Additionally, you'll only receive a `UIScreenDidConnectNotification` notification if mirroring is turned on in the AirPlay options (accessible via Control Center). If mirroring is turned off, AirPlay will route any audio your app plays to the device the user has selected, but won't send any video.

Discussion

When the user has selected an AirPlay display, iOS treats it as if a screen is attached. You can then treat it as a `UIScreen` (there's no distinction made between wireless screens and plugged-in screens).

Just like with a plugged-in screen, the contents of the primary screen will be mirrored onto the additional screen. If you give the screen to a `UIWindow` object, mirroring will be turned off and the screen will start showing the `UIWindow`. If you remove the `UIScreen` from the `UIWindow`, the screen will return to mirroring mode.

If there are more than two screens attached, only one screen will mirror the main display. The other screens will be blank until you give them to a UIWindow.

14.4. Using External Screens

Problem

You would like to display elements of your game on a screen external to the iOS device.

Solution

To get the list of available screens, you use the UIScreen class:

```
for connectedScreen in UIScreen.screens() as! [UIScreen] {
    if connectedScreen == UIScreen.mainScreen() {
        NSLog("Main screen: \(connectedScreen)")
    } else {
        NSLog("External screen: \(connectedScreen)")
    }
}
```

On iPhones, iPod touches, and iPads, there's always at least one UIScreen available—the built-in touchscreen. You can get access to it through the UIScreen's mainScreen property:

```
let mainScreen = UIScreen.mainScreen()
```

When you have a UIScreen, you can display content on it by creating a UIWindow and giving it to the UIScreen. UIWindows are the top-level containers for all views—in fact, they're views themselves, which means you add views to a screen using the addSubview: method:

```
if UIScreen.screens().count >= 2 {

    // This next step requires that there's a view controller
    // in the storyboard with the Identifier "ExternalScreen"
    let viewController = self.storyboard?
        .instantiateViewControllerWithIdentifier("ExternalScreen")
        as? UIViewController

    // Try to get the last screen..
    if let connectedScreen
        = UIScreen.screens().last as? UIScreen {

        // Create a window, and put the view controller in it
        let window = UIWindow(frame: connectedScreen.bounds)
```

```
        window.rootViewController = viewController
        window.makeKeyAndVisible()

        // Put the window on the screen.
        window.screen = connectedScreen
    }
}
```

Discussion

You can detect when a screen is connected by subscribing to the `UIScreenDidConnect Notification` and `UIScreenDidDisconnectNotification` notifications. These are sent when a new screen becomes available to the system—either because it's been plugged in to the device, or because it's become available over AirPlay—and when a screen becomes unavailable.

If you want to test external screens on the iOS Simulator, you can select one by choosing Hardware→TV Out and choosing one of the available sizes of window (see Figure 14-3). Note that selecting an external display through this menu will restart the entire simulator, which will quit your game in the process. This means that while you can test *having* a screen connected, you can't test the `UIScreenDidConnectNotifica tion` and `UIScreenDidDisconnectNotification` notifications.

Figure 14-3. Choosing the size of the external screen in the iOS Simulator

14.5. Designing Effective Graphics for Different Screens

Problem

You want your game to play well on different kinds of screens and devices, including iPhones, iPads, and large-scale televisions.

Solution

When you design your game's interface, you need to consider several factors that differ between iPhones, iPads, and connected displays. Keep the following things in mind when considering how the player is going to interact with your game.

Designing for iPhones

An iPhone:

Is very portable

People can whip out an iPhone in two seconds, and start playing a game within five. Because they can launch games very quickly, they won't want to wait around for your game to load.

Additionally, the iPhone is a very light device. Users can comfortably hold it in a single hand.

Has a very small screen

The amount of screen space available for you to put game content on is very small. Because the iPhone has a touchscreen, you can put controls on the screen. However, to use them, players will have to cover up the screen with their big, opaque fingers and thumbs. Keep the controls small—but not too small, because fingers are very imprecise.

Will be used in various locations, and with various degrees of attention

People play games on their iPhones in a variety of places: in bed, waiting for a train, on the toilet, at the dinner table, and more. Each place varies in the amount of privacy the user has, the amount of ambient noise, and the amount of distraction. If you're making a game for the iPhone, your players will thank you if the game doesn't punish them for looking away from the screen for a moment.

Additionally, you should assume that the players can't hear a single thing coming from the speaker. They could be sitting in a quiet room, but they could just as easily be in a crowded subway station. They could also be playing in bed and trying not to wake their partners, or they could be hard of hearing or deaf.

Your game's audio should be designed so that it enhances the game but isn't necessary for the game to work. (Obviously, this won't be achievable for all games; if you've got a game based heavily on sound, that's still a totally OK thing to make!)

Designing for iPads

An iPad:

Is portable, but less spontaneous
Nobody quickly pulls out an iPad to play a 30-second puzzle game, and then puts it back in his pocket. Generally, people use iPads less frequently than smartphones but for longer periods. This means that "bigger" games tend to do very well on the iPad, beacuse the user starts playing them with an intent to play for at least a few minutes rather than (potentially) a few seconds.

Has a comparatively large screen
There are two different types of iPad screens: the one present on the iPad mini, and the one present on larger-size iPads (such as the iPad 2 and the iPad Air). The mini's screen is smaller, but still considerably larger than that on the iPhone. This gives you more room to place your controls, and gives the player a bigger view of the game's action.

However, the flipside is that the iPad is heavier than the iPhone. iPads generally need to be held in both hands, or placed on some kind of support (like a table or the player's lap). This contributes to the fact that iPads are used less often but for longer sessions: it takes a moment to get an iPad positioned just how the user wants it.

Will be used in calmer conditions
For the same reason, an iPad tends to be used when the user is sitting rather than walking around, and in less hectic and public environments. The user will also be more likely to give more of her attention to the device.

Designing for larger screens

When players have connected a larger screen:

They're not moving around
An external screen tends to be fixed in place, and doesn't move around. If the screen is plugged directly into the iPad, this will also restrict movement. This means that the players are likely to play for a longer period of time—because they've invested the energy in setting up the device with their TV, they'll be in for the (relatively) long haul.

The player has two screens to look at
A player who's connected an external screen to his iOS device will still be holding the device in his hands, but he's more likely to not be looking at it. This means that

he's not looking at where your controls are. If he's not using a controller, which is likely, he won't be able to feel where one button ends and another begins. This means that your device should show *very large* controls on the screen, so that your users can focus on their wonderfully huge televisions and not have to constantly look down at the device.

Having two devices can be a tremendous advantage for your game, for example, if you want to display secondary information to your user—*Real Racing 2* does this very well, in that it shows the game itself on the external screen, and additional info like the current speed and the map on the device.

More than one person can comfortably look at the big screen
Large displays typically have a couch in front of them, and more than one person can sit on a couch. This means that you can have multiple people playing a game, though you need to keep in mind that only one device can actually send content to the screen.

Discussion

Generally, you'll get more sales if your game works on both the iPhone and the iPad. Players have their own preferences, and many will probably have either an iPhone or an iPad—it's rare to have both, because Apple products are expensive.

When it comes to supporting large screens, it's generally a cool feature to have, but it's not very commonplace to have access to one. You probably shouldn't consider external screen support to be a critical feature of your game unless you're deliberately designing a game to be played by multiple people in the same room.

14.6. Dragging and Dropping

Problem

You want to drag and drop objects into specific locations. If an object is dropped somewhere it can't go, it should return to its origin. (This is particularly useful in card games.)

Solution

Use gesture recognizers to implement the dragging itself. When the gesture recognizer ends, check to see whether the drag is over a view that you consider to be a valid *destination*. If it is, position the view over the destination; if not, move it back to its original location.

The following code provides an example of how you can do this. In this example, `CardSlot` objects create `Cards` when tapped; these `Card` objects can be dragged and dropped only onto other CardSlots, and only if those CardSlot objects don't already have a card on them, as shown in Figure 14-4.

Figure 14-4. The drag and drop example in this recipe

Additionally, card slots can be configured so they delete any cards that are dropped on them.

Create a new class called CardSlot, which is a subclass of UIImageView. Put the following code in *CardSlot.swift*:

```
@IBDesignable
class CardSlot: UIImageView {

    // @IBInspectable and @IBDesignable makes the deleteOnDrop
    // property appear in the interface builder
    @IBInspectable
    var deleteOnDrop : Bool = false

    var currentCard : Card? {
        // If we're given a new card, and this card slot is
        // 'delete on drop', delete that card instead of
        // making it be added
        didSet {
            if self.deleteOnDrop == true {

                currentCard?.delete()
                self.currentCard = nil
                return
            }
        }
    }

    private var tap : UITapGestureRecognizer?

    override func awakeFromNib() {
        self.tap = UITapGestureRecognizer(target: self, action: "tapped:")
        self.addGestureRecognizer(self.tap!)

        self.userInteractionEnabled = true
    }

    func tapped(tap: UITapGestureRecognizer) {

        if tap.state == .Ended {
            // Only card slots that aren't "delete when cards
            // are dropped on them" can create cards
            if self.deleteOnDrop == false {
                let card = Card(cardSlot: self)

                self.superview?.addSubview(card)

                self.currentCard = card
            }
        }

    }

}
```

Then, create another UIImageView subclass called Card. Put the following code in *Card.swift*:

```swift
import UIKit

class Card: UIImageView {

    // The CardSlot that this card is in.
    var currentSlot : CardSlot?

    // Detects when the user drags this card.
    var dragGesture : UIPanGestureRecognizer?

    // Prepares the card to be added
    init(cardSlot: CardSlot) {
        currentSlot = cardSlot

        super.init(image: UIImage(named: "Card"))

        dragGesture = UIPanGestureRecognizer(target: self, action: "dragged:")

        self.center = cardSlot.center

        self.addGestureRecognizer(self.dragGesture!)
        self.userInteractionEnabled = true
    }

    // Called when the drag gesture recognizer changes state
    func dragged(dragGesture: UIPanGestureRecognizer) {
        switch dragGesture.state {

        // The user started dragging
        case .Began:

            // Work out where the touch currently is...
            var translation =
                dragGesture.translationInView(self.superview!)
            translation.x += self.center.x
            translation.y += self.center.y

            // Then animate to it.
            UIView.animateWithDuration(0.1) { () -> Void in
                self.center = translation

                // Also, rotate the card slightly.
                self.transform =
                    CGAffineTransformMakeRotation(CGFloat(M_PI) / 16.0)
            }

            // Reset the gesture recognizer in preparation
            // for the next time this method is called.
```

```swift
        dragGesture.setTranslation(CGPointZero, inView: self.superview)

        // If we aren't already at the front, bring ourselves
        // forward
        self.superview?.bringSubviewToFront(self)

    // The drag has changed position
    case .Changed:

        // Update our location to where the touch is now
        var translation = dragGesture.translationInView(self.superview!)
        translation.x += self.center.x
        translation.y += self.center.y

        self.center = translation

        dragGesture.setTranslation(CGPointZero, inView: self)

    // The drag ended
    case .Ended:


        // Find out if we were dragging over a location
        var destinationSlot : CardSlot?

        // For each view in the superview..
        for view in self.superview!.subviews {

            // If it's a CardSlot..
            if let cardSlot = view as? CardSlot {

                // And if the touch is inside that view
                // AND that card slot doesn't have a card
                if cardSlot.pointInside(
                    dragGesture.locationInView(cardSlot),
                    withEvent: nil) == true
                    && cardSlot.currentCard == nil {

                        // ..Then this is our destination
                        destinationSlot = cardSlot
                        break;
                }
            }
        }

        // If we have a new card slot, remove ourselves
        // from the old one and add to the new one
        if destinationSlot != nil {

            self.currentSlot?.currentCard = nil
            self.currentSlot = destinationSlot
            self.currentSlot?.currentCard = self
```

```
        }

        UIView.animateWithDuration(0.1) { () -> Void in
            self.center = self.currentSlot!.center
        }

    // The gesture was interrupted.
    case .Cancelled:

        UIView.animateWithDuration(0.1) { () -> Void in
            self.center = self.currentSlot!.center
        }

    default:
        () // do nothing

    }

    // If the drag has ended or was cancelled, remove the
    // rotation applied above
    if dragGesture.state == .Ended ||
        dragGesture.state == .Cancelled {
        UIView.animateWithDuration(0.1) { () -> Void in
            self.transform = CGAffineTransformIdentity;
        }
    }

}

// Fade out the view, and then remove it
func delete() {

    UIView.animateWithDuration(0.1, animations: { () -> Void in
        self.alpha = 0.0
        }) { (completed) -> Void in
            self.removeFromSuperview()
    }

}

// This initializer is required because we're a
// subclass of UIImageView
required init(coder aDecoder: NSCoder) {
    super.init(coder: aDecoder)
}

}
```

Add two images to your project: one called *CardSlot*, and another called *Card*.

Then, open your app's storyboard and drag in a `UIImageView`. Make it use the *Card-Slot* image, and set its class to `CardSlot`. Repeat this process a couple of times, until you have several card slots. When you run your app, you can tap the card slots to make cards appear. Cards can be dragged and dropped between card slots; if you try to drop a card onto a card slot that already has a card, or try to drop it outside of a card slot, it will return to its original location.

You can also make a card slot delete any card that is dropped on it. To do this, select a card slot in the Interface Builder, go to the Attributes inspector, and change Delete On Drop to On.

Discussion

Limiting where an object can be dragged and dropped provides constraints to your game's interface, which can improve the user experience of your game. If anything can be dropped anywhere, the game feels loose and without direction. If the game takes control and keeps objects tidy, the whole thing feels a lot snappier.

In this example, the *dragging* effect is enhanced by the fact that when dragging begins, the card is rotated slightly; when the drag ends or is cancelled, the card rotates back. Adding small touches like this can dramatically improve how your game feels.

The `CardSlot` class is marked with the keyword `@IBDesignable` at the start of the class definition. This indicates to Xcode that certain properties, which are marked with `@IBInspectable` in the class, should appear in the Attributes inspector.

Note that if you want a property to appear in the inspector, you need to specify the property's type. For example, this won't work:

```
// a Bool, but won't appear in the inspector
@IBInspectable var someProperty = true
```

This, however, will:

```
// Explicitly giving the type will make it appear
@IBInspectable var someProperty : Bool = true
```

CHAPTER 15

Performance and Debugging

At some point during its development, every game will have performance issues, and every game will crash. Fortunately, iOS has some of the best tools around for squeezing as much performance as possible out of your games and finding bugs and other issues.

In this chapter, you'll learn about how to use these tools, how to fix problems, and how to get information about how your game's behaving.

15.1. Improving Your Frame Rate

Problem

You need to coax a better frame rate out of your game so that it plays smoothly.

Solution

To improve your frame rate, you first need to determine where the majority of the work is being done. In Xcode:

1. From the Scheme menu, select your device, so that the application will be installed to the device when you build.

2. Open the Product menu and choose Profile (or press Command-I).

   The application will build and install onto the device, and Instruments will open and show the template picker (see Figure 15-1).

3. Select the Time Profiler instrument and run your game for a while. You'll start seeing information about how much CPU time your game is taking up.

4. Turn on Invert Call Tree, Hide Missing Symbols, and Hide System Libraries, and turn off everything else in the list, as shown in Figure 15-2.

5. Take note of the name of the functions that are at the top of the list:

   a. If the top functions are the method in which you call OpenGL, the game is spending most of its time rendering graphics. To improve your frame rate, reduce the number of objects on the screen, and make fewer calls to `glDrawEle ments` and its related functions.

   b. If not, the game is spending most of its time running code on the CPU. Turn on Hide System Libraries; the function at the top of the list is your code, which the game is spending most of its time processing.

Figure 15-1. Selecting the Instruments template

If your game is spending most of its time rendering graphics, you can improve the speed by drawing fewer sprites (if you're using Sprite Kit) or drawing fewer objects (if you're using OpenGL). If most of the time is spent running code on the CPU, it's less straightforward, because different games do different things. In this case, you'll need to look for ways to optimize your code. For example, if a long-running function is calculating a value that doesn't change very often, store the result in a variable instead of recalculating it.

Figure 15-2. Instruments in action

Discussion

You improve frame rates by taking less time to do the work you need to do per frame. This means either reducing the total amount of work you need to do, or not making the rendering of frames wait for work to complete.

> You should only profile using a real device, because the simulator performs differently than the real thing. The simulator has a faster CPU, but a slower GPU.

15.2. Making Levels Load Quickly

Problem

You want to make your levels load as quickly as possible, so that the player can get into the game immediately.

Solution

There are three main techniques for making a level load faster:

Load smaller or fewer resources
> Make the images and sounds that you load smaller. Reduce the dimensions of textures, use compressed textures, and use lower-quality audio. Alternatively, load fewer resources.

Show progress indicators
> When you begin loading resources for a new level, first count the number of resources you need to load; every time one gets loaded, show progress to the user, either using a progress indicator (such as a `UILabel` or `UIProgressView`) or a text field.

Stream textures
> When level loading begins, load very small resources, such as very small textures. Once the game has begun, begin loading full-size textures in the background; once each high-resolution texture has loaded, replace the small texture with the large one.

Discussion

Half the battle is making the game *look* like it's fast. The other half is actually *being* fast.

Loading smaller resources means that less data needs to be sent. An iOS device is really a collection of small, interconnected pieces, and it takes time to transfer data from the flash chips to the CPU and the GPU. In almost all cases, "faster loading" just means "loading less stuff."

If you can't increase the speed beyond a certain point, showing progress indicators at least means the user sees some kind of progress. If you just show a static "loading" screen, the player will get bored, and it will *feel* like it's taking longer. You can see this technique outside of games, too: when you launch an iOS application, the system first shows a placeholder image while the app launches in the background. Apple encourages developers to make this placeholder image look like part of the application, but without any text or actual data to show, and the result is that the app feels like it's launching faster.

Finally, it's often the case that you just want to get *something* on the screen so that the player can start playing, and it's OK if parts of the game don't look their best for the first few seconds. This is called *texture streaming*, and the idea is that you load a deliberately small texture during the normal loading process, let the player get into the game, and then start slowly loading a better texture in the background.

Texture streaming means that your game's loading process is faster because there's less data that needs to be transferred before the game can start. However, it can lead to visual problems: when the larger, higher-quality texture is loaded, a visible "pop" can happen. Additionally, loading two versions of the same texture at the same time means that more memory is being consumed, which can lead to memory pressure problems on iOS devices.

15.3. Dealing with Low-Memory Issues

Problem

Your app is randomly crashing when images or other resources are loaded into memory.

Solution

There are several ways you can reduce the amount of memory that your application is using. For example:

Use fewer textures

> If you can reuse an image for more than one sprite or texture, it's better than having multiple images that vary only slightly.

Trim your textures

> If you have a texture that's got some transparent area around the edges, trim them. When a texture is loaded, every pixel counts toward memory usage, including ones that are entirely transparent.

Use texture atlases

> If you're using Sprite Kit, Xcode makes it pretty easy to create texture atlases. Texture atlases group multiple textures together, which is more efficient because per-texture overhead is minimized. Xcode also automatically trims your textures for you. To create a texture atlas, create a folder with a name ending in *.atlas*, and put your images into that. Once that's done, your textures will be combined into a single image, saving a little memory.

Memory-map large files

If you need to read a large file—for example, a level file, a large collection of data, or a large sound file—you'll often load it in as an NSData object. However, the usual method of doing this, with `dataWithContentsOfFile:`, copies the data into memory. If you're reading from a file that you know won't change, you can instead *memory-map* it, which means instructing iOS to pretend that the entire file has been copied into memory, but to only actually read the file when parts of it are accessed. To do this, load your files using `dataWithContentsOfFile:options:error:` and use the `NSDataReadingMappedIfSafe` option:

```
var error : NSError? = nil
let data = NSData(contentsOfFile: "path/to/file",
    options: NSDataReadingOptions.DataReadingMappedIfSafe,
    error: &error)
```

Use compressed textures

Compressed textures can dramatically reduce the amount of memory that your game's textures take up. For more information, see Recipe 15.5.

Discussion

iOS has a very limited amount of memory, compared to OS X. The main reason for this is that iOS doesn't use a *swap file*, which is a file that operating systems use to extend the amount of RAM available by using the storage medium. On OS X, if you run out of physical RAM (i.e., space to fit stuff in the RAM chips), the operating system moves some of the information in RAM to the swap file, freeing up some room. On iOS, there's no swap file for it to move information into, so when you're out of memory, you're completely out of memory.

 The reason for this is that writing information to flash memory chips, such as those used in iOS devices, causes them to degrade very slightly. If the system is constantly swapping information out of RAM and into flash memory, the flash memory gradually gets slower and slower. From Apple's perspective, it's a better deal for the user to have a faster device and for developers to deal with memory constraints.

Because there's a fixed amount of memory available, iOS terminates applications when they run out of memory. When the system runs low on memory, all applications are sent a low memory warning, which is their one and only notification that they're running low.

The amount of memory available to apps depends on the device; however, as of iOS 7, there's a hard limit of 600 MB per app. If an app ever goes above this limit, it will be immediately terminated by the operating system.

15.4. Tracking Down a Crash

Problem

You want to understand why an application is crashing, and how to fix it.

Solution

First, determine what kind of crash it is. The most common kinds of crashes are:

Exceptions

These occur when your code does something that Apple's code doesn't expect, such as trying to insert nil into an array. When an exception occurs, you'll see a backtrace appear in the debugging console.

Memory pressure terminations

As we saw in the previous recipe, iOS will terminate any application that exceeds its memory limit. This isn't strictly a crash, but from the user's perspective, it looks identical to one. When a memory pressure termination occurs, Xcode displays a notification.

Once you know what kind of crash you're looking at, you can take steps to fix it.

Discussion

The approach you take will depend on the kind of issue you're experiencing.

Fixing exceptions

To fix an exception, you need to know where the exception is being thrown from. The easiest way to do this is to add a breakpoint on Objective-C exceptions, which will stop the program at the moment the exception is thrown (instead of the moment that the exception causes the app to crash).

To add this breakpoint:

1. Open the Breakpoints navigator, and click the + button at the bottom left of the window (see Figure 15-3).

Figure 15-3. The breakpoints menu

2. Click Add Exception Breakpoint.

3. Run the application again; when the exception is thrown, Xcode will stop inside your code.

Fixing memory pressure issues

There are lots of different approaches you can take to reduce the amount of memory being consumed by your application; see Recipe 15.3 for some pointers.

15.5. Working with Compressed Textures

Problem

You want to use compressed textures to save memory and loading time.

Solution

To work with compressed textures, you need to have compressed textures to load. Xcode comes with a texture compression tool, but it's sometimes tricky to use. It's better to write a simple script that handles many of the details of using the compression tool for you:

1. Create a new, empty file called *compress.sh*. Place this file anywhere you like.

2. Put the following text in it (note that the path must all appear on one line; it's broken here only to fit the page margins):

```
PARAMS="-e PVRTC --channel-weighting-perceptual --bits-per-pixel-4"

/Applications/Xcode.app/Contents/Developer/Platforms/iPhoneOS.platform/
  Developer/usr/bin/texturetool $PARAMS -o "$1.pvrtc" -p "$1-Preview.png" "$1"
```

3. Open the Terminal, and navigate to the folder where you put *compress.sh*.

4. Type the following commands:

```
chmod +x ./compress.sh
./compress.sh MyImage.png
```

After a moment, you'll have two new images: *MyImage.png.pvrtc* and *MyImage.png-Preview.png*. The preview PNG file shows you what the compressed version of your image looks like, and the PVRTC file is the file that you should copy into your project.

Once you have your compressed texture, you load it like any other texture. If you're using Sprite Kit, you load a texture using the `textureWithImageNamed:` method, providing it with the name of your PVRTC file:

```
let texture = SKTexture(imageNamed: "MyCompressedTexture.pvrtc")
```

With GLKit, it's much the same process, though you have to get the full path of the image file using NSBundle's `pathForResource:ofType:` method. Once you have that, you use GLKTextureLoader's `textureWithContentsOfFile:options:error:` method to load the texture:

```
let textureLocation = NSBundle.mainBundle()
    .pathForResource("MyCompressedTexture", ofType:"pvrtc")
var error : NSError? = nil;
let texture = GLKTextureLoader
    .textureWithContentsOfFile(textureLocation,  options:nil, error:&error)
```

 Unfortunately, it's not possible to load a *.pvrtc* file using the `UIImage` class's methods. This means that you can't use compressed textures in `UIImageViews`, which is annoying. The only places you can use compressed textures are in OpenGL or when using Sprite Kit.

Discussion

Compressed textures use much less memory, and take less time to load (because there's less data to transfer to the graphics chip), but they look worse. How much "worse" depends on the type of image you want to compress:

- Photos and similar-looking textures do quite well with compression.

- Line art tends to get fuzzy fringes around the edges of lines.

- Images with transparent areas look particularly bad, because the transparent edges of the image get fuzzy.

On iOS, compressed textures are available as 2 bits per pixel (not bytes, *bits*) and 4 bits per pixel. Whereas a full-color 512-by-512 image would take up 1 MB of graphics memory, a 4 bpp version of the same image would take up only 128 kb of graphics memory.

The compression system used is called PVRTC, which stands for PowerVR Texture Compression (PowerVR provides the graphics architecture for iOS devices).

An image can only be compressed when it fits all of the following requirements:

- The image is square (i.e., the width is the same as the height).

- The image is at least 8 pixels high and wide.

- The image's width and height are a power of 2 (i.e., 8, 16, 32, 64, 128, 512, 1024, 2048, 4096).

Use compressed textures with care. While they can dramatically improve performance, reduce memory usage, and speed up loading times, if they're used without care they can make your game look very ugly, as in the zoomed-in images in Figure 15-4. The image on the left is the compressed version; PVRTC introduces compression artifacts, which creates a slight "noisy" pattern along the edge of the circle. There's also a subtle color difference between the image on the left and on the right, which is an additional consequence of compression. (If you're reading the print version of this book, Figure 15-4 is black and white, and the difference might be too subtle to see. The main difference is that the colors in the PVRTC-compressed image are slightly paler.) Experiment, and see what looks best in your game.

Figure 15-4. Compressed image (left) and original image (right)

15.6. Working with Watchpoints

Problem

You want to know when a specific variable changes.

Solution

To make Xcode stop your program when a variable changes from one value to another, you use a watchpoint. To set a watchpoint on a variable:

1. First, stop your program using a breakpoint.

   When the program stops, the list of visible variables appears in the debugging console.

2. Add the watchpoint for the variable you want to watch.

   Find the variable you want to watch, right-click it, and choose "Watch *name of your variable*," as shown in Figure 15-5.

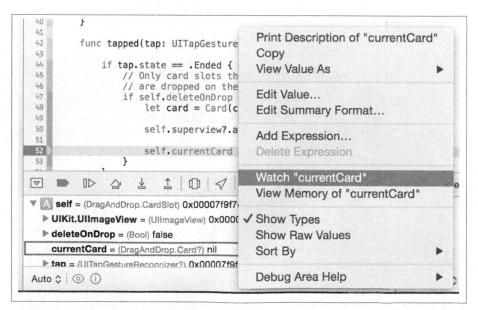

Figure 15-5. Creating a watchpoint

3. Continue the application.

   The application will stop when the variable you've watched changes value.

Discussion

Watchpoints are breakpoints that "watch" a location in memory and stop the program the moment the value stored in that location changes. Watchpoints can't be added to properties—they only watch regions of memory. If you want to watch a property, you need to locate the instance variable that that property uses, and watch it.

Keep in mind that when you stop and relaunch a program, the locations of the variables you were watching last time will have changed, and you'll need to add the watchpoints again.

15.7. Logging Effectively

Problem

You want to log additional information about what your application is doing when information is logged to the console.

Solution

You can make NSLog show additional information by overriding it.

Add the following function to one of your Swift files. Don't put it in a class—this is a global function, so put it outside any class definitions:

```
func Log(message: String,
    file: String = __FILE__,
    line : Int = __LINE__,
    function: String = __FUNCTION__) {

    NSLog("\(function) (\(file.lastPathComponent);\(line)): \(message)")

}
```

Now when you use Log, the debugging console will show the names of the class and the method that the line is in, as well as the filename and line number of the logging statement. The following command:

```
Log("Yes")
```

will produce this on the console:

```
currentCard (CardSlot.swift:31): Hello
```

Discussion

The compiler provides several "magic" variables that change based on where they're used in your code.

For example, the __LINE__ variable always contains the current line number in the file that's currently being compiled, and the __FILE__ variable contains the full path to the source code file that's being compiled. The __FUNCTION__ variable contains the name of the current function.

 When __LINE__, __FILE__, and __FUNCTION__ are used as the default values for parameters in a function, the line number, file, and function that that function was called *from* are used, instead of the line number and file at which the called function is defined.

In the solution given in this recipe, we've done a little bit of extra coding to make the logs easier to read. We mentioned that the __FILE__ variable contains the full path to the file that's being compiled, but that's often way too long—most of the time, you just want the filename. To get just the filename, you can call lastPathComponent method, which returns the last part of the path.

15.8. Creating Breakpoints That Use Speech

Problem

You want to receive audio notifications when something happens in your game.

Solution

Add a spoken breakpoint that doesn't stop the game:

1. Add a breakpoint where you want a notification to happen.
2. Right-click the breakpoint, and choose Edit Breakpoint. The Edit Breakpoint dialog box will appear, as shown in Figure 15-6.
3. Turn on "Automatically continue after evaluating actions."
4. Click Add Action.
5. Change the action type from Debugger Command to Log Message.
6. Type the text you want to speak.
7. Click Speak Message.

Figure 15-6. Making the breakpoint speak

When the breakpoint is hit, Xcode will speak the log message.

Discussion

Using spoken breakpoints is a really useful way to get notifications on what the game's doing without having to switch away from the game. Breakpoints are spoken by your computer, not by the device, which means that they won't interfere with your game's audio (don't forget to unmute your computer's speakers).

Index

Symbols

2D graphics, 143–179
  adding a sprite, 152
  adding a text sprite, 153
  and Sprite Kit, 143–179
  animating a sprite, 170
  Bézier paths for, 166
  blending modes for, 163
  creating a scene, 150–152
  creating Sprite Kit view, 149
  determining available fonts, 155
  grids, 26–29
  image effects for sprite drawing, 165
  including custom fonts, 156
  math basics for, 143–149
  moving sprites and labels around, 158–161
  noise for image creation, 178
  parallax scrolling, 171–178
  particle effects for, 167
  shaking the screen, 168
  shape nodes, 162
  texture atlases, 162
  texture sprites, 161
  transitioning between scenes, 156
2D grids, 26–29
3D graphics
  adding specular highlights, 273–274
  adding toon shading, 276
  advanced, 255–276

animating a mesh, 246–249
basics, 209–233
batching draw calls, 249
creating a movable camera object, 250–253
drawing a cube, 227–231
GLKit context for, 214–215
intermediate, 235–253
lighting a scene, 266–269
loading a mesh, 235–242
loading a texture, 224–226
making objects transparent, 271
math for, 210–213
moving camera in 3D space, 232
normal mapping, 269–271
normal maps and, 287
parenting objects, 242–246
rotating a cube, 231
shader basics, 255–258
shaders for texturing, 265
squares using OpenGL, 216–223
text as, 284
working with materials, 259–265
3D objects
  creating with Scene Kit, 280
  importing, 288
  managing with Scene Kit, 280
  rendering with Scene Kit, 280
3D rotation, 63
3D Studio Max, 289

We'd like to hear your suggestions for improving our indexes. Send email to index@oreilly.com.

3D vectors, 210

A

A* algorithm, 303
Academy Award (Ken Perlin), 179
action methods, 44
action, nodes, 158–161
active application, 10
addAnimation(_, forKey:) method, 61, 64
additive blending, 273
AirPlay, 347
alpha value, 272
ambient light objects, 282
anchor point, sprite, 153
Angry Birds, 313
animated views, UI dynamics for, 55
animation
    limits on, 284
    of sprite, 170
    pop effect for buttons, 60
    UI dynamics for, 55
app sandbox, 127
appearance proxy, 62
Apple, 313
Apple TV, 347
application music player, 114
architecture, laying out, 1
arrays, filtering with closures, 22
artificial intelligence and behavior, 293–311
    calculating a path for an object to take, 303–308
    determining if an object can see another object, 309
    enhancing game design with, 311
    finding the next best move for a puzzle game, 308
    making an object decide on a target, 300
    making an object flee when it's in trouble, 299
    making an object know where to take cover, 302
    making an object move toward a position, 295–297
    making an object steer toward a point, 301
    making object intercept moving target, 298
    making things follow a path, 297
    making vector math nicer in Swift, 293–295
assertion methods, 26
asset catalog, 51

asset(s)
    loading during gameplay, 22–24
    managing collection of, 137–139
atlases, texture, 162
attachment, adding to views, 56
audio players, multiple, 108
authenticating a player, 318
authentication handler, 318
automobiles, creating, 205
AVAudioplayer, 103–106
AVAudiorecorder, 106
AVAudioSessionCategory, 120
AVSpeechSynthesizer, 112
axis input, 346

B

background application, 10
background images, 62
background music, 119–121
background property, 53
background quality of service, 23
backgroundColor, 151
bandwidth, saving, 330
began touch state, 69
Bézier paths, 166
Blender, 289
blending function, 271
blending modes, 163
bodies, 182
breakpoints
    and watchpoints, 370
    with speech, 372
bridging, 127
brute force approach, 308
buffer, OpenGL terminology, 220
button input, 346
button(s)
    pop animation for, 60
    slicing images for, 53–54
    storyboards and, 32–37

C

CABasicAnimation, 63
CABasicAnimation objects, 283
CAKeyframeAnimation, 61
calls, batching, 249
camera objects, 281

camera(s)
    as movable object, 250–253
    in OpenGL terminology, 233
    moving in 3D space, 232
cancelled touch state, 69
cars, creating, 205
cartoon shading, 276
category, audio session, 120
CGAffineTransform, 58
CGPoint structure, 144
challenges, Game Center and, 321–325
change in time, 8
change velocity, 188
CIFilter, 165
client/server model, 327
closures
    calling, 17
    filtering an array with, 22
    method for calling, 17
    with game layout, 15–17
code, triggering segues from, 46
COLLADA files, 288
colliders, 182, 185
collision shape, 289
collision(s), 183
    adding to views, 55
    detecting, 193
    walls for scenes, 189
color
    background, 151
    of view, changing, 62
    with shape nodes, 163
color buffer, clearing, 215
combined leaderboard, 321
compass heading, 85–87
completion handler, 337
component-based layout, 4–7
compressed textures, 366–368
constraining objects, 287
constraints, view layout, 49–51
continuous gesture recognizers, 74
coordinate spaces, 253
coordinate system, 2D, 144
Core Animation system, 13
    Scene Kit and, 283
core animation, moving images with, 56
cover, taking, 302
crash, tracking down a, 365
CrazyBump, 269

creating objects, 327–329
cross-fading, 109–111
cube(s)
    drawing, 227–231
    rotating, 231
currency, in-game, 141
current state, 327
currentTime property, 105
custom fonts, 156
custom gestures, 76–80
custom shapes, Bézier paths for, 166

D

Dafont, 156
data storage, 123–142
    files vs. database for, 136
    iCloud key-value store, 132–134
    iCloud to save games, 128–132
    implementing best strategy for, 141
    in-game currency, 141
    loading structured information, 134–136
    managing collection of assets, 137–139
    saving state of game, 123–126
    storing high scores locally, 126
    storing information in NSUserdefaults, 139–141
dealloc method, 264
debugging, 363–366, 370–373
    creating breakpoints that use speech, 372
    improving your frame rate, 359–361
    logging effectively, 371
    low-memory issues, 363–364
    SKView and, 150
    tracking down a crash, 365
    working with watchpoints, 370
decoding (NSArchiver), 125
degrees, converting from radians, 147
delta time, 8
delta time calculation, 7–9
density, 188
dependency(-ies), 21
depth buffer, 229
destroying objects, 327–329
detail, normal mapping for, 269–271
detecting game controllers, 343–345
device attitude, 85
device orientation, gravity and, 201
device tilt, 83–85
diffuse map, 271

directional light objects, 283
dot product, 148–149
dragging
    images, 70–72
    objects, 202–205
dragging and dropping, 352–358
Dragon class, 3
draw calls, batching, 249
dropping out of game, 331
dull texture, 274
dynamic bodies, 184

E

easing equations, 249
edge chains, 190
edge colliders, 183, 190
edge loops, 190
elapsed time
    calculating since start of game, 14
    delta time calculation, 7–9
ended touch state, 69
entrance of user, detecting, 9
exceptions, crashes and, 365
exit of user, detecting, 9
exit segues, 48
explosions, 199–201
extended gamepad, 341
external screens, 347–358
    basics, 343
    dragging and dropping, 352–358
    effective graphics for different screens, 350–352
    iPad, 351
    iPhone, 350
    larger screens, 351
    showing content via AirPlay, 347
    using, 348

F

Facebook, posting scores/characters on, 335
fade out (cross-fading), 109–111
falling, keeping objects from, 192
field of view, 309
__FILE__ variable, 372
files
    database vs., 136
    managing collection of assets, 137–139
fill color, 163

filters, 22
findComponent(s) method, 7
finding objects, 194
fire effects, 167
fixed joints, 196
fleeing objects, 299
floors (graphics), 290
font families, 155
font(s)
    custom, 156
    determining availability of, 155
force(s), 182, 197
foreground application, 10
fragment shader, 255, 265, 268, 273
frame rate, improving, 359–361
friction, 182
friends, of local players, 321
__FUNCTION__ variable, 372
future, performing a task in, 20

G

Game Center
    and Game Kit for turn-based gameplay, 332–335
    and turn-based games, 335
    finding people to play with using, 325–327
    making leaderboards and challenges with, 321–325
    networking with, 313–320
    selection of server by, 327
    storing saved games in, 336
game controller, 341–346
    basics, 341
    detecting, 343–345
    dragging and dropping, 352–358
    external, 345
    getting input from, 345
    profiles of, 341
game controller input
    axis, 346
    button, 346
Game Kit, turn-based gameplay with, 332–335
GameObject base class, 3
gameplay
    loading assets during, 22–24
    turn-based, with Game Kit, 332–335
generics, 7
geocoding, 95, 97
geometry objects, defining, 281

gesture recognition
  custom, 76–80
  pinching gesture, 75–76
  rotation gesture, 72–74
gesture recognizers, 80
GKMatchRequest, 325, 332
glBlendFunc function, 271
GLKit
  3D vectors and, 210
  compressed texture loading, 367
  context for, 214–215
  effects, 222
  Swift compatibility problems, 209
glowing materials, 285
Goblin class, 3
GPS coordinates, for street address, 95
Grand Central Dispatch, 20, 110
graphics
  and improving game speed, 360
  effective, for different screens, 350–352
gravity
  adding to views, 55
  customizing, 191
  device orientation to control, 201
grids, 2D, 26–29
group action, 160

H

heading, compass, 85–87
headphones, 121
hiding (taking cover), 302
high scores, storing, 126
high-definition screen, 347
highlights, specular, 273–274
hinge joints, 196
hit-testing, 290
horizontal axis, 144
hosted matches, 327

I

iCloud
  containers, 128
  for saving games, 128–132
  key-value store, 132–134
identity matrix, 211
image effects, 165
image(s)
  adding, 51

dragging, 70–72
for texture sprite, 161
moving with core animation, 56
noise for texture and effects, 178
rotating, 58–59
sharing to social media sites, 335
slicing for buttons, 53–54
in-game currency, 141
information
  loading structured, 134–136
  storing in NSUserdefaults, 139–141
inheritance-based layout, 2–4
input, 67–101
  accessing user location, 87–90
  calculating user speed, 90
  creating custom gestures, 76–80
  detecting device tilt, 83–85
  detecting magnets, 99–100
  detecting pinching gestures, 75–76
  detecting rotation gestures, 72–74
  detecting shakes, 81
  detecting when view is touched, 68
  dragging image around screen, 70–72
  getting compass heading, 85–87
  looking up GPS coordinates for street address, 95
  looking up street addresses from users location, 97
  pinpointing user proximity to landmarks, 91
  receiving notifications when user changes location, 92–95
  receiving touches in custom areas of view, 80
  responding to tap gestures, 69
  using device as steering wheel, 98
  utilizing to improve game design, 101
instantiating, nib, 65
interception, moving target, 298
interpolation, object state, 329
inverse kinematics (IK) constraints, 288
iOS
  and compressed textures, 368
  background color with, 151
  memory issues, 364
  networking feature implementation, 338
  social feature implementation, 338
iOS 7, Sprite Kit and, 143
iOS Fonts, 156
iPads, 351
iPhones, 350

iTunes Connect, 315
iTunes, playing user-purchased media from, 118

J

JavaScript Object Notation (JSON), 135
joints, 183, 196–197

K

Kerbal Space Program, 191
key, 64
key path, 61, 64
key-value storage, 128
key-value store, iCloud, 132–134
keyTimes property, 61

L

labels, moving, 158–161
landmarks, user proximity to, 91
large screens, 351
latitude, of street address, 95
laying out a game, 1–29
    2D grids, 26–29
    adding unit tests, 24–26
    calculating time elapsed since start, 14
    component-based layout, 4–7
    delta time calculation, 7–9
    dependencies, 21
    detecting user entrance/exit, 9
    filtering array with closures, 22
    inheritance-based layout, 2–4
    laying out your engine, 1
    loading new assets during gameplay, 22–24
    making operations depend on each other, 21
    pausing a game, 13
    performing a task in the future, 20
    updating based on timer, 11
    updating based on when the screen updates, 11–13
    working with closures, 15–17
    working with operation queues, 18
    writing method that calls closure, 17
leaderboards, 321–325
length, vector, 145
levels, quick loading of, 362
lighting effects, 282
lighting, scene, 266–269
limit joints, 197

__LINE__ variable, 372
linear dodge, 273
loading
    assets, 22–24
    of levels, 362
    structured information, 134–136
local player, 318
location, user
    accessing, 87–90
    looking up street addresses from, 97
    notifications of change in, 92–95
    relative to landmarks, 91
logged-in player(s), information about, 320
logging, effective, 371
longitude, of street address, 95
look-at constraints, 288
low memory, 363–364

M

magic variables, 371
magnet(s), detecting, 99–100
magnetometers, 86
magnitude, vector, 145
main queue, 19
manager object, 108
mapping, normal, 269–271
mass, 182, 188
Material (class), 259–265
materials, in Scene Kit, 285
    properties of, 285
mathematics
    coordinate system, 144
    for 2D graphics, 143–149
    for 3D graphics, 210–213
    making vector math nicer in Swift, 293–295
    vectors, 144–149
matrix, 211–213
Maya, 289
measuring yaw tilt, 86
Media Player framework, 113
memory mapping, 364
memory pressure terminations, 365
memory, low, 363–364
menus
    effective, 66
    overlaying on game content, 65
Mesh object, 241
mesh(es)
    animating, 246–249

lights with, 266
    loading, 235–242
method, calling closure with, 17
model spaces, 253
model-view matrix, 212, 222, 228
money (in-game currency), 141
Monster subclass, 3
motion sickness, 178
moved touch state, 69
moving targets, 298
moving vectors, 146
MPMediaItem, 114
MPMusicController, 113
MPMusicPlaybackState, 116
music
    allowing user to select, 117–119
    controlling playback, 116
    cooperating with other audio, 119–121
    detecting track changes, 114
    getting information about, 113

N

name, for OpenGL buffer, 220
networking and social media, 313–339
    creating/destroying/synchronizing objects
        on network, 327–329
    finding people to play with using Game Cen-
        ter, 325–327
    getting information about logged-in player,
        320
    getting information about other players, 320
    implementing social networks effectively,
        338
    interpolating object state, 329
    iOS networking implementation, 338
    making leaderboards and challenges with
        Game Center, 321–325
    player disconnecting/rejoining, 331
    sharing text/images to social media sites, 335
    storing saved games in Game Center, 336
    turn-based gameplay with Game Kit, 332–
        335
    using Game Center, 313–320
nibs, 65
node
    action, 158–161
    defined, 153
    visual effects for, 165

nodes, 280
    parent/child, 281
noise textures, generating, 286
noise, visual, 178
nonphotorealistic rendering, 276
normal mapping, 269–271
normal maps, 286
normalizing, 201
normalizing vectors, 296
normals (vector), 266, 268
notifications of change in user location, 92–95
NSData object, 327
NSFileManager class, 107
NSUserdefaults, 139–141

O

object library, 32
object(s)
    adding specular highlights, 273–274
    adding toon shading, 276
    and thrusters, 198
    batching draw calls, 249
    calculating path for, 303–308
    creating, on network, 327–329
    destroying, on network, 327–329
    determining if an object can see another, 309
    dragging around, 202–205
    finding, 194
    fleeing when in trouble, 299
    following a path, 297
    interpolating state of, 329
    joining together, 196–197
    knowing where to take cover, 302
    moving target interception, 298
    moving toward another object, 295–297
    normal mapping, 269–271
    parenting, 242–246
    separating appearance from geometry, 259–
        265
    steering toward point, 301
    synchronizing, on network, 327–329
    target selection by, 300
    transparent, 271
Objective-C, Swift vs., 209
objects
    animating with Scene Kit, 283
    chaining together, 288
    constraining, 287
    physics body of, 289

reaction to light, controling, 285
texturing in Scene Kit, 286
observer object, 115
obstacles, avoiding, 303–308
omni lights objects, 283
OpenGL
    and GLKit context, 214–215
    and UIView, 65
    camera in, 233
    displaying texture with, 224–226
    for 3D graphics, 209
    scene redrawing by, 215
    squares with, 216–223
OpenGL ES, 209, 215
operation queues, 18
operation(s), as dependency, 21
operators, Swift, 148
orientation, device, 201
origin, coordinate system, 144
orthographic cameras, 282
orthographic projection transform matrix, 212
OS X
    background color with, 151
    Sprite Kit and, 143
outlet property, 44
outside input, 2
overlaying menus, 65

P

parallax scrolling, 171–178
parent, sprite, 153
parenting objects, 242–246
particle effects, 167
path(s)
    calculating, 303–308
    making objects follow, 297
    SKSceneNode and, 163
pause method, 104
pausing a game
    and detecting user entrance/exit, 9
    layout for, 13
peer-to-peer matches, 327
performance, improving, 359–363
    improving your frame rate, 359–361
    making levels load quickly, 362
    working with compressed textures, 366–368
Perlin noise, 179
Perlin, Ken, 179
perspective cameras, 282

perspective projection transform matrix, 211
Photo Booth, 165
physics, 181–206
    adding thrusters to objects, 198
    connecting objects, 196–197
    controlling gravity, 191
    controlling time, 192
    creating a car, 205
    defining collider shapes, 185
    detecting collisions, 193
    device orientation for gravity control, 201
    dragging objects around, 202–205
    explosions, 199–201
    finding objects, 194
    for sprites, 183
    for static/dynamic objects, 184
    forces, applying, 197
    in Scene Kit, 289
    joining objects together, 196–197
    keeping objects from falling over, 192
    setting velocities, 187
    terms and definitions, 181–183
    walls for collision scenes, 189
    working with mass, size, density, 188
physics body of objects, 289
physics world, 182
pin joints, 196
pinching gestures, 75–76
pitch tilt, 83, 85
pixel shaders, 215
play method, 104
playback, 116
player(s)
    disconnecting/rejoining, 331
    finding with Game Center, 325–327
    getting information about logged-in, 320
    getting information about other, 320
    profile, 314
playing sounds
    controlling music playback, 116
    with AVAudioplayer, 103–106
point light objects, 282
point lights, 266
point, object steering toward a, 301
pop animation, 60
prepareToDraw method, 263
presentation context, 38
presentScene, 152, 156
profile, player, 314

progress indicators, 362
projection matrix, 222
puzzle games, 308

Q

QuartzCore
    and pop animation, 60
    for rotating a 3D view, 63
queues, operation, 18

R

radians, 147
RAM, swap files and, 364
rasterization, 258
real-time games, 12
recording sound, 106
reference frames, 86
reflections, 290
rejoining game, 331
retaining objects, 16
reverse geocoding, 97
rewinding, 105
roll tilt, 83, 85
root node, 281
root view controller segue, 38
rotating
    cubes, 231
    images, 58–59
    keeping objects from, 192
    UIview in 3D, 63
    vectors, 147
rotation gestures, detecting, 72–74

S

sampler 2D, 266
sandbox, 314
saved games, storing, 336
saving games, iCloud for, 128–132
scaleMode, 151
scaling vectors, 147
Scene Kit, 279–291
    animating objects, 283
    appearance of objects, customizing, 285
    bumpy textures in, 286
    cameras, 281
    COLLADA files and, 288
    constraining objects, 287

    Core Animation classes and, 283
    creating scenes in, 280
    hit testing, 290
    lighting effects, 282
    material, 285
    normal mapping, 286
    physical behavior in, 289
    reflections, adding, 290
    rendering 3D objects, 280
    setting up, 279
    text, rendering with, 284
    texturing objects, 286
scene(s)
    lighting, 266–269
    moving sprites and labels in, 158–161
    OpenGL and, 215
    Sprite Kit for creating, 150–152
    transitioning between, 156
scenes, 280
SCNCamera objects, 281
SCNFloor objects, 290
SCNNode objects, 281
SCNText class, 284
SCNView class, 279
    hitTest function, 290
scores, high
    displaying with Game Center, 321–325
    storing locally, 126
screen updates, 11–13
screen(s)
    iPad, 351
    iPhone, 350
    organizing with storyboards, 32–38
    segues for moving between, 45–48
scrolling, parallax, 171–178
segues, 38, 45–48
sequence (SKAction), 159
server, best player as, 327
shader program, 255
shader(s)
    basics, 255–258
    texturing with, 265
shading, toon, 276
shaking
    detecting, 81
    screen, 168
shape nodes, 162
shiny materials, 285
shiny object, 274

show segue, 38
simulation sickness, 178
single leaderboard, 321
Siri, 112
size of objects, 188
SKAction objects, 158
  for shakes, 170
  for textures, 171
SKBlendMode, 164
SKEffectNode, 165
SKLabelNode, 154
SKScene, 150, 157
SKSceneScaleMode, 151
SKSpriteNode, 153
SKTexture, 178
SKTransition, 157
SKView, 150
slicing images, 53–54
slider joints, 197
sloping materials, 285
smoke effects, 167
smoothness parameter, 179
sound, 103–121
  allowing user to select music, 117–119
  controlling music playback, 116
  cooperating with other audio, 119–121
  cross-fading between tracks, 109–111
  detecting when currently playing track
    changes, 114
  determining how to best use in game design,
    121
  getting information about what music is
    playing, 113
  playing with AVAudioplayer, 103–106
  recording sound with AVAudiorecorder, 106
  synthesizing speech, 111
  working with multiple audio players, 108
specular highlights, 273–274
specular mapping, 274
speech
  breakpoints with, 372
  synthesizing, 111
speed
  calculating user, 90
  controlling in physics simulation, 192
spot light objects, 283
Sprite Kit
  2D graphics and, 143–179
  adding a sprite, 152
  adding a text sprite, 153
  adding a texture sprite, 161
  and UIView, 65
  animating a sprite, 170
  Bézier paths with, 166
  blending modes with, 163
  compressed texture loading, 367
  creating a scene, 150–152
  creating view with, 149
  fonts for, 155
  generating noise textures with, 286
  image effects for sprite drawing, 165
  moving sprites and labels around, 158–161
  noise for image creation, 178
  parallax scrolling, 171–178
  physics bodies in, 185
  physics simulations with, 181–206
  shaking the screen with, 168
  shape nodes, 162
  smoke, fire, particle effects with, 167
  texture atlases for, 162
  transitioning between scenes, 156
squares
  3D, with OpenGL, 216–223
  applying texture to, 224–226
  triangles and, 219–223
standard game controller, 341
state of game, saving, 123–126
state of object, 329
static bodies, 184
steering wheel, 98
steering, of object toward a point, 301
stop method, 104
storyboards, 32–38
street address
  looking up from user's location, 97
  looking up GPS coordinates for, 95
stroke color, 163
structured information, loading, 134–136
suspending apps, 10
swap files, 364
Swift
  defining operators in, 148
  making vector math nicer in, 293–295
  Objective-C vs., 209
  vector extensions in, 145
synchronizing objects, 327–329
synthesized speech, 111
system music player, 113

T

taking cover, 302
tap gestures, 69
target
    intercepting, 298
    moving toward, 295–297
    selecting, 300
tarnished object, 274
task(s), future, 20
test cases, 25
test suites, 25
text
    in Sprite Kit scene, 153
    rendering in 3D, 284
    sharing to social media sites, 335
texture atlases, 162, 363
texture coordinates, 226
texture streaming, 363
texture(s)
    compressed, 366–368
    loading for 3D graphics, 224–226
    tinting, 266
    with shaders, 265
themes/theming, 62
thrusters, 198
tilt, 83–85
time
    controlling in physics simulation, 192
    delta time calculation, 7–9
timers, 2, 11
tinting
    setting color for, 62
    textures, 266
toon shading, 276
touch states, 68
touch system
    detecting when view is touched, 68
    receiving touches in custom areas of view, 80
track, music, 114
transform constraints, 288
transform matrix, 59, 64
transform property, 58
transform(s), 246
translation, vector, 146
transparent materials, 285
transparent objects, 271
triangles
    for drawing squares, 219–223
    for faces of cubes, 228

triggering segues, 46
Tron (film), 179
turn-based games
    finding next best move for, 308
    making gameplay work with Game Kit, 332–335
Twitter, posting scores/characters on, 335
type alias, 16

U

UI dynamics, 55
UI elements, 62
UIAppearance, 62
UIAttachmentBehavior, 56
UIBezierPath objects, 166
UIDynamicAnimator, 55
UIFont class, 155
UIKit
    controls in, 31
    physics engine with, 56
UIView
    overlaying, 65
    rotating 3D, 63
UIViewController class, 37
unarchiving, 125
unit tests, 24–26
update method, 231
updating
    based on timer, 11
    delta time calculation, 7–9
    from screen updates, 11–13
user defaults, 139
user input, 1
user(s)
    accessing location of, 87–90
    calculating speed of, 90
    detecting entrance/exit, 9
    looking up street address from location of, 97
    music selection by, 117–119
    notifications of change in location, 92–95
    pinpointing proximity to landmarks, 91

V

value changed handlers, 346
values property, 61
vectors, 144–149
    3D with GLKit, 210

and dot product, 148–149
and shape nodes, 162
defined, 144
lengths, 145
math in Swift, 293–295
moving, 146
normalizing, 296
rotating, 147
scaling, 147
velocity(-ies), 182
change, 188
setting, 187
with vectors, 144
vertex shader, 255, 268
vertical axis, 144
view controllers
creating, 38–45
defined, 37
view(s), 31–66
adding images, 51
animating popping effect on view, 60
background images for, 62
changing color, 62
constraints for view layout, 49–51
creating view controllers, 38–45
detecting when touched, 68
effective game menus, 66
moving images with core animation, 56
overlaying menus over game content, 65
receiving touches in custom areas of, 80
rotating images, 58–59

rotating UIview in 3D, 63
segues for moving between screens, 45–48
slicing images for buttons, 53–54
theming UI elements with UIAppearance, 62
UI dynamics for animated views, 55
working with storyboards, 32–38
visual effects, 165
visual noise, 178

W

walls, for collision scenes, 189
watchpoints, 370
weak references, 17
weight, 188
world spaces, 253

X

x-axis, 144
Xcode, 314
texture atlases with, 162
watchpoints with, 370

Y

y-axis, 144
yaw tilt, 83, 85, 86

Z

z-axis, 144

About the Authors

Jonathon Manning is a cofounder of Secret Lab (*http://www.secretlab.com.au*), an independent game development studio based in beautiful Hobart, Tasmania, Australia (an island at the bottom of the world). He's worked on apps of all sorts, ranging from iPad games for children to instant messaging clients. Jon will soon graduate with a PhD in Computing and can be found on Twitter as @desplesda.

Paris Buttfield-Addison is also a cofounder of Secret Lab. Secret Lab builds award-winning games and apps for mobile devices. Paris formerly worked as mobile product manager for Meebo (acquired by Google) and has a PhD in Computing. Paris can be found on Twitter as @parisba.

Colophon

The animal on the cover of *iOS Swift Game Development Cookbook* is a queen triggerfish (*Balistes vetula*), so named for the two interlocking spines it can raise under threat, to firmly ensconce itself in the crevice of a reef or prevent a would-be predator from swallowing it whole. Queen triggerfish inhabit coral and rocky reefs in the Atlantic Ocean at depths of approximately 10 to 100 feet, though they have been known to seek sand- or seagrass-covered sea floors 900 feet below the surface.

Though as often found in schools as alone, queen triggerfish maintain a reputation as an aggressive fish. They fiercely defend the eggs they lay in nests on the ocean floor and use strong jaws and teeth to eat the crustaceans and other invertebrates that make up the bulk of their diet. Queen triggerfish create their nests by moving their fins quickly to direct a current of air into the sea floor. They also use this technique to avoid the longer spines on top of a sea urchin by blowing it onto its back to reach the tender meat underneath.

The queen triggerfish's appetite for invertebrates, as well as its penchant for confrontation, make it an unsuitable addition to reef aquariums. If it is placed in an aquarium, it is ideal to use a tank holding at least 500 gallons, or the queen triggerfish will attack other fish. It is also known for *redecorating* aquariums by picking up pieces of coral and moving them elsewhere.

The mood of the triggerfish is not, for all of its aggression, static. Its changing moods can be seen in the varying shade of yellow that mixes with blues and greens, which helps it blend in with its surroundings when it is stressed.

Many of the animals on O'Reilly covers are endangered; all of them are important to the world. To learn more about how you can help, go to *animals.oreilly.com*.

The origin of the cover image is unknown. The cover fonts are URW Typewriter and Guardian Sans. The text font is Adobe Minion Pro; the heading font is Adobe Myriad Condensed; and the code font is Dalton Maag's Ubuntu Mono.

Have it your way.

Get even more for your money.

Join the O'Reilly Community, and register the O'Reilly books you own. It's free, and you'll get:

- $4.99 ebook upgrade offer
- 40% upgrade offer on O'Reilly print books
- Membership discounts on books and events
- Free lifetime updates to ebooks and videos
- Multiple ebook formats, DRM FREE
- Participation in the O'Reilly community
- Newsletters
- Account management
- 100% Satisfaction Guarantee

Signing up is easy:

1. Go to: oreilly.com/go/register
2. Create an O'Reilly login.
3. Provide your address.
4. Register your books.

Note: English-language books only

To order books online:
oreilly.com/store

For questions about products or an order:
orders@oreilly.com

To sign up to get topic-specific email announcements and/or news about upcoming books, conferences, special offers, and new technologies:
elists@oreilly.com

For technical questions about book content:
booktech@oreilly.com

To submit new book proposals to our editors:
proposals@oreilly.com

O'Reilly books are available in multiple DRM-free ebook formats. For more information:
oreilly.com/ebooks